ROBERT L. MILLET AND LLOYD D. NEWELL

DRAW NEAR
Unto Me

**DAILY REFLECTIONS ON
THE DOCTRINE AND COVENANTS**

**DESERET
BOOK**

SALT LAKE CITY, UTAH

Visit us at deseretbook.com

Library of Congress Cataloging-in-Publication Data

Millet, Robert L.
  Draw near unto me : daily reflections on the Doctrine and Covenants /
Robert L. Millet, Lloyd D. Newell.
    p. cm.
  Includes bibliographical references.
  ISBN 1-59038-284-6 (hardcover : alk. paper)
  1. Doctrine and Covenants. 2. Church of Jesus Christ of Latter-day Saints—Doctrines. 3. Mormon Church—Doctrines.
I. Newell, Lloyd D., 1956- II. Title.
  BX8628.M55 2004
  289.3'2—dc22
                                2004010104

Printed in the United States of America   42316
Inland Press, Menomonee Falls, WI

10   9   8   7   6   5   4   3   2

In memory of Joseph Smith, the Prophet of
the Restoration, the head of this final dispensation,
the preeminent prophetic revealer of Christ and
the plan of salvation in these last days

PREFACE

After long centuries in which divine authority and precious truths were lost from the earth, morning broke on a beautiful spring day in 1820. God the Eternal Father and his Beloved Son, Jesus Christ, appeared to a fourteen-year-old boy who was seeking divine assurance. That First Vision marked the beginning of God's revelations in this final dispensation and the reestablishment of his kingdom on the earth. Foundational to it were the translation and publication of the Book of Mormon, which sets forth plainly the nature of fallen man and the need for redemption from the Fall and reconciliation with the Father through the gift of the Atonement.

The Lord continued to reveal his truths to the young Prophet Joseph Smith, giving him precept upon precept the instructions necessary to organize and teach a covenant people. Soon the revelations were compiled into the volume of scripture we know as the

Doctrine and Covenants. Just as the keystone of our religion, the Book of Mormon, invites all to come unto Christ, so the capstone of our religion, the Doctrine and Covenants, invites all to come unto Christ's kingdom, The Church of Jesus Christ of Latter-day Saints (Benson, *A Witness and a Warning*, 36).

We invite you to walk with us through the Doctrine and Covenants, reading the passages of scripture and reflecting upon their meaning. Intended only to add to your scripture study, not to replace it, the daily essays are our thoughts, and we encourage you to search the scriptures for your own insights and applications. Although we have sought to be in harmony with the standard works and the teachings of latter-day apostles and prophets, this work is not an official publication of either The Church of Jesus Christ of Latter-day Saints or of Brigham Young University.

As with many of our other writing projects, this book could not have been completed without the painstaking efforts of Lori Soza, who organized and prepared the manuscript. We likewise appreciate our friends at Deseret Book Company: Jana Erickson, whose encouragement never faltered, and Suzanne Brady, whose keen editorial eye has been indispensable. Most of all, we are grateful to our wives, Shauna and Karmel, and to our children for their sustaining love and support.

JANUARY

Hearken, O ye people of my church,
saith the voice of him who dwells on high.

DOCTRINE & COVENANTS

1:1

For verily the voice of the Lord is unto all men, and there is none to escape; and there is no eye that shall not see, neither ear that shall not hear, neither heart that shall not be penetrated.

DOCTRINE & COVENANTS 1:2

God's voice is unto all men and women in these last days. The Doctrine and Covenants, the Book of Mormon, the Pearl of Great Price, and the inspired utterances of latter-day prophets and apostles—these messages are delivered directly to the Latter-day Saints but have relevance and application to all the world. Our Heavenly Father is the Father of the spirits of all people, and thus his divine directives are intended for persons of every nation, kindred, tongue, and people. All who hearken to the light of Christ within them will be led, whether in this life or in the life to come, to the higher light of the Holy Ghost that comes through the gospel covenant, the fulness of the gospel of Jesus Christ. The message of salvation is now being sent forth into all the world, and the day will come when no one can profess ignorance of these saving truths.

*And the voice of warning shall be unto all people, by the mouths
of my disciples, whom I have chosen in these last days.*
DOCTRINE & COVENANTS 1:4

In the first verses of the Lord's preface to the doctrines, covenants, and commandments given in this dispensation, the Lord sounds the voice of warning to all people. His revelations will sound in every ear, proclaiming the new and everlasting covenant, admonishing each one to exercise faith, repent, and come unto Christ and his true and living Church (D&C 1:30). The Lord's authorized servants who are endowed with priesthood keys and sacred stewardships are known to the Church. They do not operate in the dark; they do not hide in the shadows. Fearlessly, these "weak things of the world," the Lord's anointed prophets, proclaim the truth of the gospel (D&C 1:19); boldly they declare the Lord's message of salvation (D&C 1:32); humbly they go forth with confidence in the commands of the Lord who watches over all (D&C 1:5). The Lord's warning voice will go throughout the world in preparation for his glorious second coming.

*Behold, this is mine authority, and the authority of my servants,
and my preface unto the book of my commandments, which I
have given them to publish unto you, O inhabitants of the earth.*
DOCTRINE & COVENANTS 1:6

Doctrine and Covenants 1 is the Lord's preface to his latter-day commandments. A preface often alerts the reader to significant points that will be covered and summarizes the important issues that will be raised. In a revelation given 1 November 1831, the Savior describes the state of things in the days of Joseph Smith (a time when the fulness of the gospel had not yet been made known), as well as the plight of humanity because individuals had chosen uninspired paths to happiness. It also contains the Lord's prescription for a generation that now wanders in darkness—the call of a modern prophet, the teachings that flow through him, and the blessings that accrue to those who heed the prophetic word.

And the day cometh that they who will not hear the voice of the Lord, neither the voice of his servants, neither give heed to the words of the prophets and apostles, shall be cut off from among the people.
DOCTRINE & COVENANTS 1:14

Some fail to hear the words of the prophets and apostles because of sin. Some are deaf because of fear, and others because of worldly preoccupation. Whatever the reason, it is a kind of pride. All who ignore the words of the Lord's servants will come to regret their deafness. If they close their hearts to prophetic counsel, they will be cut off from the Lord's promised blessings to all who humble themselves before him in righteousness. They will be cut off spiritually from the growth that comes to meek followers of Christ. They will be cut off from the abiding peace and everlasting joy that come to those who heed the prophets and turn their hearts to the Lord. Too much is at stake to treat prophetic words casually, or worse, to reject proudly the words of the prophets—ancient or modern. May we heed the admonitions of the Lord's authorized servants and sustain them with full purpose of heart.

They seek not the Lord to establish his righteousness, but every man walketh in his own way, and after the image of his own god, whose image is in the likeness of the world, and whose substance is that of an idol, which waxeth old and shall perish in Babylon, even Babylon the great, which shall fall.

DOCTRINE & COVENANTS 1:16

We need not bow down to deities of wood or stone to be guilty of idolatry. Idolatry is a sin that takes place when individuals trust themselves and devote their lives to anything other than the true and living God. In our modern age, idolatry can take the form of inappropriate hero worship, entail the inordinate quest for popularity, or be manifest in the acquisition of financial portfolios and real estate—in general, being possessed by possessions. People who worship cattle or crocodiles or cedar posts are entitled to all of the blessings such gods can confer here and hereafter. The only way, however, to obtain peace here and eternal life in the world to come is to know and worship the God of all creation, that Holy Being the knowledge of whom brings eternal life.

*That the fulness of my gospel might be proclaimed
by the weak and the simple unto the ends of the world,
and before kings and rulers.*

DOCTRINE & COVENANTS 1:23

Some wish aloud, "If only we could convert a movie star, a famous athlete, or a prominent religious leader, then people would surely pay more attention to us." In fact, never has divine truth been carried principally on the backs of the mighty and great ones of the earth. "For ye see your calling, brethren, how that not many wise men after the flesh, not many mighty, not many noble, are called: but God hath chosen the foolish things of the world to confound the wise; and God hath chosen the weak things of the world to confound the things which are mighty" (1 Corinthians 1:26–27). We who see through a glass darkly must be reminded occasionally that the Almighty has his own timetable and his own plan for how his gospel is to be presented; he is able to do his own work (2 Nephi 27:20).

*Those to whom these commandments were given, might have power
to lay the foundation of this church, and to bring it forth out of
obscurity and out of darkness, the only true and living church upon
the face of the whole earth, with which I, the Lord, am well pleased.*

DOCTRINE & COVENANTS 1:30

We need only become acquainted with individuals of other religious persuasions to recognize their goodness and the truths that they possess. It would be blatant arrogance to suppose that the Latter-day Saints are the only people on earth with whom our Heavenly Father is concerned or to whom he seeks to make known his mind and will. God loves all of his children on earth and seeks to teach all that people are prepared to receive (Alma 29:8). To state that The Church of Jesus Christ of Latter-day Saints is the only true and living church upon the face of the whole earth is neither a denunciation of others nor a denial of their truths but rather a declaration that the Latter-day Saints are custodians of divine priesthood authority and the fulness of the everlasting gospel. With those consummate blessings comes the responsibility to share, not to judge or demean those of other faiths.

What I the Lord have spoken, I have spoken, and I excuse not myself; and though the heavens and the earth pass away, my word shall not pass away, but shall all be fulfilled, whether by mine own voice or by the voice of my servants, it is the same.

DOCTRINE & COVENANTS 1:38

In his second epistle, the apostle Peter indicated that "prophecy came not in old time by the will of man: but holy men of God spake as they were moved upon by the Holy Ghost" (2 Peter 1:21). When a servant of the Lord speaks under the direction of the Holy Ghost, he is, in actuality, speaking the words of God. It is as if the Lord were himself present, telling us what he would want us to know and do. The Lord's authorized representatives are his agents, surrogates, teachers, and spokesmen; however, unlike the Lord, who is perfect in every way, these servants are themselves imperfect and striving to overcome the world—like each of us. Nevertheless, they have been called by inspiration and magnified in their callings by the Lord. Thanks be to God, who speaks to us today as in times past by the voice of his servants.

For behold, and lo, the Lord is God, and the
Spirit beareth record, and the record is true, and the
truth abideth forever and ever. Amen.

DOCTRINE & COVENANTS 1:39

God is the standard against which we measure good and evil. Jesus himself stated that "there is none good but one, that is, God" (Matthew 19:17). Thus, our beloved Father could not do other than call us to the standard of perfection (Matthew 5:48; 3 Nephi 12:48). At the same time, our perfect Lord is fully aware of the faults and foibles of his imperfect children. In that sense, as the Prophet Joseph Smith declared, "God does not look on sin with allowance, but when men have sinned, there must be allowance made for them" (*Teachings of the Prophet Joseph Smith,* 240). The gospel of Jesus Christ, the plan of salvation, has been provided to us as a means whereby we can confront our sins and be sanctified from the effects of them. We can, through the mediation and atonement of the only perfect Being to walk this earth, thus become qualified for association with holy beings.

*I will reveal unto you the Priesthood, by the hand of
Elijah the prophet, before the coming of the great and dreadful
day of the Lord. And he shall plant in the hearts of the
children the promises made to the fathers, and the
hearts of the children shall turn to their fathers.*

DOCTRINE & COVENANTS 2:1–2

When Moroni appeared to Joseph Smith on the evening of 21 September 1823, he quoted many Old and New Testament passages of scripture. Some of these he quoted quite differently from the King James text. For example, Moroni's rendition of Malachi 4:5–6 sheds a brilliant light upon an otherwise little appreciated doctrine: Elijah the prophet would be sent to plant within our hearts the promises made to our ancient fathers, Abraham, Isaac, and Jacob—the promise of the gospel, the priesthood, eternal lives, and a land inheritance (Abraham 2:8–11, 19). This prophecy was fulfilled on 3 April 1836, when Elijah visited the Kirtland Temple with Moses and Elias to confer the keys of the kingdom upon Joseph Smith and Oliver Cowdery. Because Elijah came, there comes into the hearts of God's latter-day covenant people a desire to have every blessing promised to the ancients. These blessings come only through the sacred ordinances of the house of the Lord.

The works, and the designs, and the purposes of God cannot be
frustrated, neither can they come to naught. . . .
Therefore his paths are straight, and his course is one eternal
round. Remember, remember that it is not the work of God
that is frustrated, but the work of men.
DOCTRINE & COVENANTS 3:1–3

The loss of the 116 manuscript pages of the Book of Mormon did not thwart the Lord's plan. He who knows all things knew where the manuscript was and who had taken it. He had also made provision for that eventuality in his directions to Nephi more than two thousand years earlier (1 Nephi 9:5–6). From the premortal Council in Heaven through the beginnings of mortality and forward to today, those who desired to ruin God's plan have sought for gain as they worked to tear down the standard of truth. It will ever be so until the Lord returns to reign in millennial glory. We need only remember what the Lord has said: "I will not suffer that they shall destroy my work; yea, I will show unto them that my wisdom is greater than the cunning of the devil" (D&C 10:43). Despite the dark deeds of enemies of righteousness, the Lord and his great plan of happiness will not fail or falter.

That the Lamanites might come to the knowledge of their fathers, and that they might know the promises of the Lord, and that they may believe the gospel and rely upon the merits of Jesus Christ, and be glorified through faith in his name, and that through their repentance they might be saved.

DOCTRINE & COVENANTS 3:20

The pattern for all nations is the same. Whether Jew or Gentile, Nephite or Lamanite, Ishmaelite or Zoramite, each of us must come unto Christ and rely upon his merits to be saved. That is, we must exercise saving faith in Jesus Christ, recognize our own inadequacies and limitations, and turn to him who did all things perfectly. As we learn in the Book of Mormon, "Since man had fallen he could not merit anything of himself; but the sufferings and death of Christ atone for their sins through faith and repentance" (Alma 22:14). Our good works matter very much, inasmuch as they evidence the depth of our conversion. But salvation, or eternal life, is free (2 Nephi 2:4) and is the greatest of all the gifts of God (D&C 6:13; 14:7). In the eternal scheme of things, we are saved through the merits and mercy and grace of the Holy Messiah (2 Nephi 2:8).

Now behold, a marvelous work is about to come forth among the children of men. Therefore, O ye that embark in the service of God, see that ye serve him with all your heart, might, mind and strength, that ye may stand blameless before God at the last day.
DOCTRINE & COVENANTS 4:1–2

A marvelous work and a wonder has come forth in these latter-days: the Church of Jesus Christ has been restored with all power and authority, keys and blessings essential for our eternal salvation. The Book of Mormon has been brought forth, containing the fulness of the everlasting gospel. This record of ancient inhabitants of the Americas was written to bring God's children to Christ. But the marvelous work is not finished. It continues unabated as members and missionaries spread the gospel message to the far corners of the earth, as people repent of old ways and traditions, put off the natural man, and become new creatures in a covenant relationship with Christ (Mosiah 3:19; 27:26). To move this marvelous work forward, the Lord needs us to earnestly dedicate ourselves to his work, with all our love and affections, our valor and willpower, our intelligence and reason and physical strength. If we do so, we may stand blameless before God at the last day.

Therefore, if ye have desires to serve God ye are called to the work; for behold the field is white already to harvest; and lo, he that thrusteth in his sickle with his might, the same layeth up in store that he perisheth not, but bringeth salvation to his soul.

DOCTRINE & COVENANTS 4:3–4

Every laborer in the kingdom is invited to work for the salvation of souls. By doing so, we bring salvation to our own souls, which is our foremost responsibility. Great will be our joy as we thrust in our sickle with our might to bring others to the Lord and his Church (D&C 18:15–16). Serving others and obtaining our own salvation is a lifelong process of *desiring* righteousness, earnestly *striving* to seek after others' welfare, *doing* our best to live what we know to be true, and ultimately, *relying* on the grace and goodness of the Lord. That can seem overwhelming at times, but we must not be discouraged. We must instead go forward with faith—one step at a time. Reach out in love and service to others. Share gospel light with a world desperate for truth and virtue. Live so that others can see what wonderful things Christ has done for you and what he can do for them.

Faith, hope, charity and love, with an eye single to the glory of God, qualify him for the work. Remember faith, virtue, knowledge, temperance, patience, brotherly kindness, godliness, charity, humility, diligence. Ask, and ye shall receive; knock, and it shall be opened unto you. Amen.

DOCTRINE & COVENANTS 4:5–7

Doctrine and Covenants 4 is a revelation given in 1829 through the Prophet Joseph Smith to his father, Joseph Smith Sr. Yet it is still pertinent to each of us today. In seven short verses, the Lord calls us to labor in his marvelous work and describes the attributes of godliness and the qualifications of those who desire to serve God. Because the Father's work and glory are to bring to pass the immortality and eternal life of his beloved children (Moses 1:39), we are to work with him to bring about much righteousness. We are to become like him, developing his attributes, qualities, and perfections. We are to extend brotherly kindness to others and be patient and humble, virtuous and diligent. Faith and charity are absolutes in our own spiritual rebirth and daily gospel living. The Lord will make us equal to the task, pouring out blessings from the windows of heaven, if we have faith in him and charity towards his children.

This generation shall have my word through you.
DOCTRINE & COVENANTS 5:10

Joseph Smith, mighty prophet and choice seer of the latter days, occupies a place of unique importance in our dispensation (D&C 124:58). We are indebted to him for the spiritual knowledge he restored and the Church he established (D&C 135:3). No wonder "the ends of the earth shall inquire after [Joseph's] name" (D&C 122:1). All prophets of the past have looked toward this generation when God would reveal his word anew to the Prophet Joseph. God's word is the plan of salvation; his word is the mind and will of the Lord as pertaining to his children on earth. The revelations that came through the Prophet Joseph Smith are true. And though we do not worship the Prophet, we honor him as an instrument in the hands of God in restoring the ancient truths of the gospel. We reverence his name for sealing his testimony with his blood. We raise our voices in admiration, "Praise to the man who communed with Jehovah!" (*Hymns*, no. 27).

*I command you, my servant Joseph, to repent and walk more
uprightly before me, and to yield to the persuasions of men no
more; . . . be firm in keeping the commandments wherewith I
have commanded you; and if ye do this, behold I grant
unto you eternal life, even if you should be slain.*

DOCTRINE & COVENANTS 5:21–22

The Prophet Joseph learned a painful lesson in yielding to the repeated requests of Martin Harris regarding the 116-page manuscript. Not only did it become lost but Joseph feared his soul might be lost as well. In Doctrine and Covenants 5 the Lord tutors the Prophet with clarity and kindness. He admonishes Joseph (and each of us) to be humble, to stand firm in the faith, and to look to him in all things. The Lord also foreshadowed the martyr's death awaiting Joseph but promised that he would receive a prophet's reward (Matthew 10:41). The Lord promises all the faithful that if we do not yield to the temptations and persuasions of the world, we can receive peace in this world and eternal life in the world to come (D&C 59:23). That does not mean that we will not experience trial and tribulation, heartache and anguish, but it does mean that our joy will be full and our reward everlasting.

Stop, and stand still until I command thee, and I will provide means whereby thou mayest accomplish the thing which I have commanded thee.
DOCTRINE & COVENANTS 5:34

The Lord provides a way for us to do all that he wants us to do and become all that he wants us to become, if we will "stop, and stand still." That means listening to the promptings of the Spirit and seeking the guidance of the Lord. It implies trusting the Lord, knowing that "all things work together for good to them that love God" (Romans 8:28). Nephi of old had complete confidence that the Lord would prepare a way for him to do all he needed to do (1 Nephi 3:7). He was led every step of the way because he was faithful in keeping the commandments, remained humble and receptive to the whisperings of the Spirit, and exercised sufficient courage to do the will of the Lord. Certainly, we must be proactive and anxiously engaged in good causes, but we must also "stop, and stand still," waiting patiently on the Lord and trusting his purposes.

Seek not for riches but for wisdom, and behold, the mysteries of God shall be unfolded unto you, and then shall you be made rich. Behold, he that hath eternal life is rich.

DOCTRINE & COVENANTS 6:7

Materialism, acquisitiveness, and greed never unite with the things of eternity. We are commanded to "lay aside the things of this world, and seek for the things of a better" (D&C 25:10). The Lord has said, "Wherefore, seek not the things of this world but seek ye first to build up the kingdom of God, and to establish his righteousness" (JST Matthew 6:38). Jacob, the brother of Nephi, counseled the Saints of his day: "Before ye seek for riches, seek ye for the kingdom of God. And after ye have obtained a hope in Christ ye shall obtain riches, if ye seek them; and ye will seek them for the intent to do good" (Jacob 2:18–19). Wisdom, which is better than rubies (Proverbs 8:11), is a combination of knowledge and action, spiritual insight and meek submission. Wisdom is built on the foundation of humility and gratitude and leads us to seek the riches of eternity in the kingdom of God.

*Say nothing but repentance unto this generation; keep my
commandments, and assist to bring forth my work, according to
my commandments, and you shall be blessed.*

DOCTRINE & COVENANTS 6:9

When John the Baptist laid his hands upon the heads of Oliver Cowdery and Joseph Smith, he conferred upon them the keys of the Aaronic Priesthood, which has the power to direct "the gospel of repentance" (D&C 13:1). Indeed, the gospel of Jesus Christ is a gospel of repentance, the glad tidings that we do not have to remain where we are, that change is possible, that we can become new creatures in Christ. The instruction to "say nothing but repentance unto this generation" (D&C 6:9) was a call to teach the doctrines of the gospel, to lay out the principles, practices, covenants, and ordinances that would cleanse human souls and enable them to do a work they could not do by their own strength and capacity. The gospel of Jesus Christ can do more than make bad men good and good men better, as important as that is; it is a system of salvation intended to transform humankind and renovate the whole of society.

*Behold thou hast a gift, and blessed art thou because
of thy gift. Remember it is sacred and cometh from above.*

DOCTRINE & COVENANTS 6:10

Each of us is given a gift by the Spirit of God (D&C 46:11–33). Part of our eternal quest is to discover and develop that sacred gift for the purpose of blessing others. President Gordon B. Hinckley has said, "You need never feel inferior. You need never feel that you were born without talents or without opportunities to give them expression. There is something of divinity in you. You have such tremendous potential because of your inherited nature. Every one of you was endowed by your Father in Heaven with a tremendous capacity to do good in the world. Cultivate the art of being kind, of being thoughtful, of being helpful. Refine within you the quality of mercy which comes as a part of the divine attributes you have inherited" (*Stand a Little Taller,* 185). The most significant gifts we can develop are such gifts of the Spirit as faith, humility, charity, wisdom, and testimony.

Blessed art thou for what thou hast done; for thou hast inquired of me, and behold, as often as thou hast inquired thou hast received instruction of my Spirit. . . . I tell thee these things that thou mayest know that thou hast been enlightened by the Spirit of truth.

DOCTRINE & COVENANTS 6:14–15

When schoolteacher Oliver Cowdery was invited to stay in the home of the Smith family, he soon learned of the call of Joseph Smith Jr. and, especially, the golden plates and translation of the Nephite-Jaredite record. Oliver sought the Lord in prayer and received a divine manifestation of the truthfulness of God's hand in the work of the Restoration. Later, the revelation recorded in Doctrine and Covenants 6 was given to Joseph and Oliver. In it, Oliver learned (as will many of us one day) that the Lord had been leading him along by the power of his Spirit for some time: the very fact that he was where he was served as evidence that he had received divine promptings and supernatural guidance. It is as though the Lord were saying to Oliver: "I now give you this revelation so that you may know that what you have been receiving is revelation."

Be faithful and diligent in keeping the commandments of God, and I will encircle thee in the arms of my love.

DOCTRINE & COVENANTS 6:20

God loves all of his children in a most miraculous way. He does not withhold his perfect love; rather, we withdraw from it when we are prideful, unrighteous, or lazy. To receive the blessings of eternity, we must be earnest about spiritual things. As we come to understand who and Whose we really are and hold fast to the iron rod, we will surely feel the love of God. President Gordon B. Hinckley has advised us: "Be true to your convictions. You know what is right, and you know what is wrong. You know when you are doing the proper thing. You know when you are giving strength to the right cause. Be loyal. Be faithful. Be true" (*Stand a Little Taller,* 16). We know what we must do. We are here to learn, not to remain in ignorance. We are here to keep the commandments, to conquer ourselves, to live together in love and righteousness.

*If you desire a further witness, cast your mind upon
the night that you cried unto me in your heart, that you
might know concerning the truth of these things. Did I not speak
peace to your mind concerning the matter? What greater
witness can you have than from God?*

DOCTRINE & COVENANTS 6:22–23

Latter-day Saints know of the Lord's instruction to
Oliver Cowdery concerning the need to study out a
matter, inquire of the Lord, and receive either confirmation or a stupor of thought (D&C 9:7–9). Most of
us know of open visions, or dreams, or other dramatic
manifestations of the Spirit. Too often, however, we
fail to realize that the simple manifestation of peace is
perhaps the most fundamental way by which we can
know we are on course and in harmony with God's
will. "Peace I leave with you," the Savior said at the
Last Supper, "my peace I give unto you: not as the
world giveth, give I unto you. Let not your heart be
troubled, neither let it be afraid" (John 14:27). In a
world tossed and torn by noise and warfare, the peace
of God, even the peace "which passeth all understanding" (Philippians 4:7), is a precious and priceless
gift of a loving Heavenly Father.

*Therefore, fear not, little flock; do good; let earth
and hell combine against you, for if ye are built upon
my rock, they cannot prevail.*

DOCTRINE & COVENANTS 6:34

Doubt and fear cannot coexist with true faith in
Christ. Our Lord and Master is in complete control,
and his repeated plea in scripture is for us to "fear not"
(D&C 6:34). Fear manifests doubt; faith results in
assurance. Fear leads to panic; faith leads to peace and
inner security. All the demons of earth and hell may
combine to hedge up the way against the Latter-day
Saints, but we need not fear, for the Captain of our
souls is in command. If this were the work of man, it
would fail. But it is the work of the Lord, and he does
not fail. To the extent that we build our lives upon a
solid and firm foundation—the foundation of the
Rock of our Redeemer (Helaman 5:12)—we can face
squarely and securely any and all odds. Truly, "thanks
be to God [who] giveth us the victory through our
Lord Jesus Christ" (1 Corinthians 15:57).

Look unto me in every thought; doubt not, fear not.
DOCTRINE & COVENANTS 6:36

The father of lies wins a victory when he persuades us to see our religious life as just another facet of our mortal existence. True happiness comes to those who view all aspects of their life through the lens of their religion (D&C 29:34). An angel instructed our first parents, Adam and Eve: "Wherefore, thou shalt do all that thou doest in the name of the Son, and thou shalt repent and call upon God in the name of the Son forevermore" (Moses 5:8). We look unto Christ in every thought when we seek to keep every day holy, when we strive to live close to the Spirit at all times, when we ask ourselves "What would Jesus do?" throughout the day. We look unto him in every thought when we struggle to gain an eye single to his glory and strive with all our hearts to learn his will and carry it out.

I will tell you in your mind and in your heart, by the Holy Ghost,
which shall come upon you and which shall dwell in your heart.
DOCTRINE & COVENANTS 8:2

Nothing is more important to the relationship between family members than open, honest communication," said Elder M. Russell Ballard. "This is particularly true for parents trying to teach gospel principles and standards to their children. The ability to counsel with our youth—and perhaps more importantly, to really listen to their concerns—is the foundation upon which successful relationships are built. Often what we see in the eyes and what we feel in the heart will communicate far more than what we hear or say" (*Ensign,* May 1999, 86–87). The sweet whisperings of the Holy Ghost can inspire understanding of perplexing problems. The still, small voice of the Spirit can give us strength and wisdom to work on mending strained relationships and healing wounded hearts. That is the spirit of revelation. Answers come to the mind and heart, hidden treasures are revealed, and light and knowledge are distilled upon our souls as the dews from heaven.

This is the spirit of revelation; behold, this is the spirit by which Moses brought the children of Israel through the Red Sea on dry ground. Therefore this is thy gift; apply unto it, and blessed art thou, for it shall deliver you out of the hands of your enemies.

DOCTRINE & COVENANTS 8:3–4

The spirit of revelation is the Holy Ghost. It is the same Spirit by which Moses received revelation at the Red Sea to know what to do to save ancient Israel. It is the same Spirit by which revelation comes to living prophets to guide modern Israel today. We, too, can be directed by the still, small voice of the Spirit. For Oliver Cowdery to successfully exercise his gift of revelation he had to "apply unto" this gift that the Lord had given him (D&C 8:4). If he did his part and applied himself to his gift, inquiring of the Lord in sincerity, he would be blessed. Likewise, we can be delivered in time of need by applying ourselves to the Spirit of revelation, seeking the Lord's will, acting upon the promptings that come, and having faith that "all things work together for good to them that love God" (Romans 8:28). Attuning ourselves to the spirit of revelation will deliver us from darkness and despair.

Be patient, my son, for . . . it is not expedient that you should translate at this present time. . . . Do not murmur, my son, for it is wisdom in me that I have dealt with you after this manner.
DOCTRINE & COVENANTS 9:3–6

Oliver Cowdery arrived in Harmony, Pennsylvania, on 5 April 1829 to inquire about Joseph Smith. Two days later he began to serve as scribe for the Prophet. Shortly thereafter he desired to be endowed with the gift of translation—as Joseph had been. But it was the Lord's desire that Oliver continue as scribe until the translation of the Book of Mormon was completed (D&C 9:1, 4). Then, the Lord promised Oliver, He would give him power to assist in the translation of other records (D&C 9:2–3). The Lord was not only ensuring that the work of translation went forward but was tutoring Oliver, and each of us, in the things of eternity. We are to perform well the labor to which we have been assigned and not aspire to do the work of another. We must be patient, faithful, humble, and steadfast in our callings (D&C 9:14). We must trust the Lord's purposes, without murmuring, and learn the things of eternity.

You have supposed that I would give it unto you, when you took no thought save it was to ask me. . . . You must study it out in your mind; then you must ask me if it be right . . .
DOCTRINE & COVENANTS 9:7–8

The Lord expects us to be wise, to evaluate alternatives, and to draw our own conclusions. We are to be self-reliant and resourceful and use our God-given powers of reason. At the same time, we are to inquire of the Lord and counsel with him (Alma 37:37). This is the spirit of revelation (D&C 8:3). We start the decision-making process and go to the Lord with our ideas, willing to receive direction or correction. As Oliver Cowdery learned, translating the ancient plates required rigorous spiritual and mental effort; most worthwhile endeavors do. If we have done our part and ask in prayer and faith, the Lord will answer. If our decision is right, a feeling of serenity and peace will take hold in our hearts; if it is not right, a feeling of uneasiness, confusion, or fear will signal that we should reconsider. Most assuredly, we need the guidance of the Holy Ghost to make good decisions amidst the tribulations of life.

*Do not run faster or labor more than you have
strength and means provided to enable you to translate;
but be diligent unto the end.*

DOCTRINE & COVENANTS 10:4

God does not call upon us to be truer than true, to
be excessive in our zeal, or to labor longer or harder
than we are capable. The race of life must be run with
wisdom, and it is surely an unwise participant who
pushes himself beyond the bounds of good sense or
seeks victory by giving more than he has power to give.
To pace ourselves is to maintain a steady course, to do
our duty with consistency. Like the unwise virgins of
the parable, we cannot depend upon spiritual
marathons or sudden bursts of righteousness to provide the oil for our lamps. Every prayer we offer, every
testimony we bear, every lesson we teach, every chap-
ter of scripture we ponder, every charitable act we perform adds to the reservoir of faith that equips us to
face the fiery darts of the adversary. Over time we
begin to learn what our limits are and when our offering is acceptable to our Master.

FEBRUARY

Behold, the Lord your Redeemer
suffered death in the flesh . . . , that all men
might repent and come unto him. And he
hath risen again from the dead, that he might
bring all men unto him, on conditions of
repentance. And how great is his joy
in the soul that repenteth!

DOCTRINE & COVENANTS
18:11–13

Verily, verily, I say unto you, wo be unto him that lieth to
deceive because he supposeth that another lieth to deceive,
for such are not exempt from the justice of God.
DOCTRINE & COVENANTS 10:28

One Latter-day Saint religious educator viewed a video on Mormonism in which a score of falsehoods were presented as fact. In one case, the narrator of the video purposely misquoted a passage from the Doctrine and Covenants. When the Latter-day Saint inquired why such a thing would be done, the critic of the Church replied simply, "Well, sir, we call it divine deception." From his perspective, all was fair in the war against the Latter-day Saints, even lies. Doctrine and Covenants 10:28 is a warning to those convinced that the work of restoration is false and who may use dishonesty and questionable methods in denouncing the Church. It is also a sobering reminder of the necessity for us to be accurate and honest in our presentation of gospel truths. The restored gospel is robust enough that it requires neither exaggeration nor folktales to buttress its strength, for "truth will cut its own way" (Smith, *Teachings of the Prophet Joseph Smith*, 313).

And now, behold, according to their faith in their prayers will I bring this part of my gospel to the knowledge of my people. Behold, I do not bring it to destroy that which they have received, but to build it up.

DOCTRINE & COVENANTS 10:52

The Book of Mormon was sent forth to the world for the purpose of "proving to the world that the holy scriptures are true, and that God does inspire men and call them to his holy work in this age and generation, as well as in generations of old" (D&C 20:11). Although critics of the Church often exclaim that the Book of Mormon contradicts the Bible, this assertion is patently false. The Book of Mormon is another testament of Jesus Christ, as its subtitle indicates, and it bears witness of the same sacred, saving truths as does the Bible. Thus the Lord teaches his servants that the Book of Mormon was brought forth not to supplant or put away the Old and New Testaments but rather to build them up—to support them, to sustain them, to testify of their essential truthfulness, and in places to offer clarification and correction.

And for this cause have I said: If this generation harden not their hearts, I will establish my church among them. Now I do not say this to destroy my church, but I say this to build up my church.

DOCTRINE & COVENANTS 10:53–54

Doctrine and Covenants 10 is part of a revelation given almost two years before the formal organization of the restored Church. The Church of Jesus Christ of Latter-day Saints possesses the fulness of the gospel of Jesus Christ and is the custodian of divine priesthood authority, and yet good and noble souls throughout the earth are acting under the quiet influence of God's Holy Spirit. When Nephi stated that there were two churches only—the church of the Lamb of God and the church of the devil (1 Nephi 14:10)—he was not saying that there are only two types of people in the world, namely, the Latter-day Saints and all others. Rather, the divine word affirms that The Church of Jesus Christ of Latter-day Saints was established on earth to shine additional light onto the nature of God and his plan of salvation for his children.

This I do that I may establish my gospel, that there may not be so much contention; yea, Satan doth stir up the hearts of the people to contention concerning the points of my doctrine; and in these things they do err, for they do wrest the scriptures and do not understand them.

DOCTRINE & COVENANTS 10:63

The Lord said that the publication of the Book of Mormon is "to bring to light the true points of my doctrine" (D&C 10:62), fulfilling his promise to the ancient prophets by including in it "all those parts of my gospel which my holy prophets, yea, and also my disciples, desired in their prayers should come forth unto this people" (D&C 10:46). Then, as now, true disciples of Christ desire that all may receive the glad tidings of the gospel and come into the fold of Christ. To do so we must be grounded in doctrinal truth and humble enough to be taught by the authorized servants of the Master. If we genuinely follow the Lord and his apostles and prophets, we will stay firmly on the gospel path and not be tossed to and fro with every wind of doctrine (Ephesians 4:11–14). Understanding and following the true doctrine of Christ are essential to living without contention and feeling real joy.

*Put your trust in that Spirit which leadeth to do good—yea,
to do justly, to walk humbly, to judge righteously; and this is my
Spirit. . . . I will impart unto you of my Spirit, which shall
enlighten your mind, which shall fill your soul with joy.*

DOCTRINE & COVENANTS 11:12–13

The Spirit of the Lord brings light, not darkness;
clarity, not chaos; joy, not despair; peace and assurance,
not fear and uncertainty. By this Spirit, we can know
all things pertaining to righteousness. By this Spirit,
we can also discern counterfeit spirits and evil influences. That which comes of God will always lead us to
goodness, justice, humility, and righteousness. Any
influence that fails to do so does not come from
heaven. Mormon said, "Whatsoever thing persuadeth
men to do evil, and believe not in Christ, and deny
him, and serve not God, then ye may know with a perfect knowledge it is of the devil; for after this manner
doth the devil work, for he persuadeth no man to do
good, no, not one" (Moroni 7:17). The Spirit of the
Lord always inspires us to do good as it enlightens the
mind and brings joy to the heart.

*Seek not to declare my word, but first seek to obtain my
word, and then shall your tongue be loosed; then, if you desire,
you shall have my Spirit and my word, yea, the power
of God unto the convincing of men.*

DOCTRINE & COVENANTS 11:21

There are times when individuals are inspired to
speak words that are new, original to them, words they
had not intended to deliver and even ideas they had
never before considered. Most of the time, however,
the Lord through his Spirit draws forth from us those
things which we have previously studied, learned, and
understood. The Savior taught at the Last Supper that
"the Comforter, which is the Holy Ghost, whom the
Father will send in my name, he shall teach you all
things, and bring all things to your remembrance,
whatsoever I have said unto you" (John 14:26). One
of the great keys to individual revelation is institutional revelation—the scriptures and the words of living prophets. The more we immerse ourselves in holy
writ, the more readily our thoughts, our feelings, and
our speech are directed by the word and will of the
Almighty.

Build upon my rock, which is my gospel.
DOCTRINE & COVENANTS 11:24

In the beautiful region of Caesarea Philippi, only six months before the Savior's death, Peter bore his Spirit-given witness that Jesus is the Christ, the Son of the Living God. Jesus replied, "And I say also unto thee, that thou art Peter, and upon this rock I will build my church; and the gates of hell shall not prevail against it" (Matthew 16:18). Upon what, then, was the Christian church to be built? First of all, Jesus is the Rock (1 Corinthians 10:4), the very Foundation (Helaman 5:12), the Chief Cornerstone of the Church (Ephesians 2:19–20). In addition, the Prophet Joseph Smith explained, the rock upon which the Lord's Church was to be built was the rock of revelation (*Teachings of the Prophet Joseph Smith,* 274). As individual Church members build their lives upon Jesus Christ and upon continuing revelation (both personal and institutional), the gates of hell—the power and dominion of the devil—will never prevail.

*And no one can assist in this work except he shall be humble
and full of love, having faith, hope, and charity, being temperate
in all things, whatsoever shall be entrusted to his care.*
DOCTRINE & COVENANTS 12:8

Each of us is laboring to become a better person day
by day. We strive to keep the commandments and do
the right things, and, perhaps more difficult, to do
them for the right reason. But we do not hold back our
contribution or refuse to be involved because our
hearts are not perfectly pure. Paradoxically, God's perfect work is accomplished through imperfect people.
To assist in the work of the Lord, we do our very best
with what we have, always seeking through prayer for
a purification of our motives and a gradual endowment of the divine nature. In Doctrine and Covenants
12:8 the Lord sets forth the divine ideal, an ideal
toward which we reach all the days of our life. As the
years pass and as our souls are slowly but surely sanctified by the Spirit, precious divine qualities, which
once existed only in embryonic form, begin to distill
upon us, and our labor becomes increasingly effective
and lasting.

Upon you my fellow servants, in the name of Messiah
I confer the Priesthood of Aaron, which holds the keys of the
ministering of angels, and of the gospel of repentance, and of
baptism by immersion for the remission of sins; and this shall
never be taken again from the earth . . .

DOCTRINE & COVENANTS 13:1

As the Prophet Joseph and Oliver Cowdery knelt on the banks of the Susquehanna River in Pennsylvania, it must have been a thrilling and soul-satisfying moment to hear John, the great forerunner of the Master—the prophet designated by Jesus as the greatest of all the prophets (Luke 7:28–30)—utter the words "Upon you my fellow servants." After long centuries when divine, saving authority had not been on earth, the heavens had now been opened and the keys of the priesthood of Aaron were returned to earth. Once more there were legal administrators to officiate in the affairs of God's kingdom. Once more the ministry of angels, the gospel of repentance, and the power to baptize were conferred upon mortals. The foundation was in place, and the stage was set for the later receipt of apostolic authority and the organization of the Master's own true Church.

*And, if you keep my commandments and endure
to the end you shall have eternal life, which gift is the
greatest of all the gifts of God.*
DOCTRINE & COVENANTS 14:7

The Lord's promise to David Whitmer in 1829 is the same promise given to each of us today: If we keep the commandments and endure in faith until the end, we will inherit eternal life. No gift could be greater than to enjoy the quality of life that God himself enjoys: eternal life. Nothing greater could be bestowed, nothing more supernal could be experienced, than to live as God lives. Ultimately, eternal life is a divine gift, a heavenly endowment, given by the grace of God to those who walk the gospel path with humility, integrity, and righteousness. God's work and glory is to bless us with his greatest gift: eternal life.

And now, behold, I say unto you, that the thing which will
be of the most worth unto you will be to declare repentance unto
this people, that you may bring souls unto me, that you may rest
with them in the kingdom of my Father. Amen.
DOCTRINE & COVENANTS 15:6

The Church of Jesus Christ is a vehicle for the salvation of God's children on earth. It provides the means whereby members receive the ordinances of salvation, engage together in a work of organized sacrifice, and gather to socialize with others with similar moral values. The Church offers numerous avenues for growth— various opportunities for learning, living, and sharing the gospel. The great mission of the Church is to "invite all to come unto Christ" (D&C 20:59). That mission is accomplished most directly by thousands of missionaries throughout the globe proclaiming the gospel and by our sharing personal witness with neighbors and relatives boldly but without overbearance (Alma 38:12). The Prophet Joseph Smith taught that "after all that has been said, the greatest and most important duty is to preach the Gospel" (*Teachings of the Prophet Joseph Smith*, 113). Such teaching is of greatest worth and brings the greatest satisfaction (D&C 18:10–16).

*And he has translated the book, even that
part which I have commanded him, and as your Lord
and your God liveth it is true.*

DOCTRINE & COVENANTS 17:6

Great power attends us in bearing testimony of the truthfulness of the words of God as spoken through his prophets. Faith comes by hearing the word of God as that word is preached by legal administrators, a word that is always accompanied by the spirit of prophecy and revelation (Romans 10:17; Smith, *Teachings of the Prophet Joseph Smith,* 148). Even greater power attends when God himself testifies of something. But he does more than simply bear witness. The phrase "and as your Lord and your God liveth" is an oath statement. Elder Bruce R. McConkie declared: "This is God's testimony of the Book of Mormon. In it Deity himself has laid his godhood on the line. Either the book is true or God ceases to be God. There neither is nor can be any more formal or powerful language known to men or gods" (*Ensign,* May 1982, 33).

Rely upon the things which are written; for in them
are all things written concerning the foundation of my church,
my gospel, and my rock. Wherefore, if you shall build up my
church, upon the foundation of my gospel and my rock, the
gates of hell shall not prevail against you.

DOCTRINE & COVENANTS 18:3–5

The early Saints were instructed to "rely upon the things which are written" (D&C 18:3). First, they were to rely upon the sacred teachings known to Christians and Jews throughout the world—the Holy Bible. In addition, the Saints were called upon to teach and testify of the singular truths to be found within the Book of Mormon. This "new covenant" (D&C 84:57) was foundational to the faith and essential to the establishment of the restored Church. What is true for the Church is likewise true for individual members of that Church: Our doctrinal understanding, our pattern for living, our language, and our logic ought to be grounded in the teachings of the Book of Mormon. Such a solid foundation—a foundation built upon by additional revelations and prophetic utterances—will empower us to face and thwart the fiery darts of the adversary.

*Remember the worth of
souls is great in the sight of God.*
DOCTRINE & COVENANTS 18:10

As children of a loving Father in Heaven, we are endowed with the seeds of divinity. Ours is neither a Father removed and disconnected from his children nor a spirit essence, unembodied and without affection. He is the Father of our spirits; he knows us, he loves us, he wants for us eternal happiness. His greatest joy and ultimate glory come from seeing his children become like him (Moses 1:39). We are here because a loving Father gave us life, and he provided a Savior so that we might repent and return to him. "For God so loved the world, that he gave his only begotten Son, that whosoever believeth in him should not perish, but have everlasting life" (John 3:16). We must remember who we are and Whose we are, for we were "bought with a price" (1 Corinthians 6:20). We honor our divine endowment of worth by living faithfully and becoming more like the Father and the Son.

The Lord your Redeemer suffered death in the
flesh . . . that all men might repent and come unto him.
And he hath risen again from the dead, that he might bring
all men unto him, on conditions of repentance. And how
great is his joy in the soul that repenteth!
DOCTRINE & COVENANTS 18:11–13

Our souls are precious in the sight of God. Because of the Father's great love for us, his spirit offspring, he provided a Savior, who suffered death to make it possible for us to repent and return to him in his exalted kingdom. Not only did Jesus die but he rose triumphant from the grave, victorious over death, that he might bring each of us unto him, if we repent. We must do our part; we must draw upon the powers of heaven, repent, and access the Atonement in our lives. Though it is incomprehensible to us, our Redeemer suffered the pain and sin of every person. His perfect empathy and love teach us how to find rest to the soul and everlasting happiness. His greatest joy is in seeing the sons and daughters of God humble themselves, repent, and become truly changed, "new creatures" in Christ (Mosiah 27:26). Repentance is the key that unlocks the door to eternal joy in the kingdom of God.

*Contend against no church,
save it be the church of the devil.*
DOCTRINE & COVENANTS 18:20

Elder B. H. Roberts observed that Latter-day Saints "are not brought necessarily into antagonism with the various sects of Christianity as such. So far as they have retained fragments of Christian truth—and each of them has some measure of truth—that far they are acceptable unto the Lord; and it would be poor policy for us to contend against them without discrimination. Wherever we find truth, whether it exists in complete form or only in fragments, we recognize that truth as part of that sacred whole of which the Church of Jesus Christ is the custodian. . . . All that makes for truth, for righteousness, is of God; it constitutes the kingdom of righteousness—the empire of Jehovah; and, in a certain sense at least, constitutes the Church of Christ. . . . With . . . the kingdom of righteousness . . . we have no warfare" (Conference Report, April 1906, 14–15). We are agents of the Prince of Peace, and ours is a ministry of healing and blessing.

Wherefore, all men must take upon them the
name which is given of the Father, for in that name
shall they be called at the last day.

DOCTRINE & COVENANTS 18:24

There is a name above every other name, on earth
or in heaven, save only the name of the Almighty
Elohim. The name brings joy to the desolate heart
and speaks peace to the sorrowing soul. The name falls
in hushed and hallowed tones from the lips of Saints
and angels and leads true believers on both sides of the
veil to glory everlasting. It is the name of the One sent
of God to bring salvation, the One who paid an infinite price to ransom us from Satan's grasp. It is the
blessed name of Jesus Christ. When we come unto
Christ by covenant, we take upon us his holy name,
promising to bear it with fidelity, dignity, and devotion. Like Adam and Eve, we are to "do all that thou
doest in the name of the Son, and thou shalt repent
and call upon God in the name of the Son forevermore" (Moses 5:8).

*And you shall fall down and
worship the Father in my name.*

DOCTRINE & COVENANTS 18:40

We worship God by study, prayer, meditation, sermons, lessons, service, and song. We worship God the Father and look to him as the great Governor of the universe, the Father of our spirits, and the ultimate object of our worship. It is true that we worship Christ, the Son (2 Nephi 25:29), in that we are reverentially grateful for all that he has done for us and we seek to emulate his matchless life, but our ultimate worship is reserved for the Father, "the only living and true God, . . . the only being whom [we] should worship" (D&C 20:19). This same order of worship was taught anciently. Jacob, son of Lehi, explained that the ancients "worshiped the Father in [Christ's] name, and also we worship the Father in his name" (Jacob 4:5; 2 Nephi 25:16). One day every knee will bow and every tongue "confess that Jesus Christ is Lord, to the glory of God the Father" (Philippians 2:11).

*Surely every man must repent or suffer, for I, God, am endless.
. . . Nevertheless, it is not written that there shall be no end to this
torment, but it is written* endless torment. . . . *wherefore it is
more express than other scriptures, that it might work upon the
hearts of the children of men, altogether for my name's glory.*
DOCTRINE & COVENANTS 19:4–7

All scripture attests that God is the same yesterday, today, and forever, from eternity to eternity. But what does this mean? Our God is an exalted Man of Holiness (Moses 6:57), he has a body of flesh and bones (D&C 130:22), and mortals are created in his image. Church leaders have taught that for God to be "from eternity to eternity" means that he is from one premortal existence to the next (Smith, *Doctrines of Salvation,* 1:12; McConkie, *Promised Messiah,* 166). The revelation recorded in Doctrine and Covenants 19 declares that such words as *eternal* and *endless* are descriptions, characteristics of God and of God's time; in that sense, they are nouns rather than adjectives, for God is endless and God is eternal. It was only under the influence of Greek philosophy that the words *eternal* or *eternity* came to mean timeless and without end. Eternal and endless punishment are qualitative forms of punishment, just as are eternal and endless life.

*I command you to repent. . . . For behold, I, God,
have suffered these things for all, that they might not suffer
if they would repent; but if they would not repent
they must suffer even as I.*
DOCTRINE & COVENANTS 19:15–17

The unrepentant are to be sorely punished," wrote
Elder Joseph Fielding Smith. "Our Father in heaven is
very merciful, long-suffering and forgiving. He has
promised to forgive the repentant sinner. Never has
greater love been manifest than that by our Father in
sending his Son, and by that Son in coming to the
earth, to die for man. But one of the immutable, or
eternal laws of God is that the unrepentant sinner
must suffer even as Christ suffered ([D&C 19] verses
15–18), for the blood of Christ will not cleanse those
who will not repent and in humility accept the free gift
which comes from God" (*Church History and Modern
Revelation,* 1:83). The Lord will freely forgive when we
repent with godly sorrow and sincere intent, when we
not only stop doing that which is wrong but also start
doing that which is right. If we repent, the Lord will
remember our sins no more (D&C 58:42).

Which suffering caused myself, even God, . . . to tremble
because of pain, and to bleed at every pore, and to suffer both body
and spirit—and would that I might not drink the bitter cup, and
shrink—nevertheless, glory be to the Father, and I partook
and finished my preparations unto the children of men.
DOCTRINE & COVENANTS 19:18–19

The pain and anguish that our Savior experienced so that we might be redeemed "is unfathomable by the finite minds." Great though his physical suffering was, his mental, emotional, and spiritual suffering was immeasurably greater. Truly, his agony was beyond anything in our ability to comprehend. And yet with perfect love and courageous perseverance—and with all eternity in the balance—the Savior took upon himself the burden of the sins and sorrows and pains of all humankind from Adam to the end of the world. He "overcame all the horrors that Satan . . . could inflict." He carried out his appointed mission with compassion and humility (Talmage, *Jesus the Christ*, 613). In Gethsemane and on Golgotha, he suffered for each of us, sinners one and all. He bled and died that we might live forever with God, if we would repent and come unto him. Truly, we stand all amazed at the love and grace he offers us (*Hymns*, no. 194).

Learn of me, and listen to my words; walk in the meekness
of my Spirit, and you shall have peace in me. I am Jesus Christ;
I came by the will of the Father, and I do his will.
DOCTRINE & COVENANTS 19:23–24

We are to "seek learning, even by study and also by faith" (D&C 88:118). But in the hierarchy of learning and truth, some things matter more than others. For example, it's interesting to know the plots of Shakespeare's plays, but it's vital to know the Author of eternal life. It's useful to be able to identify stars in the cosmos, but it's indispensable to know how to draw upon the powers of heaven in humble prayer. It's valuable to commit passages of scripture to memory, but it's essential that we follow the Savior by striving to become more like him. Christ did the will of his Father because of his love for him and for us. He wants us to come unto him and find peace. The Lord Jesus "so loved the world that he gave his own life, that as many as would believe might become the sons of God" (D&C 34:3). We enter into covenant kinship with him by learning of him, listening to his words, following his gospel plan, and becoming spiritually reborn.

*Of tenets thou shalt not talk, but thou shalt declare
repentance and faith on the Savior, and remission of sins
by baptism, and by fire, yea, even the Holy Ghost.*
DOCTRINE & COVENANTS 19:31

The early missionaries of this dispensation were
called to go into the world and "declare glad tidings"
(D&C 31:3). That is, they were to teach Jesus Christ
and him crucified, as revealed by a modern prophet,
Joseph Smith. Likewise today our missionaries are
called upon to teach "a portion of [Christ's] word" to
earth's inhabitants (Alma 12:9)—the first principles
and ordinances of the gospel and what investigators
must know in order to inquire of God and learn the
truth for themselves by revelation. Tenets are doctrines, teachings, or dogma. Doctrine and Covenants
19:31 essentially teaches us that in delivering the message of the Restoration to the world, we need not (and
should not) dot every doctrinal "i" or cross every theo-
logical "t." It is the simple and straightforward proclamation of divine truth that leads to lasting conversion.

Pay the debt thou hast contracted. . . .
Release thyself from bondage.
DOCTRINE & COVENANTS 19:35

Prophets have long counseled the Saints to live within their means and stay out of debt. Materialism and acquisitiveness are slavery; they lead only to disappointment and misery. Crippling debt can destroy a marriage and drain the joys out of family life. President Gordon B. Hinckley has said: "We have been seduced into believing that borrowed money has no penalty, that financial bondage is an acceptable way to live. I suggest that it is not. We would do well to be modest and prudent in our expenditures, to discipline our purchasing and avoid debt to the extent possible, to pay off debt quickly, and to free ourselves from the bondage of others" (*Stand a Little Taller,* 74). Just as we desire to be spiritually free from the bondage of sin, so we must strive to be temporally free from the bondage of debt. We are to be industrious and self-reliant, wise stewards of our resources, and humble enough to live prudently.

*After it was truly manifested unto this first elder
that he had received a remission of his sins, he was
entangled again in the vanities of the world.*
DOCTRINE & COVENANTS 20:5

Young Joseph Smith went into the grove of trees in
the spring of 1820 for two reasons. He wanted to know
which of all the churches was right, for the thought that
the true church was not on the earth had not occurred
to him (Joseph Smith–History 1:18). In addition,
Joseph went into the grove seeking a remission of his
sins and striving to improve his standing before the
Almighty. In two of the dictated accounts of that great
theophany (1832, 1835), Joseph was told: "Thy sins are
forgiven thee" (Backman, *Joseph Smith's First Vision,* 157,
159). It was after he had learned that his sins had been
remitted and that he would be an instrument in the
hands of God in restoring the true church to earth
again that young Joseph found himself "entangled again
in the vanities of the world" (D&C 20:5). Thus, he
sought God once more, was visited by Moroni, rein-
stated in the divine favor, and readied for the manifestations, revelations, and visitations to come.

[The Book of Mormon] contains a record of a
fallen people, and the fulness of the gospel of Jesus Christ
to the Gentiles and to the Jews also.
DOCTRINE & COVENANTS 20:9

The Doctrine and Covenants testifies that the Book of Mormon is a "record of a fallen people" (D&C 20:9), a chronicle of the rise and fall of two major civilizations—the Jaredites and the Lehites. In both cases these powerful nations allowed themselves to become ensnared by secret combinations and succumbed to pride and arrogance, which are destructive to individual souls and entire nations. Perhaps less obvious, the Book of Mormon is a haunting reminder of the nature of fallen man, a sobering testimonial that unless people put off the natural man and put on Christ, unless they acknowledge their weakness and seek his strength, they remain lost and fallen forever. The message of the Book of Mormon is clear and penetrating, that "salvation was, and is, and is to come, in and through the atoning blood of Christ, the Lord Omnipotent" (Mosiah 3:18).

There is a God in heaven, who is infinite and eternal, from everlasting to everlasting the same unchangeable God, the framer of heaven and earth, and all things which are in them.

DOCTRINE & COVENANTS 20:17

Joseph Smith taught that God "changes not, neither is there variableness with him; but that he is the same from everlasting to everlasting, being the same yesterday, to-day, and for ever; and that his course is one eternal round, without variation" (*Lectures on Faith,* 3:15). God's plan for the creation and redemption of his children is eternal; his work and glory—"to bring to pass the immortality and eternal life of man" (Moses 1:39)—is forever the same. Nephi taught that God is unchanging, "and the way is prepared for all men from the foundation of the world, if it so be that they repent and come unto him" (1 Nephi 10:18). Policies and procedures in the administration of the Lord's Church may change, but the principles are eternal, for "God doth not walk in crooked paths, . . . neither doth he vary from that which he hath said, therefore his paths are straight, and his course is one eternal round" (D&C 3:2).

*As many as would believe and be baptized in his holy name, and
endure in faith to the end, should be saved—not only those who
believed after he came in the meridian of time, in the flesh, but all
those from the beginning, . . . as well as those who should come after.*

DOCTRINE & COVENANTS 20:25–27

Jesus Christ brought to pass an infinite atonement.
It is infinite because it overcomes the most universal
fact of mortality: physical death (2 Nephi 9:7). It is
infinite because it was performed by an infinite Being,
One who had within himself the powers of Godhood,
the powers of immortality (John 10:17–18; Alma
34:14). It is infinite because it reaches beyond this
earth to the untold numbers of worlds created by the
Lord Jehovah: Jesus redeems all that he creates (D&C
76:24; Moses 1:33–35). It is infinite because it is timeless: Christ is the Lamb slain from the foundation of
the world (Revelation 13:8; Moses 7:47). His atoning
sacrifice in the meridian of time reached back to take
effect from the days of Adam and forward through
time until the last person is born, lives, and is
redeemed.

MARCH

*Wherefore, meaning the church, thou shalt
give heed unto all his words and commandments which he shall give unto you as he
receiveth them, walking in all holiness before
me; for his word ye shall receive, as if from
mine own mouth, in all patience and faith.*

DOCTRINE & COVENANTS
21:4–5

Father, Son, and Holy Ghost are one God,
infinite and eternal, without end. Amen.
DOCTRINE & COVENANTS 20:28

Some have thought that Doctrine and Covenants 20:28 seems to convey the notion that there are not three Gods but one. Joseph Smith's first vision represents the beginning of the revelation of God to man in our day, and it shows clearly that the Father and the Son are distinct personages and distinct Gods. And yet there is a unity, a divine indwelling relationship that exists among the members of the Godhead such that they are infinitely more one than they are separate. Their oneness may be described as follows: They are three separate persons, each of whom possesses all the attributes of godliness in perfection. Further, they are a completely united, divine community of beings whose oneness is occasionally expressed in the scriptural formula "they are one God" (2 Nephi 31:21; Alma 11:44; 3 Nephi 11:23–25; Mormon 7:7). Their oneness is a lesson, a signal, a call for all true disciples to likewise be one.

*And we know that justification through the grace
of our Lord and Savior Jesus Christ is just and true.*
DOCTRINE & COVENANTS 20:30

To be justified before God is to be made right, declared innocent, pronounced clean. If it were possible, one way to attain God's justification would be to live God's law perfectly, traversing life's paths without error. Anyone who so lived could be described as one who was justified by works or by law; however, Jesus alone lived a perfect life (Hebrews 4:15; 1 Peter 2:22). Truly, "by the deeds of the law there shall no flesh be justified" (Romans 3:20; 2 Nephi 2:5). Thus, the only real way to attain justification from God is to lean upon the One who did live the law of God perfectly. We must exercise faith in Jesus Christ—have complete confidence in him and maintain a ready reliance upon him. Though we strive to do good works and show our conversion by our deeds, in the end it is by the grace of God that we are pronounced clean and thus prepared to dwell in the Holy Presence.

And we know also, that sanctification through the grace of our Lord and Savior Jesus Christ is just and true, to all those who love and serve God with all their mights, minds, and strength.

DOCTRINE & COVENANTS 20:31

As we come unto Christ by covenant and receive the ordinances of salvation, we are justified by him— our slate is wiped clean, and we are treated as if we had never sinned. Justification thus deals with our legal standing before God. Thereafter, we cultivate the influence of the Holy Spirit in our lives so that his divine influence can direct, empower, and cleanse us from the effects of sin. To be so cleansed is to be sanctified, to enjoy a change of state. This change also is a gift, a manifestation of God's grace. "Therefore they were . . . sanctified, and their garments were washed white through the blood of the Lamb. Now they, after being sanctified by the Holy Ghost, having their garments made white, being pure and spotless before God, could not look upon sin save it were with abhorrence; and there were many, exceedingly great many, who were made pure and entered into the rest of the Lord their God" (Alma 13:11–12).

And the members shall manifest before the church, and also before the elders, by a godly walk and conversation, that they are worthy of it, that there may be works and faith agreeable to the holy scriptures—walking in holiness before the Lord.
DOCTRINE & COVENANTS 20:69

The apostle Paul taught that the natural man, the unregenerated individual, brings forth the "works of the flesh" (Galatians 5:19), the sins and spiritual flaws that are only so obvious in the life of one who has spurned the gracious gift of the Atonement. On the other hand, Paul taught, those who have put on Christ enjoy the "fruit of the Spirit" (Galatians 5:22), the sweet manifestations of righteousness that follow naturally from a changed heart. Paul concluded, "If we live in the Spirit, let us also walk in the Spirit" (Galatians 5:25). In today's parlance, if we talk the talk we really ought to walk the walk. There's something different about individuals who have been born again, who have given themselves to the Lord and his work and whose highest aspiration is to learn the will of God and do it. They evidence that they are worthy of membership in the Lord's Church, and their walk and talk are uplifting to everyone they meet.

For his word ye shall receive, as if from mine own mouth, in all patience and faith. For by doing these things . . . the Lord God will disperse the powers of darkness from before you, and cause the heavens to shake for your good, and his name's glory.

DOCTRINE & COVENANTS 21:5–6

The importance of the law of the prophets was underscored by its being revealed at the organization of The Church of Jesus Christ of Latter-day Saints at Peter Whitmer's farmhouse, 6 April 1830. This law, like the law of the Sabbath or the law of tithing or the law of chastity, sets forth an admonition and an associated blessing: follow the prophet and be blessed; reject him and suffer. If we heed the words and commandments that the Lord's anointed prophet gives us, we will receive transcendent blessings both here and hereafter. Hell and its damning effects will have no power over us. The darkness of sin and arrogance will be dispersed. Heaven will pour out blessings of peace and joy as we walk in holiness before the Lord and humbly follow his prophet. In all ages, the Lord works through choice seers and inspired prophets who are foreordained to their appointed missions (Amos 3:7). Our responsibility is to patiently, faithfully, and wholeheartedly follow them.

This is a new and an everlasting covenant. . . . Wherefore, although a man should be baptized an hundred times it availeth him nothing, for you cannot enter in at the strait gate by the law of Moses, neither by your dead works.

DOCTRINE & COVENANTS 22:1–2

Early converts to the Church wondered if they needed to be baptized again if they had previously been baptized by immersion in another church. The Lord instructed the Saints that his house is a house of order and that certain principles and practices are eternal and cannot be bypassed. An ordinance performed without the Lord's true authority is invalid; no covenant is established; no sealing by the Spirit takes place. Dead works are just that—dead, without power or efficacy. Every ordinance depends upon the presence of the Spirit for life. The Holy Ghost must ratify, or seal, an ordinance for it to be a valid, living covenant (D&C 132:7). For that to be possible, both proper priesthood authority to transact the ordinance and worthiness on the part of the covenant maker are necessary (Articles of Faith 1:5). Thus, baptism is both a new and an everlasting covenant, revealed anew to the Saints in the dispensation of the fulness of times and binding in all dispensations.

Be patient in afflictions, for thou shalt have many; but endure them, for, lo, I am with thee, even unto the end of thy days.
DOCTRINE & COVENANTS 24:8

The persecution of Joseph Smith had become intense by the summer of 1830 and would only increase. But the Lord, ever mindful of his prophet and his faithful associates, continued to strengthen, encourage, and instruct. From the earliest days of the Prophet's ministry, the Lord told him forthrightly that he would have many afflictions. With honesty, authenticity, and perfect empathy, the Lord—who understands better than anyone what persecution and affliction mean—encouraged his latter-day prophet to remain steadfast and faithful, looking to the Lord for comfort, guidance, and strength. Likewise, when we feel weighed down by despair and discouragement, the Lord beckons us to come unto him. When we feel we cannot go on, the Lord offers rest to our souls. When we are true and faithful, the Lord is with us every step of the way.

Thou shalt lay aside the things of this world,
and seek for the things of a better.
DOCTRINE & COVENANTS 25:10

The world crowds upon us, enticing and beckoning us to partake of its allurements. Power, prestige, and possessions are what matter on the worldly scoreboard. But the Lord, ever encouraging us toward Zion and treasures in heaven, admonishes us to step out of the worldly mainstream and seek for that which is of everlasting worth. Elder Boyd K. Packer has said, "The choice of life is not between fame and fortune, nor between wealth and poverty, but between good and evil" (*Memorable Stories and Parables,* 47). The things that matter to the Lord are the things that should matter to us. Certainly, the Lord of the universe is not impressed by wealth or celebrity. He cares greatly about the integrity of our hearts, our willingness to love and to forgive, our selfless service to others, our obedience to truth, our faithfulness to God and his Son. Where our treasure is, there will our hearts be also (Matthew 6:19–21).

*For my soul delighteth in the song of the heart; yea,
the song of the righteous is a prayer unto me, and it shall be
answered with a blessing upon their heads.*
DOCTRINE & COVENANTS 25:12

The song of a righteous heart is a prayer unto the Lord. He delights when we sing with love, reverence, and worship. Music is the universal language of the Saints. Since the earliest days of this dispensation (and we suppose in every dispensation beginning with Adam), inspiring, worshipful music and singing have been part of the everlasting gospel. In meetings large and small, at home and in congregations, in conferences and solemn assemblies, the Saints have lifted their voices in praise and thanks. Oftimes, the soul's sincere desire is more fully expressed in song. Music can invite the Spirit and touch hearts with a power that transcends the spoken word. It matters not if our voice is beautiful or our pitch perfect. What matters is that we lift our voices in song with righteous hearts and sincere expression.

*Behold, I say unto you that you shall let your time
be devoted to the studying of the scriptures, and to preaching,
and to confirming the church at Colesville, and to performing
your labors on the land, such as is required.*

DOCTRINE & COVENANTS 26:1

In June 1830 Joseph Smith began a serious study of the King James Version of the Bible. Acting by appointment and direction (D&C 42:56; 76:15), the Prophet and his scribes read the Bible and made alterations according to the promptings of the Spirit. In the process, more than 3,400 verses were altered. This branch of Joseph Smith's calling as a translator (Smith, *History of the Church,* 1:238) was a significant means by which plain and precious truths were restored, as prophesied in the Book of Mormon (1 Nephi 13:20–40). This work was an important part of the Prophet's spiritual education and became the impetus for the receipt of several revelations in the Doctrine and Covenants (D&C 74; 76; 77; 91; 132). Joseph Smith's inspired translation of the Bible is one of the great evidences of his prophetic call, a vital means by which the Bible has begun to be restored to its pristine purity.

*Wherefore, lift up your hearts and rejoice, and gird up
your loins, and take upon you my whole armor, that ye may be
able to withstand the evil day, having done all,
that ye may be able to stand.*

DOCTRINE & COVENANTS 27:15

The apostle Paul taught the Ephesian Saints to put on the whole armor of God, "that ye may be able to stand against the wiles of the devil" (Ephesians 6:11). The doctrine of morality and the principles of chastity and virtue have been given to assist us and our posterity to remain free from moral taint. We fend off the blows of the evil one through personal righteousness and stand among those whose feet are considered beautiful because they proclaim the message of salvation. Our faith in the Lord Jesus Christ empowers us to withstand and overcome temptation (Alma 37:33). We fight against orchestrated evil by wielding the sword of the Spirit, cultivating that sacred influence in our life that directs our path and cleanses our soul. The helmet of salvation, or, more specifically, the helmet of the hope of salvation (1 Thessalonians 5:8), is the sweet assurance that our lives are in order and we are on course to gain eternal life.

*No one shall be appointed to receive commandments and
revelations in this church excepting my servant Joseph Smith,
Jun., for he receiveth them even as Moses. . . . And thou shalt not
command him who is at thy head, and at the head of the church.*
DOCTRINE & COVENANTS 28:2–6

In the fall of 1830, the Church was a young and inexperienced organization. When Hiram Page professed to receive revelations concerning the Church, some members became confused. The Prophet Joseph Smith inquired of the Lord, and line upon line, the Lord revealed the order and structure of his latter-day kingdom. One fundamental governing principle is that the Lord reveals his will for members of the Church through a duly authorized prophet (D&C 28:7). Another is that "all things must be done in order" and by common consent (D&C 28:13). Each of us is to seek the spirit of revelation for our own lives and for those in our stewardship, but the prophet is the Lord's sole mouthpiece for the Church, his only spokesman on the earth. He is the one who presides over the whole Church. He is the one who possesses the keys of the priesthood (D&C 107:91–92; 132:7). We are to keep our eyes firmly fixed on the Lord and his prophet.

*Listen to the voice of Jesus Christ, your Redeemer, the
Great I Am, whose arm of mercy hath atoned for your sins.*
DOCTRINE & COVENANTS 29:1

Jesus Christ wrought the infinite and intimate atonement for each of us individually and all of us collectively. Drawing upon the power of the Atonement begins when we listen to his voice and reach for his outstretched hand. In sickness and in health, in good times and bad, our lives improve and become more peaceful and joyous when we turn to our Redeemer. Although we, like Nephi, "do not know the meaning of all things," yet we may always have the full assurance that God "loveth his children" (1 Nephi 11:17). His love and mercy toward us are constant and everlasting. The Savior beckons: "Come unto me, all ye that labour and are heavy laden, and I will give you rest. Take my yoke upon you, and learn of me; for I am meek and lowly in heart: and ye shall find rest unto your souls" (Matthew 11:28–30). Listen to his voice; accept his atoning invitation.

And ye are called to bring to pass the gathering of mine elect; for mine elect hear my voice and harden not their hearts.

DOCTRINE & COVENANTS 29:7

Latter-day Saints go into all the world to preach the gospel to every creature, striving to do so by the power of the Holy Ghost. When these servants of the Lord speak by the power of the Spirit, those who are listening with real intent will hear the voice of their Master, a voice that they had come to know very well in the premortal life that preceded this life on earth. That is what the Savior meant when he taught in the meridian of time: "My sheep hear my voice, and I know them, and they follow me" (John 10:27). The elect of God thus identify themselves by accepting the proclamation of truth when it is delivered by legal administrators of God's church and kingdom.

*For I will reveal myself from heaven with power and
great glory, with all the hosts thereof, and dwell in righteousness with
men on earth a thousand years, and the wicked shall not stand.*

DOCTRINE & COVENANTS 29:11

Despite the challenges and pains of mortality, life
is good and is meant to be enjoyed. And yet, in a not
too distant future, the Lord Jesus will return to earth
in power and great glory. The Prophet Joseph Smith
taught: "Christ and the resurrected Saints will reign
over the earth during the thousand years. They will
not probably dwell upon the earth, but will visit it
when they please, or when it is necessary to govern it"
(*Teachings of the Prophet Joseph Smith,* 268). The wicked
will be destroyed, the righteous will be lifted up, and
the earth will become for a thousand years a paradise.
Pain and death and heartache and tears will be no
more. Righteousness will prevail. Though there is
much in this life that brings satisfaction and enjoyment, the righteous look forward with an eye of faith
to the future. They echo the plea of John the
Revelator: "Even so, come, Lord Jesus" (Revelation
22:20).

*But, behold, verily I say unto you, before the earth
shall pass away, Michael, mine archangel, shall sound his
trump, and then shall all the dead awake, for their graves shall
be opened, and they shall come forth—yea, even all.*

DOCTRINE & COVENANTS 29:26

Jesus was the "firstfruits of them that slept" (1 Corinthians 15:20). After he rose from the tomb, the righteous dead from the days of Adam to the meridian of time came forth from the grave (Mosiah 15:21). The first resurrection will resume when the Savior returns to the earth in power and glory. Michael (or Adam, the Ancient of Days) has been delegated "the keys of salvation under the counsel and direction of the Holy One, who is without beginning of days or end of life" (D&C 78:16). Joseph Smith taught that as the father of the human family, Adam (or Michael) oversees angelic ministrations and the proper administration of the keys of the priesthood and the ordinances of salvation (*Teachings of the Prophet Joseph Smith,* 167–68). Thus, when Christ returns in glory and at Michael's signal, the graves will once again be opened, the righteous dead will have body and spirit joined forever, and the blessings of immortality and eternal life will be theirs.

*But behold, I say unto you, that little children
are redeemed from the foundation of the world through
mine Only Begotten; wherefore, they cannot sin, for power
is not given unto Satan to tempt little children, until they
begin to become accountable before me.*

DOCTRINE & COVENANTS 29:46–47

Are little children innocent? The obvious answer is yes. Less obvious is why. The humanistic explanation is that little children are innocent by nature—they're just that way. They are always kind and patient, eager to share, and never cross or irritable. So much for that explanation. But the scriptural explanation is clear: Little children are innocent because they are decreed so by and through the atonement of Jesus Christ. They may be guilty of deeds that you and I might consider sins, but "they cannot sin" in the sense that such sins are covered by the Savior until the children reach the age of accountability. In addition, the sweet message of revelation tells us that those who never become mentally accountable are open to the tender mercies of a loving Savior who treasures all the children of his Father (D&C 29:49–50).

You have feared man and have not relied on me
for strength as you ought. But your mind has been on the
things of the earth more than on the things of me, your Maker,
and the ministry whereunto you have been called; and
you have not given heed unto my Spirit.

DOCTRINE & COVENANTS 30:1–2

Trusting in the arm of flesh is akin to fearing the world. If we are afraid of what we might miss out on by holding fast to the iron rod of the gospel, if we focus so much on this world because the hereafter seems so far away, if we rely on present gratifications rather than eternal rewards, we show fear and faithlessness. We cannot be passive in our covenant relationship with the Savior. We must be actively involved in growing spiritually. Each of us has been called and elected to live worthily so that we might enjoy the quality of life that God himself enjoys—eternal life. To do so, we must humbly heed the promptings of the Spirit of the Lord, meekly center our hearts on everlasting things, and steadfastly follow the prophet and other authorized leaders.

Lift up your heart and rejoice, for the hour of your mission is come; and your tongue shall be loosed. . . . You shall declare the things which have been revealed to my servant, Joseph Smith, Jun. You shall begin to preach from this time forth, yea, to reap in the field which is white already to be burned.

DOCTRINE & COVENANTS 31:3–4

The instruction given to Thomas B. Marsh regarding how to proclaim the restored gospel is true for us today as well. Elder Marsh was called upon to lift up his heart and rejoice, to "declare glad tidings of great joy" (D&C 31:3). What was he to do? Was he to deliver again the Sermon on the Mount? Was he to teach once again the Bread of Life sermon? Was he to go into all the world quoting hundreds of passages from the Old and New Testaments? No, he was to declare the glad tidings of the Restoration, to make known the things that had been revealed through Christ's preeminent, prophetic revealer, Joseph Smith. In short, Thomas B. Marsh was instructed to be true and loyal to the message of the Restoration. In so doing, he would avoid the condemnation, scourge, and judgment that come to those who treat lightly that which God has revealed in these latter days (D&C 43:15–16; 49:1–4; 84:56–58).

Be patient in afflictions, revile not against those that
revile. Govern your house in meekness, and be steadfast.
DOCTRINE & COVENANTS 31:9

Doctrine and Covenants 31 is a revelation given
through the Prophet Joseph to Thomas B. Marsh in
1830, five years before the first Quorum of the Twelve
Apostles in this dispensation was organized. Had
Brother Marsh, who later served as president of the
Twelve, continued to follow the Lord's counsel, his subsequent apostasy from the Church could have been
averted. The Lord foresaw potential problems and gave
him relevant counsel. Thomas needed to be patient with
the decisions of priesthood leaders; he needed to set his
house in order and govern it in meekness; he needed to
remain faithful and obedient to the end. This counsel is
for each of us. We must be meek and humble, patient
and faithful. Sometimes we are given trials and afflictions
to test our faithfulness. These are the tests of discipleship. Will we taste the bitter cup without becoming bitter? Will we endure our adversities well, unto the end?
Will we hold fast to the iron rod even in affliction?

*Pray always, lest you enter into temptation and lose
your reward. Be faithful unto the end, and lo, I am with you.*
DOCTRINE & COVENANTS 31:12–13

Loved and respected by the early Saints, Thomas B.
Marsh served as the first president of the Quorum of
the Twelve in this dispensation, went on missions, and
faithfully defended the Prophet Joseph Smith against
dissidents. But pride and the spirit of apostasy pushed
the Spirit of the Lord from his heart. He became
estranged from the Church because of leaders' decisions
regarding his wife's dishonest domestic dealings. For
nineteen years he remained away. At last he begged for
forgiveness and asked to be rebaptized. Aged beyond his
fifty-seven years from the afflictions of apostasy, Brother
Marsh was a broken man when he stood before a congregation in Salt Lake City and pleaded with the Saints
to avoid the mistakes he had made. We can learn from
his example. We can pray that we will be obedient and
faithful to the end. We can seek for the strength to
avoid temptation, to be humble, and to stand by the
Brethren who lead the Lord's Church today.

*Declare my gospel and learn of me, and be meek
and lowly of heart. . . . give heed to that which is written,
and pretend to no other revelation; and they shall pray always
that I may unfold the same to their understanding.*
DOCTRINE & COVENANTS 32:1–4

Some early members of the Church expressed interest in preaching the gospel to the Lamanites. The Lord, who directs the missionary work of his Church, granted their desires and gave counsel and instruction regarding their efforts. These missionaries were to learn the gospel, be humble, go forth in the strength of the Lord, knowing that he would be with them and protect them (D&C 32:3), and preach the words given to the Lord's prophet and none other. This is a model for all who desire to spread the gospel message. Yes, we are entitled to receive revelation in our own callings and stewardships, but only the prophet is authorized by the Lord to speak to the entire membership of the Church (D&C 21:4–6; 28:2–3). This first mission to the Lamanites found success in unexpected, unplanned places. Like all faithful missionary labors, it bore rich fruit that is still being harvested today.

Repent and be baptized, every one of you, for a remission of your sins; yea, be baptized even by water, and then cometh the baptism of fire and of the Holy Ghost. . . . and remember that they shall have faith in me or they can in nowise be saved.

DOCTRINE & COVENANTS 33:11–12

Ordinances themselves do not save us; rather, Christ the Person saves us. Yet ordinances are outward expressions of our inward covenant to come unto Christ. Baptism by water symbolizes our acceptance of the Atonement, our willingness to go down into the watery tomb by burying the old man of sin and coming forth unto "newness of life" (Romans 6:4). Though we speak of our sins being washed away through baptism by water (Acts 22:16; D&C 39:10), a remission of sins comes only after we have received the gift of the Holy Ghost, who is the Sanctifier (2 Nephi 31:17). The Prophet taught: "You might as well baptize a bag of sand as a man, if not done in view of the remission of sins and getting of the Holy Ghost. Baptism by water is but half a baptism, and is good for nothing without the other half—that is, the baptism of the Holy Ghost" (*Teachings of the Prophet Joseph Smith*, 314; see also 360).

*Be faithful, praying always, having your lamps
trimmed and burning, and oil with you, that you may
be ready at the coming of the Bridegroom.*
DOCTRINE & COVENANTS 33:17

When the tests of life inevitably come, cramming does little good. Either we are prepared, or we are not. Either our loved ones are prepared, or they are not. "The kind of oil that is needed to illuminate the way and light up the darkness is not shareable," said President Spencer W. Kimball. "How can one share obedience to the principle of tithing; a mind at peace from righteous living; an accumulation of knowledge? How can one share faith or testimony? How can one share attitudes or chastity, or the experience of a mission? How can one share temple privileges? Each must obtain that kind of oil for himself" (*Faith Precedes the Miracle,* 255–56). When a priesthood blessing is needed, the time of preparation is over for that priesthood bearer. Spiritual preparedness takes time, effort, righteous choices, and willing sacrifice. Spiritual strength that endures over time comes from humble submission and faithful obedience to the Lord's plan of happiness.

*Who so loved the world that he gave his own
life, that as many as would believe might become the
sons of God. Wherefore you are my son.*
DOCTRINE & COVENANTS 34:3

This verse, a restatement of John 3:16 for the benefit of Elder Orson Pratt, sets forth one of the grand purposes of the gospel of Jesus Christ. The gospel is intended to do far more than help people get along with each other, as important as that is. It is intended to do more than make bad people into good people, although that is also important. The gospel is "the power of God unto salvation" (Romans 1:16), a power that not only forgives our sins and cleanses our souls but also reinstates us in the royal family of God. Acceptance of the fulness of the gospel and faithful participation in the ordinances of exaltation empower us to become the sons and daughters of God. As such, when Jesus "shall appear, we shall be like him; for we shall see him as he is" (1 John 3:2).

I say unto my servant Sidney, I have looked upon
thee and thy works. I have heard thy prayers, and prepared
thee for a greater work. . . . Behold thou wast sent forth, even
as John, to prepare the way before me, and before Elijah
which should come, and thou knewest it not.

DOCTRINE & COVENANTS 35:3–4

Marvelous things happen when we surrender our lives and submit our wills to an omniscient God. The prophets have repeatedly taught us that God can do far more with us than we can do with ourselves, especially if we are left to our own limited resources. As intelligent a man as Sidney Rigdon was, he had no idea that the Lord, through his Holy Spirit, was working upon him and preparing him and those within his congregations for the richer blessings of the fulness of the gospel. Truly, Sidney was an Elias, a forerunner, one who was sent to lay the foundation and prepare the hearts of hundreds of people to receive the everlasting gospel when it was preached by the early Latter-day Saint missionaries. Like Sidney, many of us do good things, but if we will open ourselves to divine guidance, the Almighty can accomplish even greater things through us.

*And there are none that doeth good except those
who are ready to receive the fulness of my gospel,
which I have sent forth unto this generation.*
DOCTRINE & COVENANTS 35:12

A lawyer once asked Jesus: "Good Master, what good thing shall I do, that I may have eternal life? And he said unto him, Why callest thou me good? there is none good but one, that is, God" (Matthew 19:16–17). God's perfection is the standard against which we judge all things. To achieve anything less than the highest standard is to fall short of the divine ideal. And so it is with our response to hearing the fulness of the gospel. Clearly, the Lord is not saying that there are no good people outside The Church of Jesus Christ of Latter-day Saints. There are many devoted, God-fearing, Christ-seeking individuals in the world who are striving to live in harmony with the light they possess. But our Heavenly Father cannot be completely satisfied with their standing before him until they have the opportunity to get on the path that leads to the divine ideal.

*And I have sent forth the fulness of my gospel by the hand
of my servant Joseph; and in weakness have I blessed him.*
DOCTRINE & COVENANTS 35:17

Joseph Smith never claimed to be perfect (*History of
the Church,* 6:366). Like us, he was human, with
strengths and weaknesses, imperfections and flaws. In
fact, he was blessed with weaknesses so that he might
be humble, teachable, and dependent on the Lord. He
was no more than a man but no less than a prophet of
God: the one called from the foundation of the world
to restore the truth, to translate the ancient record
containing the fulness of the gospel, to usher in the
last and greatest of all dispensations. Because no perfect person but Jesus has ever walked the earth, the
Lord has always done his work through the weak and
the simple. It is reassuring to know that the Lord
works through imperfect people. Whom the Lord
calls, he qualifies—when they are steadfast, diligent,
and have their eye single to his glory.

*And a commandment I give unto thee—that thou shalt
write for him; and the scriptures shall be given, even as they are
in mine own bosom, to the salvation of mine own elect.*
DOCTRINE & COVENANTS 35:20

Sidney Rigdon was called by God to act as a scribe to
the Prophet in what we know now as the Joseph Smith
Translation of the Bible. Although others served as
scribes in this great prophetic enterprise (Oliver
Cowdery, Emma Smith, John Whitmer, and Frederick
G. Williams), Sidney was the principal scribe; he was to
the Joseph Smith Translation what Oliver Cowdery was
to the Book of Mormon. The Lord said the scriptures
would be given to the translators "even as they are in my
own bosom" (D&C 35:20). That is, God would give
through Joseph Smith scriptural insight that mirrored
the thinking and feelings of the Almighty. Because we
are commanded to live by every word that proceeds
from the mouth of God (D&C 84:44), the inspired
translation of the Bible serves as more than a helpful
commentary, more than a useful historical device, more
even than an alternative version of scripture. Receiving it
in faith would lead to the salvation of souls.

*And I will lay my hand upon you by the hand of my
servant Sidney Rigdon, and you shall receive my Spirit,
the Holy Ghost, even the Comforter, which shall
teach you the peaceable things of the kingdom.*

DOCTRINE & COVENANTS 36:2

Those who are called to bear the priesthood receive
a divine investiture of authority. God is our Principal,
and as bearers of the priesthood, we are his agents. In
a very real sense, as agents we do not have the right to
do things our way; we must do things his way, for
"whatever ye do according to the will of the Lord is the
Lord's business" (D&C 64:29). The truest exercise of
our moral agency is therefore in learning and carrying
out the will of our Principal. Those who act by divine
authority act in his name. Those who speak by divine
authority speak in his name. Thus, when a priesthood
bearer is properly ordained and living so as to qualify
for the promptings and guidance of the Holy Spirit,
his deeds—whether prayers or sermons or ordinances—are His deeds; it is as though the Almighty
were performing the acts himself.

*Again, a commandment I give unto the church,
that it is expedient in me that they should assemble
together at the Ohio, against the time that my servant
Oliver Cowdery shall return unto them.*
DOCTRINE & COVENANTS 37:3

Individuals and nations are scattered when they reject the true Messiah and forsake his Church and doctrine. Conversely, they are gathered when they come unto Christ by covenant, accept his doctrine, and congregate with the faithful. The gathering is first to Christ, the Person, and second, to a place, a location. That is, first we are gathered spiritually and then temporally. Once we have been baptized into the true Church, receive the gift of the Holy Ghost, and are thereby qualified to associate with the household of faith, we then prepare to participate in the final phase of gathering. "What was the object of gathering the Jews, or the people of God in any age of the world? . . . The main object was to build unto the Lord a house whereby He could reveal unto His people the ordinances of His house and the glories of His kingdom, and teach the people the way of salvation" (Smith, *Teachings of the Prophet Joseph Smith,* 307–8).

APRIL

It shall not be given to any one to go forth to
preach my gospel, or to build up my church,
except he be ordained by some one who has
authority, and it is known to the church that
he has authority and has been regularly
ordained by the heads of the church.

DOCTRINE & COVENANTS
42:11

But behold, verily, verily, I say unto you that mine eyes are upon you. I am in your midst and ye cannot see me.
DOCTRINE & COVENANTS 38:7

Our God is not, as the deists proclaimed, the divine watchmaker who winds up the universe and lets it run down on its own. He is not a distant Deity, nor is he an absentee God. He is close to his people, as close as they will allow him to be. The Prophet Joseph Smith taught that the disembodied spirits of the just are not far from us, and so it is with him who is the Lord of the living and the dead (*Teachings of the Prophet Joseph Smith,* 326). We may see him now only with the eye of faith, but the day is coming when we will see him even as he now sees us. This sobering reality ought to affect our speech, our actions, and our attitudes, for we know full well that we live and move and have our being in the midst of those charged to look after us and oversee the work of God's kingdom.

And let every man esteem his brother as himself,
and practice virtue and holiness before me.
DOCTRINE & COVENANTS 38:24

The brotherhood and sisterhood of faithful Latter-day Saints is one of the sweetest aspects of the restored gospel of Jesus Christ. We are united in our devotion to the Lord; united in faith, belief, and doctrine; united in our desire to serve others and build Zion. As fellow believers, we are to hold our brothers and sisters in the gospel in high esteem, to be concerned for their welfare, and to look after them with kindness and respect. We are to follow the admonition of Paul that "no one of you be puffed up for one against another" (I Corinthians 4:6). Christ gave us the vital commandment "that ye love one another; as I have loved you, that ye also love one another. By this shall all men know that ye are my disciples, if ye have love one to another" (John 13:34–35). We demonstrate the virtues of holiness most vividly in how we regard and treat our fellow beings.

If ye are prepared ye shall not fear.
DOCTRINE & COVENANTS 38:30

The chief weapon in Satan's arsenal is fear. The father of lies whispers to us that authentic gospel living is too hard, that life is essentially hopeless, that all people are ultimately hypocrites, that we cannot *really* change or be forgiven. The Master, conversely, speaks the truth and wants for us everlasting happiness and eternal life. Despite the trials and temptations of life, we need to have hope in the Lord and trust his promises. To live in peace and joy, here and hereafter, we must go forward with faith. Life is never easy. But we can do our part to be prepared. We can stand faithful with the Saints. We can earnestly keep our covenants. We can be humble and prayerful. We can feast upon the words of eternal life from the scriptures and the living prophets. We can be anxiously engaged in serving others. We will then have no need to fear the coming day of the Lord but will look forward with eagerness.

*If ye seek the riches which it is the will of the Father
to give unto you, ye shall be the richest of all people, for ye shall
have the riches of eternity; and it must needs be that the riches
of the earth are mine to give; but beware of pride.*

DOCTRINE & COVENANTS 38:39

The Book of Mormon is a vivid account of the pride cycle. The Lord pours out blessings upon his people and yet in time many of those people become proud and wicked, ultimately turning against the gospel verities that once touched their hearts. The lust for riches has been present in every dispensation, but the love of money, obsession with material things, acquisitiveness in all its varieties, will have no place in the glorious hereafter. Those who do the works of righteousness will receive the riches of eternity—peace in this life and "eternal life in the world to come" (D&C 59:23). What can worldly wealth possibly mean to him who is Eternal? What can the things of this earth mean to him who is Everlasting, without beginning or end? We are to be humble and content with what the Lord has given us (Alma 29:3).

*And this is my gospel—repentance and baptism
by water, and then cometh the baptism of fire and the Holy
Ghost, even the Comforter, which showeth all things, and
teacheth the peaceable things of the kingdom.*

DOCTRINE & COVENANTS 39:6

The gospel of Jesus Christ is the glad tidings that the Son of God came into the world to ransom us from death and sin and eternal unhappiness (D&C 76:40–42). It is the good news that redemption from the Fall and deliverance from the effects of individual sins are available to every accountable person on conditions of repentance. But the gospel is also described in scripture as the good news that can be appropriated into our personal lives through receiving what the Prophet Joseph called "the articles of adoption": those actions and rites that enable us to be adopted into the family of the Lord Jesus Christ (*Teachings of the Prophet Joseph Smith*, 328). These articles of adoption we know as the first principles and ordinances of the gospel (Articles of Faith 1:4; D&C 33:11–12). These simple principles and ordinances lead the obedient disciple to understand and experience profound truths.

He that receiveth my law and doeth it, the same is my disciple;
and he that saith he receiveth it and doeth it not, the same is
not my disciple, and shall be cast out from among you.
DOCTRINE & COVENANTS 41:5

True disciples of Jesus Christ strive to become even as he is and thereby receive his image in their countenances (Alma 5:14). They do more than believe—they *do.* "Believing requires action," said President James E. Faust. "If you prepare to walk down the path of life, you can be rewarded beyond your dreams and expectations. But to achieve this, you must work hard, save, be wise, and be alert. You must learn to deny yourselves of worldly gratification. You must be faithful in paying tithes; you must keep the Word of Wisdom; you must be free from other addictions. You must be chaste and morally clean in every respect. You should accept and be faithful in all of the calls that come to you. Steadiness and toil will serve you better than brilliance" (*New Era,* July 1998, 4). With all their hearts, faithful followers of Christ do their utmost to live with inside-out congruence as they both believe and live the gospel.

It shall not be given to any one to go forth to preach my gospel, or to build up my church, except he be ordained by some one who has authority, and it is known to the church that he has authority and has been regularly ordained by the heads of the church.

DOCTRINE & COVENANTS 42:11

No one can preach the gospel as a missionary ("go forth to preach") or serve or teach in any way in the Church ("build up my church") without having first been called and ordained or set apart by the acknowledged authorities of the Church, sustained publicly by the membership, and then set apart appropriately (D&C 42:11). Secret ordinations or clandestine callings have no part in the Lord's Church. This law protects the Saints both personally and institutionally. We can trust the authority and callings of those who have been ordained or set apart by the leaders of the Church. We are protected from imposters who seek to deceive Church members and lead the Church astray. For this reason, we regularly raise our arm in sustaining votes. We manifest our support of the priesthood authority of our leaders and all who are called to serve. We extend the hand of fellowship and support in behalf of those who are called.

*[They] shall teach the principles of my gospel,
which are in the Bible and the Book of Mormon, in the
which is the fulness of the gospel. And they shall observe the
covenants and church articles to do them, and these shall be
their teachings, as they shall be directed by the Spirit.*

DOCTRINE & COVENANTS 42:12–13

All who teach in the Church are to teach the fulness
of the gospel: faith in Christ, repentance, baptism, and
the gift of the Holy Ghost as found in the standard
works of the Church (D&C 33:12; 39:6; 3 Nephi
27:20–21; Hebrews 6:1–2). We are also blessed to continue to receive further light as part of the new and
everlasting gospel covenant, light that expands our
understanding of God's plan of happiness (for example,
the ordinances of the temple). Nevertheless, we are not
to cast gospel pearls before unprepared or unapprecia-
tive individuals (D&C 41:6). We are to teach from the
scriptures, bear testimony of the scriptures, and feast
upon the doctrines and transcendent teachings found
therein. We are to follow the living prophet and bear
witness in word and deed of his counsel and teachings.
We who teach—and every member of the Church is a
teacher—must focus on gospel essentials and not stray
away into speculative interests or gospel hobbies.

And the Spirit shall be given unto you by the prayer
of faith; and if ye receive not the Spirit ye shall not teach.
DOCTRINE & COVENANTS 42:14

Teaching and learning spiritual truth can only be done spirit to spirit, as a transaction between the spirit of the teacher, the spirit of the hearer, and the Spirit of the Lord. Righteous teachers pray for the Spirit to be with them so that a confirmation will come to their hearers of the truthfulness of what they teach. Because all who are members of the Church are teachers in one way or another, ours is a continual process of studying and preparing, repenting and overcoming, as we humbly do our best to be "an example of the believers" (1 Timothy 4:12). We cannot fake, shortcut, or cram. If we do not have the Spirit, we can talk, but we do not teach; we can speak, but we do not inspire with the influence of the Spirit. Both hearer and teacher can usually feel the difference. It is both a commandment and a statement of fact: If we do not have the Spirit, we cannot teach.

*Thou shalt love thy wife with all thy heart, and
shalt cleave unto her and none else. And he that looketh
upon a woman to lust after her shall deny the faith, and shall
not have the Spirit. . . . Thou shalt not commit adultery.*

DOCTRINE & COVENANTS 42:22–24

Prophets of God have spoken clearly about chastity in thought, word, and deed. President Ezra Taft Benson admonished: "Decide now to be chaste. The decision to be chaste and virtuous need only be made once. Make that decision now, and let it be so firm and with such deep commitment that it can never be shaken" (*New Era,* January 1988, 6). The powers of creation are most sacred and are to be employed only as the Lord has directed. The greatest joys of life come when husband and wife love each other with all their hearts, when they are trustworthy and loyal to each other, when they bridle their thoughts and actions. President Gordon B. Hinckley counseled, "You should recognize, you *must* recognize, that both experience and divine wisdom dictate virtue and moral cleanliness as the way that leads to strength of character, peace in the heart, and happiness in life" (*Ensign,* May 1987, 48). Husband and wife are to cleave to each other in love and faithfulness.

Behold, thou wilt remember the poor, and consecrate of thy properties for their support that which thou hast to impart unto them, with a covenant and a deed which cannot be broken.

DOCTRINE & COVENANTS 42:30

Once individuals have enjoyed the outpouring of the Holy Spirit in their lives, even "that Spirit which leadeth to do good—yea, to do justly" (D&C 11:12), they feel compelled to look to the welfare of their fellow beings. Because "the earth is the Lord's, and the fulness thereof" (Psalm 24:1), because all things really do belong to God, it is natural that regenerated souls desire to confess the hand of God and to surrender all that they possess to the proper Owner. This is the principle of consecration. Because we are agents, not owners, we are designated as stewards, assigned to manage our affairs in a way that would be fruitful and beneficial to the larger kingdom. The pure in heart rejoice in this system, "every man seeking the interest of his neighbor, and doing all things with an eye single to the glory of God" (D&C 82:19).

*And the elders of the church, two or more, shall
be called, and shall pray for and lay their hands upon
them in my name; and if they die they shall die unto
me, and if they live they shall live unto me.*

DOCTRINE & COVENANTS 42:44

We live in a fallen world, a world in which things break down. None of us is immortal, and it is inevitable that no matter how prudently we eat and exercise, we will eventually come to the end of our mortal existence. Thankfully, our benevolent Lord steps into history occasionally and brings to pass a miracle. People are healed, the sick are made well, the blind are made to see, and the dead are raised. But knowing as we do that death is a significant part of "the merciful plan of the great Creator" (2 Nephi 9:6), we humbly acknowledge that not all of the sick will be healed, and not all of our prayers and administrations will be answered affirmatively. We trust in the Almighty, in his eternal purposes and timetable. He alone knows who should live and who should die. Surely that is a burden, an overwhelming responsibility that no mortal would want to bear. Mercifully, such decisions rest with our Heavenly Father.

Thou shalt live together in love.
DOCTRINE & COVENANTS 42:45

Love is the essence of the gospel. "Let us love one another: for love is of God; and every one that loveth is born of God. . . . if God so loved us, we ought also to love one another" (1 John 4:7–11). The plan of happiness was established by a loving Father, who wants ultimate joy and eternal life for his children. Because of love, Heavenly Father "sent his Son to be the propitiation for our sins" (1 John 4:10). Because of love, Jesus laid down his life that we might live again (John 10:17–18; 11:25–26). A caring Father dispersed the darkness of apostasy to speak to mankind anew and usher in the last and greatest of gospel dispensations. All this and so much more was done because of love. When the love of God fills our souls, we feel more inclined to forgive, we desire to live with our family in love, and we seek to bless all people.

*Thou shalt weep for the loss of them that die, and
more especially for those that have not hope of a glorious
resurrection. . . . those that die in me shall not taste
of death, for it shall be sweet unto them.*

DOCTRINE & COVENANTS 42:45–46

When we experience the loss of loved ones, our hearts are tender with emotion, our feelings subdued, and our thoughts turn heavenward. That is the time when our beliefs come face to face with the final reality of our mortal life: We all must die. Questions of life and death are in the Lord's hands. But it is *how* we die, what is in our heart and reflected in our actions, wherein we can exercise agency. Jesus said, "I am the resurrection, and the life: he that believeth in me, though he were dead, yet shall he live: and whosoever liveth and believeth in me shall never die" (John 11:25–26). Those who die in the Lord will find joy everlasting. But for those who die without the Lord, much will have to be done on the other side of the veil. The Lord loves his children and will, within the constraints imposed by human agency and the immutable laws of divine justice and mercy, work out these eternal judgments to the fullest blessing possible of all involved.

*And now, behold, I give unto you a commandment, that when ye
are assembled together ye shall instruct and edify each other, that
ye may know how to act and direct my church, how to act upon
the points of my law and commandments, which I have given.*
DOCTRINE & COVENANTS 43:8

There is much value in meeting together as Saints to
renew friendships and reinforce relationships, but
there is more to the gospel of Jesus Christ than sociality. A sobering responsibility rests upon the shoulders
of those called to teach in the Church, namely, to see
that meetings are instructive, inspirational, and edifying. A person's time is sacred, and to waste that time
dealing with trivia or focusing upon the unimportant
is counter to the Spirit. Faith comes by hearing the
word of God (Romans 10:17). The messengers of salvation should constantly strive to be equal to the sublime message they are called to teach through the
Spirit. In short, we need to be taught the gospel, we
need to be taught our duty, and our witness needs to be
strengthened in the meetings of the Church.

Again I say, hearken ye elders of my church,
whom I have appointed: Ye are not sent forth to be
taught, but to teach the children of men the things which
I have put into your hands by the power of my Spirit.

DOCTRINE & COVENANTS 43:15

It is healthy and worthwhile to learn of others' religious views and doctrines, for such learning not only stimulates our minds but broadens our horizons and allows us to speak intelligently with persons of other religious persuasions. None of us knows so much that he or she cannot learn from what another knows or believes and be benefited by it. At the same time, the Saints of God, particularly those called as missionaries, are sent forth not to be taught but rather to teach the principles of salvation. Such counsel should not lead us to be either insular or arrogant but rather cause us to be careful stewards over our time and talents and testimony.

*For the great Millennium, of which I have spoken
by the mouth of my servants, shall come. For Satan shall be
bound, and when he is loosed again he shall only reign for a
little season, and then cometh the end of the earth. . . .
and the earth shall pass away so as by fire.*

DOCTRINE & COVENANTS 43:30–32

The wickedness long prophesied by the ancients is now upon us (2 Timothy 3:1–7). The number of fatherless homes increases, violence spreads rampantly, and immorality becomes an accepted way of life. One day this all will change, however, for the King of Kings will come with mighty power and cleanse the earth of all wickedness. That will be the end of the world, meaning the end of worldliness. Then the Millennium will be ushered in by power and maintained by righteousness (1 Nephi 22:26). At the end of the thousand years, some mortals will once more deny God (D&C 29:22), and the forces of good and evil will once again war against one another in what we know as the battle of Gog and Magog (Smith, *Teachings of the Prophet Joseph Smith,* 280). And once again, Michael and his forces will achieve the victory, and the final end of the earth will come. This earth will then be glorified and become the celestial kingdom.

*Behold, I am Jesus Christ, the Savior of the world. Treasure
these things up in your hearts, and let the solemnities of eternity
rest upon your minds. Be sober. Keep all my commandments.*
DOCTRINE & COVENANTS 43:34–35

The scriptures point us to the Lord and his righteousness. They are given so that we might prepare for
eternity while in this mortal probation. "This life is
the time . . . to prepare to meet God" (Alma 34:32). In
the next life there will be no lenience for those who
paid no attention to gospel study because of laziness
or apathy or for those who had no time for the things
of eternity because of worldly preoccupations. There
will be no special arrangements or acceptable rationalizations—neither for the gifted and talented nor for
the wealthy and powerful. We must each give an
accounting to the Lord's unchangeable, nonnegotiable
realities of the universe, the solemnities of eternity. If
we treasure these truths in our hearts, if we more fully
strive to live with an eternal perspective, if we keep the
commandments with soberness, the Lord will bless us
with "peace in this world, and eternal life in the world
to come" (D&C 59:23).

Listen to him who is the advocate with the Father, who is pleading your cause before him—Saying: Father, behold the sufferings and death of him who did no sin . . . ; wherefore, Father, spare these my brethren that believe on my name, that they may come unto me and have everlasting life.

DOCTRINE & COVENANTS 45:3–5

Amulek taught that the atonement of Jesus Christ is an infinite atonement: It defies man's sense of justice, for the blood of an innocent victim atones for an offender (Alma 34:10–12). The plan of salvation is not what we would call a plan of fairness, because, thankfully, none of us will receive hereafter exactly what we deserve. None of us could qualify for exaltation in the highest degree of the celestial kingdom if we had to depend totally upon our own perfect righteousness. The plan of salvation is very much about mercy and goodness and grace, even the grace that makes up the difference, for indeed, it is grace that makes all the difference! In the end, we are saved by "the merits, and mercy, and grace of the Holy Messiah" (2 Nephi 2:8). Our task is to believe on the name of him who offered for us his atoning blood, the name that stands above all other names (Philippians 2:9), the blessed name of Jesus.

When the times of the Gentiles is come in, a light shall break forth among them that sit in darkness, and it shall be the fulness of my gospel; but they receive it not; for they perceive not the light, and they turn their hearts from me because of the precepts of men.

DOCTRINE & COVENANTS 45:28–29

We live in the day of the Gentile, the day when the gospel goes first to those who are Gentile by culture (though most are Israelite by descent) and then to the Lehites and the Jews. A light, a marvelous light, has burst upon the world as a result of the Restoration. Too many, however, do not perceive the light because they have been blinded by the precepts of men. Having trusted in the arm of flesh, they cannot perceive the all-powerful arm of the Lord in the midst of this marvelous work and a wonder. Deliverance from such blindness comes only through trusting in the Almighty. "O Lord," Nephi exulted, "I have trusted in thee, and I will trust in thee forever. . . . Yea, I know that God will give liberally to him that asketh. . . . I will cry unto thee, my God, the rock of my righteousness" (2 Nephi 4:34–35).

*Then shall the Jews look upon me and say: What are these
wounds in thine hands and in thy feet? Then shall they know that
I am the Lord; for I will say unto them: . . . I am Jesus that was
crucified. I am the Son of God. And then shall they weep.*

DOCTRINE & COVENANTS 45:51–53

The day of the Jew, the time when a nation will be born again in a day, is yet ahead. In fact, it is millennial. Though it is true that many of our Jewish brothers and sisters will receive the fulness of the gospel before the Lord returns, the day of mass conversion will begin with the Master's appearance on the Mount of Olives. And what a day it shall be! It is difficult to imagine the pain and disappointment and even frustration in the hearts and minds of many of God's chosen people as they discover that for more than two millennia they have rejected the Anointed One of Israel. In that day, the Jews will see the tokens of the crucifixion in the resurrected Lord and hear from his own mouth that he is indeed the Savior and Redeemer of all humankind.

*When I shall come in my glory, shall the parable be fulfilled
which I spake concerning the ten virgins. For they that are wise
and have received the truth, and have taken the Holy Spirit for
their guide, . . . shall not be hewn down . . . but shall abide the day.*

DOCTRINE & COVENANTS 45:56–57

No doubt many have read the parable of the ten
virgins (Matthew 25:1–13) and asked themselves, Why
don't the wise virgins simply share what they have with
the foolish virgins so that they can all go to the wed-
ding feast? We can hardly imagine that Jesus would
not encourage people to share with one another. But
some things simply cannot be shared. For example,
individuals may share their testimonies, but they
cannot actually give their testimony to another person. They may share doctrinal truths, but they cannot
convey to someone else the knowledge they have
gained over a lifetime of study. Spiritual marathons
will not do. Sudden bursts of spiritual energy will not
suffice. Rather, every prayer we offer, every passage of
scripture we ponder, every act of Christian service we
render fills our spiritual lamps gradually, one drop at
a time. Spiritual preparation cannot be rushed.

*But notwithstanding those things which are written,
it always has been given to the elders of my church from the
beginning, and ever shall be, to conduct all meetings as
they are directed and guided by the Holy Spirit.*

DOCTRINE & COVENANTS 46:2

Almost always, organizations that expand at a rapid rate eventually suffer from stagnation, regimentation, and fossilization. They begin to emphasize rules and regulations rather than principles. Though the Church of the Lamb of God will grow to fill the entire earth, it will maintain the spiritual spontaneity required for the revelation necessary to the Lord's living Church. Handbooks and other formal guides are useful aids in directing the affairs of the kingdom, but life and light are breathed into the souls of the Saints through the direction and animation of the Holy Spirit of God. There can be no written constitution for the kingdom of God, no rigid system of theology, for growth and development are the hallmark of a church led by the living Lord.

For all have not every gift given unto them; for there are many gifts, and to every man is given a gift by the Spirit of God. To some is given one, and to some is given another, that all may be profited thereby.

DOCTRINE & COVENANTS 46:11–12

All spiritual gifts come from God, and he gives them for the benefit of his children (D&C 46:26). That he bestows gifts of the Spirit upon his children is another sign of his divine generosity and loving fatherhood. Each of us is given a gift—not for our own gratification or self-aggrandizement but to bless other people and to build up the kingdom of God. Gifts are given to those who are spiritually prepared, who are diligently seeking righteousness. The Giver of all gifts knows our hearts, our desires and intents, and he gives us our agency in developing and exercising the spiritual gifts he has given us. In humility we are to "covet earnestly the best gifts" (1 Corinthians 12:31) and seek "the best gifts, always remembering for what they are given" (D&C 46:8; 1 Corinthians 12–14; Moroni 10; D&C 46).

To some it is given by the Holy Ghost to know that Jesus Christ is the Son of God, and that he was crucified for the sins of the world. To others it is given to believe on their words, that they also might have eternal life if they continue faithful.

DOCTRINE & COVENANTS 46:13–14

The first of the gifts of the Spirit named in Doctrine and Covenants 46 is the gift of testimony, the gift of knowing with certainty of the truthfulness and divinity of this work (see also 1 Corinthians 12; Moroni 10). It is by the spirit of prophecy, which is the spirit of revelation, that we come to know that Jesus is the Christ, the Son of the living God, and that his was an infinite and eternal sacrifice. Not everyone comes to this knowledge with the same certainty or at the same pace. Many have the gift of a believing heart, the gift to believe on the testimony of those who do know. They have taken seriously the command to "search diligently, pray always, and be believing" (D&C 90:24) and to lean upon the faith of others while they are in the process of gaining their own.

*Unto such as God shall appoint and ordain to
watch over the church and to be elders unto the church, are
to have it given unto them to discern all those gifts lest there
shall be any among you professing and yet be not of God.*
DOCTRINE & COVENANTS 46:27

It would be wonderful if all who profess to have
spiritual gifts were indeed inspired by God. Such is
not always the case, however, for some manifestations
are of God, some are of men, and some are of the devil
(D&C 46:7). In the Church, the presiding elder, or
bishop, is given the right to discern the source of such
gifts. Further, the prophet, seer, and revelator is given
the right to all the spiritual gifts, "which [God]
bestows upon the head of the Church" (D&C 107:92).
"The devil is an orator," the Prophet Joseph Smith
declared. "He is powerful. . . . The gift of discerning
spirits will be given to the Presiding Elder. Pray for
him that he may have this gift" (*Teachings of the Prophet
Joseph Smith,* 162). We need not fear nor be confused,
for God has set in place a system for discerning spiritual gifts, whereby we may uphold the true and discard
the false.

APRIL 27

*Behold, it is expedient in me that my
servant John should write and keep a regular history.*
DOCTRINE & COVENANTS 47:1

In 1831 the Lord called John Whitmer, one of the Eight Witnesses of the Book of Mormon plates, to write the history of the Church. The Lord told him "that he shall continue in writing and making a history of all the important things which he shall observe and know concerning my church" (D&C 69:3). Before this call, he had served as a scribe to the Prophet Joseph in Fayette, New York. Although he later became disaffected from the Church, he remained true to his testimony of the Book of Mormon plates until his death in 1878. His early history of the Church is a significant treasure today. Record-keeping has always been commanded by the Lord. When the Church was organized in this dispensation, the Lord commanded that a record be kept of people and events, doctrines and covenants (D&C 21:1). We are also to keep individual and family records. These records and journals will be among our most precious possessions for us and for generations yet unborn.

*Whoso forbiddeth to marry is not ordained of God,
for marriage is ordained of God unto man, . . . and they
twain shall be one flesh, and all this that the earth
might answer the end of its creation.*

DOCTRINE & COVENANTS 49:15–16

Joseph Smith inquired of the Lord in March 1831 regarding the Shakers' belief that a celibate life was superior to marriage. The Lord answered that marriage is ordained of God. After the restoration of the sealing keys by Elijah (D&C 110:13–16), Joseph Smith gave greater emphasis to the "new and everlasting covenant of marriage." This covenant, the Lord revealed, is a requirement to attain the highest degree in the celestial kingdom (D&C 131:1–2) and the means of becoming like God (D&C 132:19–24). "The Family: A Proclamation to the World," issued by the First Presidency and the Quorum of the Twelve Apostles, reaffirmed "that marriage between a man and a woman is ordained of God" (*Ensign,* November 1995, 102). Husband and wife are to cleave unto each other and none else in thought, word, and deed (D&C 42:22). In the oneness of marriage, we fill the measure of our creation, and, as we do so, the earth fulfills its foreordained purpose.

*But it is not given that one man should possess that
which is above another, wherefore the world lieth in sin.*
DOCTRINE & COVENANTS 49:20

One sign that all is not well on earth is that there is such a polarization between the wealthy and the poor. Millions go to sleep hungry each night, and millions wander the streets homeless. We know, because the Lord has told us, that "the earth is full, and there is enough and to spare" (D&C 104:17). The problem is not a lack of resources but a lack of individual unselfishness. Imagine what could happen if everyone lived the law of the fast, once each month, and contributed the value of those two meals to the care of the poor. We could doubtless solve the problem of starvation throughout the world in no time at all. Though that may be beyond our power, we can make a difference in the life of one person or one family. We could well take as our motto: "When ye are in the service of your fellow beings ye are only in the service of your God" (Mosiah 2:17).

Be not deceived, but continue in steadfastness, looking forth for the heavens to be shaken, and the earth to tremble and to reel to and fro as a drunken man . . .—and all this when the angel shall sound his trumpet.

DOCTRINE & COVENANTS 49:23

The unusual revelation recorded in Doctrine and Covenants 49 is addressed to the Shakers, the United Society of Believers in Christ's Second Appearing. Some of their beliefs are set forth in the headnote to this revelation, including their belief that the Savior had returned already in the form of a woman, Ann Lee. In this revelation, the Savior assures us that he will not return as a woman and that when he does return it will not be a secret. One neighbor will not have to call a friend down the street and ask if the Second Coming has taken place yet, for all shall know. Although our Lord will make some preliminary appearances that are known only to select groups, his coming in glory will be welcomed and feared and known by the entire world.

MAY

Listen to him who is the advocate with the
Father, who is pleading your cause before
him—Saying: Father, behold the sufferings
and death of him who did no sin . . . ; where-
fore, Father, spare these my brethren that
believe on my name, that they may come
unto me and have everlasting life.

DOCTRINE & COVENANTS
45:3–5

There are many spirits which are false spirits, which have gone forth in the earth, deceiving the world. And also Satan hath sought to deceive you, that he might overthrow you.

DOCTRINE & COVENANTS 50:2–3

We must be on guard against the wiles of the adversary and his minions who want misery and spiritual death for all of God's children. Said President Boyd K. Packer: "'There are many spirits which are false spirits.' There can be counterfeit revelations, promptings from the devil, temptations! As long as you live, in one way or another the adversary will try to lead you astray. 'For after this manner doth the devil work, for he persuadeth no man to do good, no, not one; neither do his angels; neither do they who subject themselves unto him.' The Prophet Joseph Smith said that 'nothing is a greater injury to the children of men than to be under the influence of a false spirit when they think they have the Spirit of God'" (*Ensign,* November 1994, 61, citing Smith, *Teachings of the Prophet Joseph Smith,* 205). Stay on the Lord's side of the line. Reject Satan and other evil spirits, and stand firmly on gospel bedrock with the prophets and the faithful Saints.

*But blessed are they who are faithful and endure,
whether in life or in death, for they shall inherit eternal life.*
DOCTRINE & COVENANTS 50:5

We make our calling and election sure by receiving the more sure word of prophecy, the assurance that our exaltation is secure (D&C 131:5–6). That, of course, is something all of the faithful long to receive, for it would serve as an anchor to the soul, a constant and consistent steadying influence for the remainder of one's earthly stay. But we need not receive an overwhelming divine manifestation or even a communication from those holding the keys of the kingdom in order to be secure in our faith. Those in this life who live to enjoy the companionship of the Holy Ghost receive the peace that is the harbinger of eternal life, the quiet personal and peaceful assurance that their life is in order, and that in the world to come they will inherit eternal life (D&C 59:23). Whether we receive such a realization of the promise here or hereafter is immaterial, for the promise is sure.

There are hypocrites among you, who have deceived some, which has given the adversary power; but behold such shall be reclaimed; but the hypocrites shall be detected and shall be cut off, either in life or in death, even as I will; and wo unto them who are cut off from my church, for the same are overcome of the world.

DOCTRINE & COVENANTS 50:7–8

The hypocrite puts on a mask, so to speak, seeking to appear to be what he is not so that he may deceive others. Unless we are careful, we may fall prey to the enticements of one who parades a hyperspirituality but conceals malicious motives within. Though we strive to enjoy the gift of discernment—to readily recognize the false and the unimportant—none of us is perfect in that spiritual gift, and we may be led astray for a time. Thankfully, God judges us by the desires of our heart as well as by our actions (Alma 41:3; D&C 137:9), and those who follow the living prophets, keeping themselves in the mainstream of the Church, will eventually open their ears to sound doctrine and take corrective action (2 Timothy 3:16). Though we may be deceived, he who views the universe with an all-seeing eye cannot be deceived. Whether in this life or the next, the hypocrite will be exposed to face the consequences of his deceit.

*Wherefore, I the Lord ask you this question—unto
what were ye ordained? To preach my gospel by the Spirit, even
the Comforter which was sent forth to teach the truth.*
DOCTRINE & COVENANTS 50:13–14

Doctrine and Covenants 50:13–14 might well be called "the law of the teacher." The Savior asks us what we have been appointed, or set apart, to do. The answer is simple—to teach the gospel of Jesus Christ by the power of the Holy Ghost. A gospel teacher, as an agent, acts according to the mind and will of his Principal; it is as though the Lord himself is teaching. To teach by "some other way" is not of God (D&C 50:18, 20). For example, to deliver a sermon or teach a lesson that is wholly an intellectual endeavor and does not represent that which the Lord wants to have taught is not of God. Even if what was said is true— no error at all in the teaching—it is not of God. True learning comes and conversion is deepened when gospel teachers first obtain their "errand from the Lord" (Jacob 1:17) and then carry it out as the Lord has prescribed (D&C 50:22).

That which doth not edify is not of God, and is darkness.
That which is of God is light; and he that receiveth light, and
continueth in God, receiveth more light; and that light groweth
brighter and brighter. . . . know the truth, that you may
chase darkness from among you.
DOCTRINE & COVENANTS 50:23–25

If a person, teaching, or influence does not build and
bless us or somehow inspire us to be better, then it is
not of God and should be shunned. Edification and
enlightenment always come from God. That which
brings anxiety, alienation, temptation, loss of faith, and
confusion is darkness and does not come from God.
Where there is light, there is the Spirit of the Lord.
"Light cleaveth unto light" (D&C 88:40), and "light
and truth forsake that evil one" (D&C 93:37). Light
and truth chase darkness from us; light and truth free
us to enjoy the blessings of the gospel here and a
crown of righteousness hereafter. We are to seek light
and truth. As we do, we will come to the embodiment
of light and truth, our Savior: "I am the light of the
world: he that followeth me shall not walk in darkness,
but shall have the light of life" (John 8:12).

If ye are purified and cleansed from all sin, ye shall ask whatsoever you will in the name of Jesus and it shall be done. But know this, it shall be given you what you shall ask; and as ye are appointed to the head, the spirits shall be subject unto you.

DOCTRINE & COVENANTS 50:29–30

It is easy to fall into the trap of uttering the same words in our prayers over and over, with little or no feeling, and thus succumbing to the sin against which the Master warned when he spoke of vain repetition (Matthew 6:7). On the other hand, as we clear our minds of distractions, speak directly from our hearts, and open ourselves to divine direction, we may find our words reaching beyond our thoughts to pray for persons or circumstances that were not part of our original intention. The apostle Paul taught that the Spirit of God helps us in knowing what to pray for; because we are not always certain what we should pray for, because we cannot always discern between needs and wants, the Spirit makes intercession for us with strivings that cannot be expressed (Romans 8:26; Smith, *Teachings of the Prophet Joseph Smith,* 273). In so doing, we pray for what we ought, and a gracious Lord is eager to hear and respond.

And the Father and I are one. I am in the
Father and the Father in me; and inasmuch as ye have
received me, ye are in me and I in you.
DOCTRINE & COVENANTS 50:43

Joseph Smith learned in the First Vision that the
Father and Son are distinct beings and separate Gods.
Over the years, however, as a result of his translation
of the Book of Mormon and his receipt of subsequent
revelations, the Prophet came to know that the members of the Godhead are infinitely more one than they
are separate, though they are separate beings. There is
more than a closeness between the Father and the
Son; it is rather what might be called a divine
indwelling relationship. To say that the Father is in the
Son or that the Son is in the Father is to state that they
are agreed, united, and one in all things, including all
of the attributes of godliness. In a like manner, as we
enjoy the guidance and enabling power of the Holy
Spirit, it could be said of us that we are in Christ and
he is in us. We thereby enjoy "the mind of Christ"
(1 Corinthians 2:16).

*And let them journey from thence preaching the
word by the way, saying none other things than that which the
prophets and apostles have written, and that which is taught
them by the Comforter through the prayer of faith.*

DOCTRINE & COVENANTS 52:9

The apostle Paul bore witness to King Agrippa of his divine vision and commission on the road to Damascus: "Having therefore obtained help of God, I continue unto this day, witnessing both to small and great, saying none other things than those which the prophets and Moses did say should come: that Christ should suffer, and that he should be the first that should rise from the dead" (Acts 26:22–23). In one sense, to say "none other things than that which the prophets and apostles have written" (D&C 52:9) is to bear witness of the central, saving verity that Jesus Christ is the Son of God and that he was crucified for the sins of the world. In a broader sense, we are to teach the gospel—both content and emphasis—according to the pattern established by living apostles and prophets (D&C 52:36).

*I will give unto you a pattern in all things, that ye
may not be deceived; for Satan is abroad in the land, and he
goeth forth deceiving the nations. . . . by this pattern ye shall
know the spirits in all cases under the whole heavens.*

DOCTRINE & COVENANTS 52:14–19

Doctrine and Covenants 52:14–19 provides a clear pattern for those whose actions and attributes are acceptable to the Lord. This unmistakable pattern will help us to discern and identify those who would mislead us, whether with subtle or with blatant deceptions. Those who are accepted of God are those whose spirits are contrite, whose prayers are humble, and whose language is meek and edifying. Those who are of God receive and recognize the Lord's power and bring forth righteous fruits; they follow the revealed truths (D&C 52:9, 36) and obey the ordinances of the gospel. The faithful and humble will be made strong, and the Lord will be with them (D&C 66:8). This perfect pattern of righteousness is both a beacon to those who seek the Lord and his kingdom and a protection against the liars and deceivers among us.

*And remember in all things the poor and the
needy, the sick and the afflicted, for he that doeth not
these things, the same is not my disciple.*
DOCTRINE & COVENANTS 52:40

The phrase "the sick and the afflicted" (D&C 52:40)
is used numerous times in scripture to exhort the
Saints. From Jacob to Moroni, prophets have warned
that those who love money more than they love the
poor and needy, the sick and afflicted, will stand condemned at the last day (see, for example, Jacob 2:19;
Alma 4:12; 34:28; Mormon 8:37). In our own day, the
Lord has likewise declared: "If any man shall take of
the abundance which I have made, and impart not his
portion . . . he shall, with the wicked, lift up his eyes in
hell" (D&C 104:18). To impart willingly means that
we look with compassion upon the less fortunate—not
in condescension but with love unfeigned. We remember always that we all are beggars who depend upon
God for everything (Mosiah 4:19–26). True disciples
seek to be like Christ, who said, "By this shall all men
know that ye are my disciples, if ye have love one to
another" (John 13:35).

Behold, I, the Lord, who was crucified for the sins of the world, give unto you a commandment that you shall forsake the world. . . . he only is saved who endureth unto the end.
DOCTRINE & COVENANTS 53:2–7

Those who take upon them the name of Christ as part of the new and everlasting covenant of the gospel distance themselves from the world. They live in the world and breathe its air, but they are not of the world. They have separated themselves by covenant to be a peculiar people, to take upon them the luster of Christ, to seek out the righteous, the uplifting, and the praiseworthy. Sometimes in our efforts to be accepted by those in the world or because of the insidious and slow stain of worldliness, we walk within only a step or two of Babylon. The world ever beckons with its enticements. But those committed to Christ hope for a better world and strive to live worthy of a glorious eternal reunion with the Infinite. Life is a constant battle to forsake the allurements of the world, to put off the natural man, to stay focused with Spirit-enhanced discernment on everlasting things.

*My servant William . . . thou art called and chosen; and after
thou hast been baptized by water, which if you do with an eye
single to my glory, you shall have a remission of your sins and
a reception of the Holy Spirit by the laying on of hands.*

DOCTRINE & COVENANTS 55:1

William Wines Phelps purchased a copy of the
Book of Mormon from Parley P. Pratt in Canandaigua,
New York, and became convinced of the truth of the
Restoration. He and his family arrived at Kirtland in
June 1831, and the Prophet Joseph sought the Lord's
will for him. The Lord knew what the Church needed
at this time, and W. W. Phelps was the right man at
the right time. His experience as a writer and editor
was put to great use as he served as clerk and scribe to
Joseph Smith and as publisher of the Church's first
newspaper, *The Evening and the Morning Star.* He also
wrote several well-known hymns, including "The
Spirit of God," "Praise to the Man," and "Redeemer of
Israel." But the essential things he did for his eternal
welfare were humbly to enter the waters of baptism,
receive the gift of the Holy Ghost, receive the priesthood, preach repentance, and die a faithful member
of the Church.

And he that will not take up his cross and follow me,
and keep my commandments, the same shall not be saved.
DOCTRINE & COVENANTS 56:2

Following the Savior entails more than lip service to the truth of his divine Sonship, more than a mere expression that one has accepted Jesus as Savior and Lord of his life. True faith in Him always results in faithfulness, in that disciplined walk we know as Christian discipleship. The Saints of the Most High are thus commanded to take up the Lord's cross and follow him. "And now for a man to take up his cross, is to deny himself all ungodliness, and every worldly lust, and keep my commandments" (JST Matthew 16:26). To accept Christ is to come unto Christ. To come unto Christ is to covenant to follow him and keep his commandments. This is a work not of a moment but of a lifetime.

*Wo unto you rich men, that will not give your
substance to the poor, for your riches will canker your souls;
and this shall be your lamentation in the day of visitation, and
of judgment, and of indignation: The harvest is past,
the summer is ended, and my soul is not saved!*

DOCTRINE & COVENANTS 56:16

Being rich is not a sin; the sin is in being proud and unwilling to share one's abundance with the less fortunate. Jacob taught: "Wo unto the rich, who are rich as to the things of the world. For because they are rich they despise the poor, and they persecute the meek, and their hearts are upon their treasures; wherefore, their treasure is their god. And behold, their treasure shall perish with them also" (2 Nephi 9:30). If we squander our second estate in acquisitive materialism, the door to celestial glory will be closed to us. Both rich and poor and everyone in between take the same amount of money with them to the other side—none. But our heart, our mind, our desires, and our testimony accompany us hereafter. What can the treasures of the earth mean to Him who is eternal? The closer we draw to the Lord with an eternal perspective, the less we will strive for the material things of this earth.

*Blessed are the poor who are pure in heart, whose hearts
are broken, and whose spirits are contrite, for they shall see the
kingdom of God coming in power and great glory unto their
deliverance; for the fatness of the earth shall be theirs.*

DOCTRINE & COVENANTS 56:18

The poor will be blessed by virtue not of their
poverty but by their purity in heart, by their meekness.
Poverty itself does not redound to eternal life. It is our
true character, our pure and humble heart, that gives
us the fatness of the earth. Fatness means that we have
abundance, more than we need. The poor who are
humble and faithful will have all they need, all they can
use, of the bounties of this earth—and more besides.
When the law of consecration is lived to its fulness by
a Zion people, all who live under it will have enough
and to spare—not just to supply their needs but their
wants as well (D&C 51:3; 82:17). The Savior said that
the poor in spirit and pure in heart will receive the
kingdom of heaven and shall see God (Matthew 5:3,
8). In a sense, the worthy poor may be last in this
earthly realm but receive mansions beyond compare
hereafter (Matthew 19:30).

Hearken, O ye elders of my church, saith the
Lord your God, who have assembled yourselves together,
according to my commandments, in this land, which is the land
of Missouri, which is the land which I have appointed
and consecrated for the gathering of the saints.

DOCTRINE & COVENANTS 57:1

People are gathered first to Christ and his kingdom and then to the congregations of the faithful. Early in the history of the restored Church, Jehovah made known that Independence, Jackson County, Missouri, was to be at the time the central place of gathering and eventually the center stake of the New Jerusalem. Although the gathering places of the early Saints changed through the years (Kirtland, Far West, Nauvoo, Salt Lake City), the scriptures of the Restoration testify that the day will come when the headquarters of the restored Church will once more be established in Jackson County. But until that day comes, until those holding the keys provide clear and adequate instruction to do otherwise, members of The Church of Jesus Christ of Latter-day Saints are instructed to gather to their respective wards and stakes and to build up the tent of Zion wherever they live (Isaiah 54:2; 3 Nephi 22:2).

Ye cannot behold with your natural eyes, for the present time, the design of your God concerning those things which shall come hereafter, and the glory which shall follow after much tribulation. For after much tribulation come the blessings.

DOCTRINE & COVENANTS 58:3–4

Who among us has not suffered the adversities and vicissitudes of life? To one degree or another, life holds difficulties for all people. But with our limited perspective, we do not see how the Master is touching us for greater good, refining and enlarging our souls for the abundant life he offers us, giving us the greatest opportunity to exercise our agency in developing the attributes of godliness. We see so little with our myopic mortal eyes. But the Lord's wide-angle viewfinder of the eternal worth of his children sees that we must be stretched and schooled to receive an "eternal weight of glory" (D&C 63:66). While the pioneer Saints were camped at Winter Quarters in 1847, the Lord revealed to President Brigham Young: "My people must be tried in all things, that they may be prepared to receive the glory that I have for them, even the glory of Zion" (D&C 136:31). Blessings surely come to those who endure with faith the tribulations of life.

*Whoso standeth in this mission is appointed to be
a judge in Israel, like as it was in ancient days, . . . to judge his
people by the testimony of the just, and by the assistance of
his counselors, according to the laws of the kingdom.*

DOCTRINE & COVENANTS 58:17–18

Few callings or assignments in the Church carry a greater burden of responsibility than that of bishop. Those called and ordained as bishops are given the commission to serve as judges in Israel. As Doctrine and Covenants 58 indicates, bishops are to discern how best to meet the needs of their flock, including the poor and needy. Not only are they to meet with those who come for special assistance but they are also to search after the poor (D&C 84:112). In addition, they are to judge the righteousness of the Saints through personal interviews and thereby determine individuals' standing in the Church, including worthiness to serve and worship in the house of the Lord. They are to love and teach and direct the transgressor, according to the principles and doctrines laid down in holy scripture and in the general handbooks of the Church.

*Let no man break the laws of the land, for he that keepeth
the laws of God hath no need to break the laws of the land.
Wherefore, be subject to the powers that be, until he reigns whose
right it is to reign, and subdues all enemies under his feet.*

DOCTRINE & COVENANTS 58:21–22

Because all things are spiritual unto God (D&C 29:34), it is impossible to fully separate heavenly law from the laws of the land. Stated more bluntly, in striving for spirituality, we cannot seek to obey all the commandments of God and at the same time ignore or spurn the laws of the land. In the United States, we have a system of government that can maintain decency and morality in society only as its citizens observe the laws. Because we do not now live in a theocracy does not mean that we do not have a spiritual obligation to be good citizens and thereby uphold "that law of the land which is constitutional" (D&C 98:5). "Let every soul be subject unto the higher powers. For there is no power but of God: the powers that be are ordained of God" (Romans 13:1).

He that is compelled in all things, the same is a slothful and not a
wise servant; wherefore he receiveth no reward. . . . men should be
anxiously engaged in a good cause, and do many things of their
own free will, and bring to pass much righteousness.

DOCTRINE & COVENANTS 58:26–27

Our greatest endowment in life is the freedom to choose. "Whosoever perisheth, perisheth unto himself; and whosoever doeth iniquity, doeth it unto himself; for behold, ye are free; ye are permitted to act for yourselves; for behold, God hath given unto you a knowledge and he hath made you free" (Helaman 14:30). God will not force us to be good; the devil cannot compel us to be bad. We are free to choose. If we were compelled to be good, what would our righteous choices mean? We are to give that which he would never take by force by offering our free will on the altar of God. We are to use our agency to bless others and build the kingdom. "For the power is in them, wherein they are agents unto themselves. And inasmuch as men do good they shall in nowise lose their reward" (D&C 58:28). Mansions on high await those who are anxiously engaged in good causes, who use their agency in righteousness.

*Behold, he who has repented of his sins, the same
is forgiven, and I, the Lord, remember them no more.
By this ye may know if a man repenteth of his sins—
behold, he will confess them and forsake them.*

DOCTRINE & COVENANTS 58:42–43

The great principle of the Savior's infinite atonement is that we can be cleansed of our iniquities and they will be blotted out, never to be remembered again. We are truly made clean through the atoning blood of the Lamb (Alma 5:21; D&C 76:69). There would be no salvation without repentance, no peace without divine forgiveness. Elder Boyd K. Packer has said, "I would find no peace, neither happiness nor safety, in a world without repentance. I do not know what I should do if there were no way for me to erase my mistakes. The agony would be more than I could bear" (*Memorable Stories and Parables,* 30). The gospel is a message of hope. The Savior has shown us the way out of the slavery of sin and the prison of transgression; it is in godly sorrow, sincere repentance, and contrite confession. There would be no sweet assurance, no lasting peace, no eternal life, without repentance, a gift of the Atonement.

*For, behold, they shall push the
people together from the ends of the earth.*
DOCTRINE & COVENANTS 58:45

The Abrahamic covenant entailed transcendent and profound promises to the posterity of the father of the faithful (Genesis 13:14–16; 15:5–6; JST Genesis 17:3–12). Abraham and his descendants were promised the blessings of the gospel of Jesus Christ, the priesthood, the eternal continuation of the family, and a land inheritance. In addition, sobering responsibilities attended the Abrahamic covenant, including the duty of taking the message of salvation to all the world and gathering the faithful to the lands of their inheritance (Abraham 2:8–11, 19). Of ancient Joseph, great-grandson of Abraham, the powerful and symbolic word of Jehovah came through Moses: "His glory is like the firstling of his bullock, and his horns are like the horns of unicorns; with them he shall push the people together to the ends of the earth: and they are the ten thousands of Ephraim and they are the thousands of Manasseh" (Deuteronomy 33:17).

*For those that live shall inherit the earth, and those
that die shall rest from all their labors, and their works shall
follow them; and they shall receive a crown in the mansions
of my Father, which I have prepared for them.*

DOCTRINE & COVENANTS 59:2

Both ancient and modern scripture teach the importance of good works. Once individuals become true followers of the Lord Jesus Christ, they begin to embody Christlike characteristics and manifest their conversion by the way they live day by day. Good works thus become a gauge, a measuring rod, by which to assess believers' depth of devotion to God. When the scriptures say that we will be judged by our works, they do not mean we will be judged by the merits of our works but rather that our works demonstrate what we have become through the transforming powers of Christ. In the end, it will be "through the merits, and mercy, and grace of the Holy Messiah" (2 Nephi 2:8) that we are saved. Our good works are necessary, but they are not sufficient for salvation (2 Nephi 31:19; Moroni 6:4; 10:32). Rather, works of righteousness help to make us even more righteous—they help us to become conformed to the image of our Master.

*Thou shalt thank the Lord thy God in all things. Thou
shalt offer a sacrifice unto the Lord thy God in righteousness,
even that of a broken heart and a contrite spirit.*
DOCTRINE & COVENANTS 59:7–8

The Master's parable of the talents teaches that we demonstrate gratitude by using well the gifts we are given (Matthew 25:14–30). When we are thankful for the treasures of time, talents, and means that bless our lives, we exhibit gratitude not by burying these treasures in our hearts for our enjoyment alone but by sharing them with others. We convey gratitude by expressing and, more importantly, demonstrating our thanks: by using gifts to give again, doubling rewards by investing them in others. We show our thankfulness by placing on God's altar the sacrifice of our will, our broken and humble hearts, our ready submission to whatever the Lord requires. Those who are righteous love the Lord. They meekly seek to follow him and do his will. Gratitude is more than giving thanks—it is *living* thanks.

*That thou mayest more fully keep thyself unspotted
from the world, thou shalt go to the house of prayer and
offer up thy sacraments upon my holy day; for verily this
is a day appointed unto you to rest from your labors,
and to pay thy devotions unto the Most High.*

DOCTRINE & COVENANTS 59:9–10

The Sabbath is a day set apart to strengthen us in our resolve to keep unspotted from the world. The First Presidency has stated: "We urge all Latter-day Saints to set this holy day apart from activities of the world and consecrate themselves by entering into a spirit of worship, thanksgiving, service, and family-centered activities appropriate to the Sabbath. As Church members endeavor to make their Sabbath activities compatible with the intent and Spirit of the Lord, their lives will be filled with joy and peace" (*Ensign,* January 1993, 80). When we are honest with the Lord and our hearts are right, we will heed the promptings of the Spirit and know what is worthy or unworthy for the Sabbath. It is meant to be a day of worship, devotion, rest, rejuvenation, service, and meaningful time with family and loved ones. True Sabbath observance helps us to forsake worldliness and center our hearts on the Lord and the real purpose for our existence.

*Nevertheless thy vows shall be offered
up in righteousness on all days and at all times.*
DOCTRINE & COVENANTS 59:11

An integral part of a lifetime of worship is the proper observance of the Sabbath day. On this day we rest in at least two ways. First, we refrain from activities we would normally perform during the week and thus allow our minds and bodies to be refreshed. Second, we strive to enter more fully into the "rest of the Lord," the quiet peace and settled conviction that enable us to engage a complex and confusing world with confidence. In a sense, the Sabbath is a pattern of what each day should be. Ours is a seven-day-a-week religion, and the Lord expects us to keep our covenants and act in holiness "on all days and at all times" (D&C 59:11). "Wherefore the Sabbath was given unto man for a day of rest; and also that man should glorify God, . . . for the Son of Man made the Sabbath day, therefore the Son of Man is Lord also of the Sabbath" (JST Mark 2:26–27).

*On this day thou shalt do none other thing, only let thy food be
prepared with singleness of heart that thy fasting may be perfect,
or, in other words, that thy joy may be full. Verily, this is fasting
and prayer, or in other words, rejoicing and prayer.*

DOCTRINE & COVENANTS 59:13–14

Fasting is much more than merely going without
food and drink. True fasting is a consecrated attitude,
a conscious sacrifice of our fleshly susceptibilities, so
that we can draw closer to God. As we do, we rejoice
in love and gratitude to the Giver of life. On the day
of fasting, our food should be prepared in the spirit of
fasting—with reverence and love. The Sabbath is itself
a kind of fast, a day set aside to separate ourselves
more fully from the world, to commune more effectively with God and take pleasure in the Lord's holy
day. President Joseph F. Smith said: "As fasting should
always be accompanied by prayer, this law would bring
the people nearer to God, and divert their minds once
a month at least, from the mad rush of worldly affairs
and cause them to be brought into immediate contact
with practical, pure and undefiled religion" (*Gospel
Doctrine*, 237–38). A true fast is a prayer of rejoicing.

MAY 28

*Do these things with thanksgiving, with cheerful hearts
and countenances, not with much laughter, for this is a sin,
but with a glad heart and a cheerful countenance.*
DOCTRINE & COVENANTS 59:15

In three verses in the Doctrine and Covenants, the
Lord teaches the Saints regarding laughter. We are to
avoid "much laughter" on the Sabbath, which is a day
of fasting and prayer (D&C 59:15). In other words, we
are to cast away "excess of laughter," to cease from "all
laughter" (D&C 88:69, 121). The Lord is not demand-
ing woeful countenances and perpetual melancholy for
the Saints, but there are appropriate expressions of
laughter and humor as well as proper places and times
for lightheartedness. Laughter in its suitable time and
place is encouraged and enjoyed. How often have we
chuckled at an anecdote told in general conference or
an appropriate joke in a Sunday School class? We
ought to look on the bright side, cultivate a sense of
humor, and be cheerful and buoyant in our faith.
Always we are to take on the luster of Christ and be
an example of the believers in thought, word, and
deed (1 Timothy 4:12).

And in nothing doth man offend God, or against none is his wrath kindled, save those who confess not his hand in all things, and obey not his commandments.

DOCTRINE & COVENANTS 59:21

Ingratitude and disobedience offend God. Two sides of the same weakness, ingratitude and disobedience reflect selfishness. Hardheartedness, or arrogance, closes the windows of heaven and shuts out the Spirit of the Lord. God, who has given us everything, asks only that we gratefully acknowledge his hand and obey his commandments. "All that he requires of you is to keep the commandments; and he has promised you that if ye would keep his commandments ye should prosper in the land" (Mosiah 2:22). From Sinai the Lord declared, "I the Lord thy God am a jealous God" (Exodus 20:5). The Hebrew word translated as *jealous* also means "possessing sensitive and deep feelings" (v. 5, note b). The Lord surely has deep feelings about his children, his greatest creation. He cares a great deal about our hearts, about our willingness to obey, about our meekness in showing gratitude to the Giver of life.

But learn that he who doeth the works of
righteousness shall receive his reward, even peace in
this world, and eternal life in the world to come.

DOCTRINE & COVENANTS 59:23

To live in peace despite tribulations and turmoil is an immeasurable reward. To inherit everlasting life, peace, and joy when we put aside this temporal realm is the greatest gift vouchsafed to mortals (D&C 14:7). That does not mean life for the righteous will be easy or carefree. Life for all people—the good and the bad—is difficult at times, filled with challenges and heartache. But for those who strive to follow Christ, for those who do the works of righteousness and live with humble, grateful hearts, the heavens will pour out blessings of peace and comfort, regardless of circumstance. The wicked and lazy, the apathetic and slothful have no promise (D&C 82:10). But the devout Saints, those who manifest in their lives the works of righteousness in covenant relationship with Christ, are assured: "This is the promise that he hath promised us, even eternal life" (1 John 2:25).

*With some I am not well pleased, for they will not
open their mouths, but they hide the talent which I have
given unto them, because of the fear of man. Wo unto such.
. . . If they are not more faithful unto me, it shall be
taken away, even that which they have.*

DOCTRINE & COVENANTS 60:2–3

Because of social pressure or embarrassment, some
of us are afraid to share the good news of the gospel
with others. We hold back, intimidated or self-
conscious, because we fear what others may say or
think. Those who live the gospel and share it may not
necessarily be popular with the world or the worldly.
But our concern must be the Lord's opinion of us. We
must use our testimonies or lose them; we must raise
our voices—respectfully and humbly—to extend to
others the truths and blessings of the restored gospel.
The consequence of refusing to bear testimony is los-
ing our own testimony. The result of giving in to fears
is the dimming of the light and zeal we once felt. Both
with believing Saints and people not of our faith, we
must share our testimonies and talents. If we do so
with a pure heart and willing mind, the Lord will
strengthen and inspire us (D&C 64:34).

JUNE

*For thus saith the Lord—I, the Lord, am
merciful and gracious unto those who fear
me, and delight to honor those who serve
me in righteousness and in truth unto the
end. Great shall be their reward and
eternal shall be their glory.*

DOCTRINE & COVENANTS
76:5–6

Behold, verily thus saith the Lord unto you, O ye elders of my church, who are assembled upon this spot, whose sins are now forgiven you, for I, the Lord, forgive sins, and am merciful unto those who confess their sins with humble hearts.

DOCTRINE & COVENANTS 61:2

Confession of sin is necessary before the miracle of forgiveness can take place. Serious sins that could affect our standing in the Church are to be confessed to the appropriate priesthood leader. Bishops and stake presidents can then counsel with the individual and oversee the process of spiritual renewal. All sins must be confessed to the Almighty. It is vital that we learn to speak openly, frankly, and freely to our Heavenly Father; to acknowledge the nature of our misdeeds; and to express our desire to forsake those sins for the rest of our days. Confession is not just a form of catharsis, for if this were the case, we could merely confide to our best friends or shout our sins from the housetops. Rather, confession is a private, personal acknowledgment of responsibility, a sober recognition of what we have done and what we must now do to make things right insofar as we can and rely on the Savior and his atonement to make up the difference.

*I, the Lord, was angry with you
yesterday, but today mine anger is turned away.*
DOCTRINE & COVENANTS 61:20

Through the revelations of the Restoration, we have come to know that God, our Heavenly Father, is a man, a Man of Holiness (Moses 6:57), an exalted and immortal Being who possesses a body of flesh and bones (D&C 130:22), in whose image we are created. We know that he is more than a force, more than a great First Cause, more than an Unmoved Mover, more than the Wholly Other. He is the Father of the spirits of all mankind (Numbers 16:22; 27:16; Hebrews 12:9). Like his Son, he is "touched with the feeling of our infirmities" (Hebrews 4:15). In other words, our God is not just a machine, a robotic instrument, a celestial computer that records good and bad deeds. Thankfully, he is a Being with body, parts, and passions, one whose justice is real but whose mercy is from everlasting to everlasting.

It mattereth not unto me, after a little, if it so be that they fill their mission, whether they go by water or by land; let this be as it is made known unto them according to their judgments hereafter.

DOCTRINE & COVENANTS 61:22

President Brigham Young taught that if after we have pleaded with the heavens long and hard for divine direction and still no clear answer comes, we should proceed according to our best judgment and know that the Lord is bound to honor that decision (*Journal of Discourses,* 3:205). Further, as time passes and as we strive to cultivate the spirit of inspiration in our lives, that spirit will educate our desires, shape our consciences, and enhance our wisdom. When we are allowed to look back upon our lives, to look more closely even at those times when we felt so very alone, we will learn that the Spirit was refining and honing our feelings and desires, thus leading us to make the wise choices God would have had us make.

Behold, and hearken, O ye elders of my church, saith the Lord your God, even Jesus Christ, your advocate, who knoweth the weakness of man and how to succor them who are tempted.

DOCTRINE & COVENANTS 62:1

The apostle Paul wrote that as Christians "we have not an high priest which cannot be touched with the feeling of our infirmities; but was in all points tempted like as we are, yet without sin" (Hebrews 4:15). Alma similarly taught that the Savior would "go forth, suffering pains and afflictions and temptations of every kind. . . . and he will take upon him their infirmities, that his bowels may be filled with mercy, according to the flesh, that he may know according to the flesh how to succor his people according to their infirmities" (Alma 7:11–12). Jesus can assist us through our trials because he has been there before us. He has the cognizance and compassion to empower us to withstand the fiery darts of the adversary, because he has faced and withstood them. Having "descended below all things" (D&C 88:6), our seasoned Savior is also an experienced Exemplar. He can run to our aid because he knows what we are going through.

*Nevertheless, ye are blessed, for the testimony which
ye have borne is recorded in heaven for the angels to look upon;
and they rejoice over you, and your sins are forgiven you.*
DOCTRINE & COVENANTS 62:3

No matter how deep our testimony or how well
expressed, if we share our testimony of truth with others, we will be greatly blessed. How inspiring to know
that our testimonies are recorded in heaven for the
angels to look upon and rejoice over! A testimony is a
precious endowment from on high. It develops as we
respond to truth with humility and obedience and
then feel the sweet promptings of the Spirit confirm
that what we are feeling in our hearts and expressing
to others is real and true. Our testimonies become
stronger, more clear and profound, the more we share
them with others. Perhaps the greatest manifestation
of a sincere testimony is the heartfelt desire to turn
away from sin, push back the world, and walk with
righteousness before the Lord. By doing so, our hearts
are turned toward repentance, and our sins are forgiven. Those who bear witness of truth, those who live
truthfully, will find joy and rejoicing in forgiveness.

*Faith cometh not by signs,
but signs follow those that believe.*

DOCTRINE & COVENANTS 63:9

The word *signs* as used in scripture refers to tangible, physical evidence. Jesus taught that great signs and wonders would follow those who came into his Church and were baptized (Mark 16:15–18). But true faith, saving and sustaining faith, cannot rest on signs alone. The flame of faith must be lit and fed by scripture study, pondering, prayer, and personal revelation. Those who join the true Church because of a notable miracle and then do not seek the quiet confirmation of the Spirit have built a house of faith upon a sandy foundation. Inevitably, that house will be beaten by the winds of skepticism and the rains of cynicism and doubt. On the other hand, those who have gained the witness of the Spirit watch with wonder as internal and external evidences fan the flame of faith and thus brighten the light that came from above. Their house of faith is built upon the rock and will withstand the tempests of life.

*But unto him that keepeth my commandments I will give
the mysteries of my kingdom, and the same shall be in him a
well of living water, springing up unto everlasting life.*
DOCTRINE & COVENANTS 63:23

Keeping the commandments of God brings to us
light and truth (D&C 93:28). Light and truth forsake
the evil one (D&C 93:37) and also open us to an
understanding of principles, doctrine, and profound
understanding that can only come through obedience.
The mysteries of the kingdom are truths that the
world cannot fathom; they are as the gibberish of alien
tongues. Such truths need not be deep and penetrating, only beyond the realm of the unillumined, beyond
the reach of the uninspired. In short, the mysteries of
God are those truths that can be known only by the
power of the Holy Ghost. From such persons flow
feelings, impressions, insights, wisdom, and words that
bless and enlighten not only themselves but those with
whom they come in contact.

*For behold, verily I say, that many there be who
are under this condemnation, who use the name of the
Lord, and use it in vain, having not authority.*

DOCTRINE & COVENANTS 63:62

Because God is above and over all things, it is a serious thing to invoke the name of the Lord. Condemnation awaits those who use that name in vain. Doctrine and Covenants 63:62 does not seem to be a specific warning against profanity or vulgarity, as serious as those are, but rather a warning against using the name of the Lord without proper authorization. We use the name of the Lord in vain when we attribute our own motives or ideas to God, perhaps to gain approval or respect. We use the name of the Lord in vain when in an attitude of high-mindedness we say to another, "The Lord would have you do this or that," when in truth the Lord has said no such thing. We use the name of the Lord in vain when we exercise unrighteous dominion. When we use the name of the Lord in vain, we cannot have his Spirit with us, and thus our works and words are for naught.

Remember that that which cometh from above is sacred,
and must be spoken with care, and by constraint of the Spirit.

DOCTRINE & COVENANTS 63:64

That which comes from the heavenly realm is holy to the Father and Son. They care very much about how we discuss and treat sacred things. To Heavenly Father, we are his children, his spirit sons and daughters; for us the world and everything therein was created. To the Son, our Savior Jesus Christ, we are the beneficiaries of his atonement and redemption, his mercy, love, and divine grace as we enter into a covenant relationship with him. The supernal truths of the gospel and of our relationship with Deity are not to be bandied about casually or inappropriately. Some things are too sacred, too special, to be treated lightly. The Spirit of the Lord will manifest to us when we may appropriately use the names of God and Christ and speak of sacred things. The Holy Spirit will direct us through the whisperings of the still, small voice and through earnest prayer as we humbly seek heavenly guidance.

Ye ought to forgive one another; for he that forgiveth not his brother his trespasses standeth condemned before the Lord; for there remaineth in him the greater sin. I, the Lord, will forgive whom I will forgive, but of you it is required to forgive all men.

DOCTRINE & COVENANTS 64:9–10

Life is a journey in forgiveness. During our mortal sojourn, we will be injured and treated unfairly, but we are nonetheless commanded to forgive. Nothing clutters the soul more than resentment and enmity toward another. Nothing enlarges the soul more than genuine forgiveness as we leave justice to the Lord. It has been said that vindictiveness toward another is like consuming poison ourselves and then waiting for the other person to die. The Lord, who is perfect in his understanding and judgment, knows our hearts and every situation. Because he sees the whole picture, he alone is able to forgive whom he—in his divine wisdom—will. The Lord wants our hearts to be soft and forgiving. That doesn't mean we ignore the hurt, but if we desire forgiveness of the Lord for our own shortcomings, we must forgive others. Forgiveness is the greatest gift we can give to others and to ourselves.

And him that repenteth not of his sins, and confesseth them not, ye shall bring before the church, and do with him as the scripture saith unto you, either by commandment or by revelation. And this ye shall do that God may be glorified.

DOCTRINE & COVENANTS 64:12–13

Church disciplinary councils are convened for the purpose of blessing the individual and protecting the Church. They do not exist to inflict punishment or to cause embarrassment but rather to bring spiritual discipline into the life of the transgressor once again, to make of him or her a true disciple. Disciplinary councils are in no way an indication that the Church or its leaders have no compassion or forgiveness; rather, the councils are a statement that "the worth of souls is great in the sight of God" (D&C 18:10). In such councils, revelations come, burdens are lifted, and love and peace are felt. Alma the Elder, faced with members of the Church who were guilty of serious transgression, "went and inquired of the Lord what he should do concerning this matter, for he feared that he should do wrong in the sight of God" (Mosiah 26:13). Disciplinary councils are councils of love that bless the transgressor and bless the Church.

*It is called today until the coming of the Son of Man,
and verily it is a day of sacrifice, and a day for the tithing
of my people; for he that is tithed shall not be burned at
his coming. For after today cometh the burning.*

DOCTRINE & COVENANTS 64:23–24

The Saints would do well to turn a deaf ear to those who claim special insight into the signs of the times or who profess to predict the exact day of our Lord's coming. Jesus was emphatic in his warning that no person will know the precise day of his return, not even the angels of heaven (Matthew 24:36). And yet, the people of the covenant whose ears are attuned to the words of living oracles and the promptings of the Spirit will be able to read the signs of the times and know the season of the Master's return. Jesus will return to the world as a thief in the night—but not to the Saints, for they will recognize the signs that warn of his approaching return (1 Thessalonians 5:2–5; D&C 106:4). The scriptures teach precisely when he will come—tomorrow. *Today* is the time of preparation for *tomorrow.* "Wherefore, if ye believe me, ye will labor while it is called today" (D&C 64:25).

*Wherefore, as ye are agents, ye are on the
Lord's errand; and whatever ye do according to
the will of the Lord is the Lord's business.*

DOCTRINE & COVENANTS 64:29

Whether our assignment is to leave the country on a mission, give a talk in sacrament meeting, or teach a class to energetic six-year-olds, we all have been called to serve. We understand that those who serve in the Church are on the Lord's errand, and our service in the kingdom is the Lord's business. When with willing hearts we accept a call, we go forward as agents of the Lord with faith, courage, and authority, knowing that, as the Lord's representative, we are supported by him. For this reason, we must serve with humility, dedication, and willingness, whatever our calling and responsibility. President Gordon B. Hinckley has said: "Within your sphere of responsibility you have as serious an obligation as do I within my sphere of responsibility. Each of us should be determined to build the kingdom of God on the earth and to further the work of righteousness" (*Ensign,* November 2003, 82). All callings in the Church are important to the Lord.

All things must come to pass in their time. Wherefore, be not weary in well-doing, for ye are laying the foundation of a great work. And out of small things proceedeth that which is great.
DOCTRINE & COVENANTS 64:32–33

The Lord sees all things in an ever-present now. His timetable is not ours, and he is perfectly patient, ever enduring. He sees the beginning and the end and everything in between. Indeed, the Lord slumbers not nor sleeps as he watches over his children (Psalm 121:4). Our part in the Lord's work and glory is to be resolute in righteousness, to forsake worldliness, and to reach out in love and kindness to all people. We must each do our part to build the kingdom and "seek to bring forth and establish the cause of Zion" (D&C 6:6). We may feel that what we are doing is just a tiny drop in the gospel ocean; our service may seem small, our contribution minute. But if our part were not there, the whole Church would be lessened by that missing drop. We do not need to think in terms of numbers or of mighty achievements. We just simply and steadfastly go about doing good.

The Lord requireth the heart and a willing mind; and the willing and obedient shall eat the good of the land of Zion in these last days. And the rebellious shall be cut off out of the land of Zion, and shall be sent away, and shall not inherit the land.

DOCTRINE & COVENANTS 64:34–35

The Lord requires "the hearts of the children of men" (D&C 64:22). If our hearts are pure, our minds will be open to truth; if our hearts are obedient, our minds are willing to surrender to the Lord. Those who are accepted of the Lord "know their hearts are honest, and are broken, and their spirits contrite, and are willing to observe their covenants by sacrifice—yea, every sacrifice which I, the Lord, shall command" (D&C 97:8). Will we come unto the Lord with full purpose of soul, with humble and broken hearts? Will we come unto the Lord with a mind eager to embrace truth and obey the commandments? Those with hard hearts and closed minds will be cut off from the Lord and his blessings of truth, light, and joy—here and hereafter. The "good of the land of Zion" is reserved for the faithful and obedient (D&C 64:34).

*Behold, I, the Lord, have made my church in these
last days like unto a judge sitting on a hill, or in a high place, to
judge the nations. For it shall come to pass that the inhabitants
of Zion shall judge all things pertaining to Zion.*
DOCTRINE & COVENANTS 64:37–38

In many ways, The Church of Jesus Christ of Latter-day Saints is a service agency, a support, an auxiliary to assist individuals and families to gain eternal life. Through the Church, we receive the ordinances of salvation and the doctrinal teachings that help us to become acquainted with our God and his plan of salvation. Through the Church, the Lord's legal administrators, his apostles and prophets, both inspire and inform us; as living revelators, they make known the mind and will and voice of the Lord concerning today's challenges and circumstances. Zion, the society of the pure in heart, has no counterpart on this earth, nor do the people of Zion take their cues from the loud janglings of Babylon. In a world founded upon the shifting sands of secularity, the Church grounds its members in solid and sacred absolute truths, in principles and practices that reflect the higher ethic, the elevated perspective of our Lord and Savior.

*Zion shall flourish, and the glory of the Lord shall
be upon her; and she shall be an ensign unto the people, and
there shall come unto her out of every nation under heaven.*

DOCTRINE & COVENANTS 64:41–42

An ensign is a flag or standard around which people gather in a unity of purpose or identity; it also served anciently as a rallying point for soldiers in battle. In effect, the Church is an ensign to all nations of the earth in the battle for truth and righteousness. President Gordon B. Hinckley said: "If we are to hold up this Church as an ensign to the nations and a light to the world, we must take on more of the luster of the life of Christ individually and in our own personal circumstances. In standing for the right, we must not be fearful of the consequences" (*Ensign,* November 2003, 84). Isaiah's prophecy is fulfilled as people come to a stake of Zion and enter a covenant relationship with Christ. We are ensigns to others when we exemplify virtue and goodness. Zion will prosper and spread as the pure in heart gather within her walls and seek to live and share the gospel.

*The keys of the kingdom of God are committed unto man
on the earth, and from thence shall the gospel roll forth unto the ends
of the earth, as the stone which is cut out of the mountain without
hands shall roll forth, until it has filled the whole earth.*

DOCTRINE & COVENANTS 65:2

Centuries before the coming of Jesus Christ, the Babylonian king Nebuchednezzar dreamed a dream that had prophetic implications for the whole of humankind. Not only did he see symbolically the formation and destruction of the kingdoms of the world throughout history but he also saw the establishment of the ultimate kingdom, God's kingdom, in the latter days (Daniel 2). Doctrine and Covenants 65, a prayer offered by the Prophet Joseph Smith, affirms that The Church of Jesus Christ of Latter-day Saints is indeed the little stone that was cut out of the mountain without hands—meaning, it was initiated and empowered by the Almighty—and that it would grow to fill the whole earth. The Prophet Joseph stated, "I calculate to be one of the instruments of setting up the kingdom of [God foreseen by] Daniel by the word of the Lord, and I intend to lay a foundation that will revolutionize the whole world" (*Teachings of the Prophet Joseph Smith,* 366).

Blessed are you for receiving mine everlasting covenant,
even the fulness of my gospel, sent forth unto the children of men,
that they might have life and be made partakers of the glories
which are to be revealed in the last days.

DOCTRINE & COVENANTS 66:2

In October 1831 William McLellin requested that the Prophet Joseph inquire of the Lord concerning him. The Lord commended him for accepting the restored gospel, reminded him of the glories to come, and exhorted him to repent: "You are clean, but not all; repent, therefore, of those things which are not pleasing in my sight" (D&C 66:3). Brother McLellin went on to serve a mission in the Midwest and helped to build Zion in Missouri. In 1835 he was called as one of the original members of the Quorum of the Twelve Apostles. Unfortunately, he struggled with faithfulness and did not remain true to the truth. In 1838, after years of devoted service, he was excommunicated for apostasy. Nevertheless, until his death more than four decades later, he maintained that the Book of Mormon was true. The lesson for us from William McLellin's life is to stay faithful to the Church, follow its leaders, be humble, and stay in our covenant relationship with Christ to the end.

He that is faithful shall be made strong in every place;
and I, the Lord, will go with you. . . . Be patient in affliction.
. . . Forsake all unrighteousness. . . . magnify thine office. . . .
Continue in these things even unto the end, and you shall have
a crown of eternal life at the right hand of my Father.

DOCTRINE & COVENANTS 66:8–12

The Lord cares greatly about his missionaries sent out across the world. He knows what they need to do to be successful, and he knows who they need to be to find the honest in heart. Those who desire to share the gospel must be true to the truth, they must be humble and teachable, they must endure well the difficulties of missionary work, they must forsake worldliness and magnify their callings as ambassadors of the Lord. The promised crown is variously described as a crown of righteousness (D&C 25:15), joy (D&C 52:43), glory (D&C 58:4), and immortality and eternal life (D&C 20:14; 81:6). It is the reward of those who overcome through Jesus Christ and sit with him in his throne in the kingdom of God (Revelation 3:21). The Lord's promise to his preachers of righteousness who remain steadfast and true is sure: "Well done, thou good and faithful servant: . . . enter thou into the joy of thy lord" (Matthew 25:21).

Behold and hearken, O ye elders of my church, who have assembled yourselves together, whose prayers I have heard, and whose hearts I know, and whose desires have come up before me.

DOCTRINE & COVENANTS 67:1

At a conference of the Church in November 1831, the Lord—as is his pattern with the righteous—comforted his small group of elders: "Behold and lo, mine eyes are upon you, and the heavens and the earth are in mine hands, and the riches of eternity are mine to give" (D&C 67:2). When we're discouraged and want to give up, when we feel that the buffetings and temptations of the world are too much to withstand, we must remember the words of the Lord in Doctrine and Covenants 67: he knows our hearts and our desires. He is not deceived by externals or explanations. He *knows.* His eyes are upon us—not in a condemning, punitive way, but in a loving, merciful, encouraging way. He wants to endow us with the riches of eternity that are reserved for the faithful, the humble, and the obedient. Our loving Lord wants for us all that he has.

Your eyes have been upon my servant Joseph Smith, Jun.,
and his language you have known, and his imperfections you have
known; and you have sought in your hearts knowledge that you
might express beyond his language; this you also know.
DOCTRINE & COVENANTS 67:5

Although we sustain those charged to guide the destiny of the Lord's kingdom, we do not believe they are perfect; we do not believe in prophetic infallibility. President Gordon B. Hinckley stated: "I have worked with seven Presidents of this Church. I have recognized that all have been human. But I have never been concerned over this. They may have had some weaknesses. But this has never troubled me. I know that the God of heaven has used mortal men throughout history to accomplish His divine purposes" (*Ensign,* May 1992, 53). On another occasion, President Hinckley reminded us that "there was only one perfect man who ever walked the earth. The Lord has used imperfect people in the process of building his perfect society. If some of them occasionally stumbled, or if their characters may have been slightly flawed in one way or another, the wonder is the greater that they accomplished so much" (*Ensign,* April 1986, 5).

For no man has seen God at any time in the flesh, except quickened by the Spirit of God. Neither can any natural man abide the presence of God, neither after the carnal mind.

DOCTRINE & COVENANTS 67:11–12

One result of the Hellenizing influence on ancient Christianity is the distancing of man from God, the placing of God in the realm of the unknowable and unreachable. Through mistranslation, faulty transmission, or the work of designing persons, the notion evolved that mortal man cannot behold God face to face (John 1:18; 1 John 4:12). By modern revelation through Joseph Smith and as a part of his inspired translation of the King James Bible, we learn that "the fool hath said in his heart, There is no man that hath seen God" (JST Psalm 14:1). Further, we learn more fully that "no man hath seen God at any time, except he [God the Father] hath borne record of the Son; for except it is through him [the Son] no man can be saved" (JST John 1:19). Indeed, "no man hath seen God at any time, except them who believe" (JST 1 John 4:12). God lives, knows, feels, loves, and interacts with his children. This we know.

And whatsoever they shall speak when moved upon by the Holy Ghost shall be scripture, shall be the will of the Lord, shall be the mind of the Lord, shall be the word of the Lord, shall be the voice of the Lord, and the power of God unto salvation.

DOCTRINE & COVENANTS 68:4

The standard works are the collective, binding, doctrinal word of God for the Church. They are the standard against which all else is judged, and they are scripture for the entire Church. The word *scripture* may also be used in a broader sense. Whenever a person speaks as moved upon by the power of the Spirit, then that message is the word of God, or *scripture,* for those who hear it and are also moved upon by the Spirit. The inspiration received is individual, whereas the inspiration of the standard works is collective and binding upon all Saints. A priesthood blessing is individual scripture, but it is not scripture for the whole Church, even though it was inspired. How blessed we are to have an open canon, regular writings and teachings from the prophets and others moved upon by the Spirit, whereby we can receive the mind and will of the Lord for ourselves individually and for the Church collectively.

*Inasmuch as parents have children in Zion, . . . that
teach them not to understand the doctrine of repentance, faith
in Christ the Son of the living God, and of baptism and the
gift of the Holy Ghost . . . when eight years old,
the sin be upon the heads of the parents.*

DOCTRINE & COVENANTS 68:25

Where is the first line of defense in the Church? Is it the Primary? Is it the Sunday School?" asked President Harold B. Lee as he spoke to parents and Primary workers. "That is not the way our Heavenly Father has revealed it. . . . The Lord placed squarely on the forefront of the battlefields against the powers which would break down these defenses the home, the first line of defense (D&C 68:25–32). . . . We must never think of ourselves as trying to supplant the home. Ours should be a conscious, everyday effort to supplement and to reinforce and to strengthen the homes which are our Heavenly Father's first line of defense" (*Teachings of Harold B. Lee*, 262). Parents are accountable to God to fulfill a sacred and wonderful obligation to teach the gospel to their children.

*And their children shall be baptized for the remission
of their sins when eight years old, and receive the laying on
of the hands. And they shall also teach their children to
pray, and to walk uprightly before the Lord.*
DOCTRINE & COVENANTS 68:27–28

The First Presidency and the Quorum of the Twelve
Apostles declared in the Proclamation on the Family:
"Parents have a sacred duty to rear their children in
love and righteousness, to provide for their physical
and spiritual needs, to teach them to love and serve
one another, to observe the commandments of God
and to be law-abiding citizens wherever they live.
Husbands and wives—mothers and fathers—will be
held accountable before God for the discharge of these
obligations" (*Ensign,* November 1995, 102). As parents,
our sacred stewardship involves not just teaching truth
but living truth. When children see parents sincerely
striving to overcome the world and change and
improve as fellow children of God, they will be nur-
tured with powerful, vivid examples of the gospel's
transforming power. The great plan of happiness will
not only be taught from the scriptures but from the
lives of parents.

I, the Lord, am not well pleased with the inhabitants of Zion, for there are idlers among them; and their children are also growing up in wickedness; they also seek not earnestly the riches of eternity, but their eyes are full of greediness. These things . . . must be done away from among them.

DOCTRINE & COVENANTS 68:31–32

Too many of us have grown accustomed to self-indulgence and idleness, believing that life is a series of entertainments and entitlements and acquiring more than our neighbor. But the Lord is not pleased with laziness and greed. As Latter-day Saints, we believe in the gospel of work, of purposeful action, of anxious engagement for good. Work and charity spell the difference in the disciple of Christ. President Gordon B. Hinckley has said: "Let not selfishness canker your relationship. Let not covetousness destroy your happiness. Let not greed, for that which you do not need and cannot get with honesty and integrity, bring you down to ruin and despair" (*Teachings of Gordon B. Hinckley*, 252). Parents are to teach by both example and precept that greed and idleness have no place in the Lord's kingdom. Together, parents and children, we are ever to keep our eyes on the things of lasting worth: the riches of eternity.

*And a commandment I give unto them—that he that
observeth not his prayers before the Lord in the season thereof,
let him be had in remembrance before the judge of my people.*
DOCTRINE & COVENANTS 68:33

A Church leader stood before a congregation of
Saints and stated that any member of the Church who
neglects his prayers should be brought before a disciplinary council and tried for his membership. This was
quite a startling announcement, and many in the congregation wondered whether the Church leader was
not overstating the need for prayer. Yet Doctrine and
Covenants 68:33 suggests that the need for prayer is
serious—God expects his people to pray, to call upon
him in times of need, to express gratitude in times of
prosperity, and to seek divine direction in their myriad decisions. Prayer not only "rests the weary" (*Hymns,*
no. 140) but provides a way by which the will of
heaven is conveyed to individuals on earth, a means
whereby finite mortal persons come to know the
wishes of an infinite and eternal God. It does us little
good to have the gift of the Holy Ghost and access to
spiritual gifts if we do not use them.

Behold, this is what the Lord requires of every man in his stewardship, even as I, the Lord, have appointed or shall hereafter appoint unto any man. And behold, none are exempt from this law who belong to the church of the living God.

DOCTRINE & COVENANTS 70:9–10

Each of us is given various stewardships by the Lord. Whether our stewardship is temporal or spiritual, the same principle applies: everyone will be required to give an accounting of his or her stewardship. "And an account of this stewardship will I require of them in the day of judgment" (D&C 70:4). As parents, we have a sacred stewardship to bring up our children in light and truth (D&C 93:40). We are accountable for the discharge of our duties in our Church callings. We have been given stewardships in our careers and in our communities to live with integrity and make the world better. Because we have been given much, much is required (D&C 82:3). In our homes, wards and branches, and neighborhoods, we have a sacred stewardship to be a light to others as we seek to live and share the gospel (Matthew 5:14–15). Active membership in the Lord's Church involves a ready willingness to enlarge our talents, serve others, and fulfill our stewardships.

Behold, thus saith the Lord unto you . . . that the time has verily come that it is necessary and expedient in me that you should open your mouths in proclaiming my gospel, . . . according to that portion of Spirit and power which shall be given unto you.

DOCTRINE & COVENANTS 71:1

The angel Moroni had promised the young Prophet much discomfort and even persecution: laying the foundation of the final dispensation would not come without a significant price. Opposition to the newly restored faith came early, and it was often necessary for the Prophet Joseph and his associates to interrupt their ministerial labors to deal directly with that opposition. In this, as in all other matters, the teaching of sound and solid doctrine has done more to soften hard feelings and correct misrepresentations than anything else. Such correction has not come necessarily by delving into deep doctrine but rather through teaching the simple principles and doctrines that God wanted delivered at a given time. Our task is to deliver that "portion of [Christ's] word" (Alma 12:9) that suits the occasion and meets the need.

JULY

*Draw near unto me and I will draw near
unto you; seek me diligently and ye shall
find me; ask, and ye shall receive; knock,
and it shall be opened unto you.*

DOCTRINE & COVENANTS
88:63

*Wherefore, confound your enemies; call upon them
to meet you both in public and in private; and inasmuch as
ye are faithful their shame shall be made manifest.*

DOCTRINE & COVENANTS 71:7

We confound our enemies not by arguing with them or debating them but by cultivating the power of God that accompanies the simple and humble proclamation of the message of salvation. We have no time for contention with those who attack the Church (3 Nephi 11:29). We have only time to be about the business of spreading the divine word. In addition, we pray with earnestness for those who proclaim themselves our enemies, and in his own time, God will turn those enemies to us (Alma 33:4). We teach and we testify. We declare the truth, we seek to show its reasonableness, and we bear witness. We then let truth "cut its own way" (Smith, *Teachings of the Prophet Joseph Smith,* 313).

*Verily, thus saith the Lord unto you—there is no weapon
that is formed against you shall prosper; and if any man lift his
voice against you he shall be confounded in mine own due time.*

DOCTRINE & COVENANTS 71:9–10

President Heber J. Grant declared: "Our enemies have never done anything that has injured this work of God, and they never will. . . . Where are the men who have assailed this work? Where is their influence? They have faded away like dew before the sun. We need have no fears, we Latter-day Saints. God will continue to sustain this work; he will sustain the right. If we are loyal, if we are true, if we are worthy of this gospel, of which God has given us a testimony, there is no danger that the world can ever injure us. We can never be injured, my brethren and sisters, by any mortals, except ourselves" (*Gospel Standards,* 85–86). No effort to disrupt the work of the Lord will succeed. The Church will continue to grow and prosper as it fills the world and ushers in the return of our Lord.

*In this thing ye have done wisely, for it is required
of the Lord, at the hand of every steward, to render an
account of his stewardship, both in time and in eternity. For
he who is faithful and wise in time is accounted worthy to
inherit the mansions prepared for him of my Father.*

DOCTRINE & COVENANTS 72:3–4

Each of us will give an accounting for what we have done with our earthly stewardship (Matthew 25:14–30). We report our stewardship to our bishop or other authorized Church leader while we live upon the earth. And we will give an accounting for our stewardship to the Lord when our mortal probation is over (D&C 70:4). The Lord desires for us all that he has. We are here to prove ourselves worthy of celestial mansions, because what we do here in our second estate determines what we inherit in eternity. We are here to exercise our ability to make righteous choices, so that we can be trusted with an everlasting inheritance hereafter. "For behold, this life is the time for men to prepare to meet God; yea, behold the day of this life is the day for men to perform their labors" (Alma 34:32). Performing well our temporal stewardship opens us to the rich blessings of eternity.

For verily, thus saith the Lord, it is expedient in me that they should continue preaching the gospel, and in exhortation to the churches in the regions round about, until conference.

DOCTRINE & COVENANTS 73:1

The elders of the Church in 1832 desired to know what the Lord wanted them to do while they were waiting to learn his will through his prophet at conference. He told them they should be anxiously engaged in productive labor and to continue doing their duty. That is good counsel for us all: while waiting, do something constructive. President Joseph F. Smith admonished "the Latter-day Saints everywhere to cease loitering away their precious time, to cease from all idleness. . . . there is far too much precious time wasted by the youth of Zion, and perhaps by some that are older and more experienced and who ought to know better. . . . Learn to sing and to recite, and to converse upon subjects that will be of interest to your associates. . . . Read . . . anything that is good, that will elevate the mind and will add to your stock of knowledge" (*Gospel Doctrine*, 235). Let us use moments of waiting productively.

*It is expedient to continue the work
of translation until it be finished.*
DOCTRINE & COVENANTS 73:4

Did the Prophet Joseph Smith finish his inspired translation of the King James Version of the Bible? The answer is a simple yes—and no. Yes, he finished it in the sense that from June 1830 to July 1833 he and his scribes gave attention to every book in the Bible, and he made changes in the verses the Lord prompted him to change. No, he did not finish the translation in that he did not alter or delete or harmonize every passage that was in need of clarification or correction. Is the Joseph Smith Translation therefore an unfinished work? No more than is the Book of Mormon. We have only a portion of the Jaredite and Nephite record and do not expect to receive the remainder until that millennial day when our faith will have been properly tried (3 Nephi 26:9), when we will have penetrated the damning veil of unbelief and matured in our faith, like unto the brother of Jared (Ether 4:7, 15).

And again, verily I say unto you, that every man who is obliged to provide for his own family, let him provide, and he shall in nowise lose his crown; and let him labor in the church.

DOCTRINE & COVENANTS 75:28

The apostle Paul in writing to his beloved Timothy pointed out, "If any provide not for his own, and specially for those of his own house, he hath denied the faith, and is worse than an infidel" (1 Timothy 5:8). The Proclamation on the Family declares: "By divine design, fathers are to preside over their families in love and righteousness and are responsible to provide the necessities of life and protection for their families. Mothers are primarily responsible for the nurture of their children. In these sacred responsibilities, fathers and mothers are obligated to help one another as equal partners" (*Ensign,* November 1995, 102). Unless incapacitated, the husband or father should feel a sense of responsibility as the chief breadwinner. In addition, the Lord reminds us of our accompanying responsibility to be active and involved in the labors of the Church. Our occupation need not preclude Church service or personal and intimate involvement with the family.

Let every man be diligent in all things. And the idler shall not have place in the church, except he repent and mend his ways.

DOCTRINE & COVENANTS 75:29

It is through purposeful labor that we progress toward salvation. That does not mean we earn our way to heaven, for we are saved by the grace of God, "after all we can do" (2 Nephi 25:23). But we access the Lord's enabling power by doing the works of righteousness. The work of the Church is done by those with willing hearts, who thrust in their sickle with their might and serve the Lord with all their might, mind, and strength (D&C 6:4; 4:2). Ours is a gospel of work, of effort. There is no place for the idler, the lazy, the onlooker. In all our labors, whether spiritual or temporal, we are to be diligent as we "put [our] shoulder to the wheel" (*Hymns,* no. 252). Our contribution may seem insignificant, but he who knows all hearts knows what our efforts are and what we are capable of. Let us work joyfully alongside our brothers and sisters as we serve each other and build the kingdom.

Hear, O ye heavens, and give ear, O earth,
and rejoice ye inhabitants thereof, for the Lord is
God, and beside him there is no Savior.

DOCTRINE & COVENANTS 76:1

As a part of Joseph Smith's inspired translation of the Bible, and more specifically his pondering upon John 5:29, a vision burst upon him and Sidney Rigdon, a revelation so significant in our dispensation that it is called the Vision. It is a marvelous commentary on the statement of the Master at the Last Supper that "in my Father's house are many mansions: if it were not so, I would have told you" (John 14:2). In other words, the concept that there is more than heaven and hell, that no two individuals live their lives in exactly the same way, and that rewards hereafter must be as varied as the quality of individuals' mortal lives—this concept is so plain, so straightforward, so obvious, that if it were any other way, Jesus would have told us so. The Vision is one of the most far-reaching of any revelation ever received. Surely it brought joy and rejoicing to persons on earth and beyond the veil.

*By the power of the Spirit our eyes were opened
and our understandings were enlightened, so as to
see and understand the things of God.*

DOCTRINE & COVENANTS 76:12

Joseph Smith and Sidney Rigdon were working on Joseph's translation of the Gospel of John at the Johnson farmhouse in Hiram, Ohio, when the magnificent vision was received. "For what man knoweth the things of a man, save the spirit of man which is in him? even so the things of God knoweth no man, but the Spirit of God" (1 Corinthians 2:11). The power of the Spirit opened the heavens to Joseph and Sidney, as their eyes gazed upon the glories of eternity and knowledge was poured out concerning life after death. Glorious in scope and precept, the Vision is one of the greatest revelations ever given to man. The Prophet said, "Could you gaze into heaven five minutes, you would know more than you would by reading all that ever was written on the subject" (*History of the Church,* 6:50). When a dispensation of light and truth is needed, the Lord opens the windows of heaven to those who diligently seek him.

*The record which we bear is the
fulness of the gospel of Jesus Christ, who is the Son,
whom we saw and with whom we conversed.*

DOCTRINE & COVENANTS 76:14

Joseph Smith summed up the Vision: "Nothing could be more pleasing to the Saints upon the order of the kingdom of the Lord, than the light which burst upon the world through the foregoing vision. Every law, every commandment, every promise, every truth, and every point touching the destiny of man, from Genesis to Revelation, where the purity of the scriptures remains unsullied by the folly of men, go to show the perfection of the theory [of different degrees of glory in the future life] and witnesses the fact that that document is a transcript from the records of the eternal world. . . . every honest man is constrained to exclaim: '*It came from God*'" (*History of the Church*, 1:252–53). Through the power of the Spirit, the eyes of Joseph Smith and Sidney Rigdon were opened, as seers they gazed upon the glories of eternity, and they saw and spoke with the Savior as had Adam, Enoch, Noah, Abraham, and Moses before them.

After the many testimonies which have been given of him, this is the testimony last of all, which we give of him: That he lives! For we saw him, even on the right hand of God; and we heard the voice bearing record that he is the Only Begotten of the Father.

DOCTRINE & COVENANTS 76:22–23

Joseph Smith and Sidney Rigdon were witnesses of the living reality of the Father and the Son. With strong faith and perfect knowledge, they saw God seated on his heavenly throne and Jesus Christ at his right hand, surrounded by the celestial inhabitants who were worshipping God and the Lamb (D&C 76:20–21). Their knowledge and faith combined as they bore sure witness and testimony to the world. A testimony is a precious endowment of heavenly truth distilled upon the souls of humble seekers by the power of the Holy Ghost. It is a witness that Jesus is the Christ, who came to earth to provide an infinite atonement for all those who come unto him. It comes as a result of obedience and humility, of desiring with all our hearts to know truth and live it. The saving truths that resonate in the hearts of all believers and true disciples are based on this one vital truth—that he lives!

*That by him, and through him, and of him,
the worlds are and were created, and the inhabitants
thereof are begotten sons and daughters unto God.*
DOCTRINE & COVENANTS 76:24

Doctrine and Covenants 76:24 refers to our becoming sons and daughters of God by regeneration, redemption, and spiritual rebirth. Truly, "as many as received him, to them gave he power to become the sons of God" (John 1:12). Christ's substitutionary offering is an infinite atonement because it reaches beyond this earth. What our Lord creates, he redeems. Thus, he is both Creator and Redeemer of worlds without number (Moses 1:30–33). In a poetic version of the Vision, the Prophet spoke of the Lord's ransoming work: "He's the Savior, and only Begotten of God—by him, of him, and through him, the worlds were all made, even all that careen in the heavens so broad, whose inhabitants, too, from the first to the last, are sav'd by the very same Savior of ours; and, of course, are begotten God's daughters and sons, by the very same truths, and the very same pow'rs" ("The Vision," *Times and Seasons* 4, no. 6 [1 February 1843]: 82–83; line breaks omitted).

*[Jesus Christ] glorifies the Father, and saves all
the works of his hands, except those sons of perdition
who deny the Son after the Father has revealed him.*

DOCTRINE & COVENANTS 76:43

In scripture the word *salvation* almost always means
"exaltation" or "eternal life." We sometimes distinguish
between *salvation* and *exaltation* to emphasize our need
to obey the commandments, including receiving the
covenants and ordinances of the house of the Lord, but
the words may generally be used synonymously.
Doctrine and Covenants 76:43 is one of the few places
in scripture where *salvation* conveys something other
than the highest of eternal rewards, for it teaches that
all of God's children (save only those who defect to
perdition) will attain some level of salvation hereafter
(compare D&C 76:88; 132:17). In that sense, *salvation*
means a kind of universal salvation, although we must
understand that only those who inherit the celestial
kingdom will live in the presence of God the Father.
The God and Father of us all loves all of his children
and, likewise, his prophets yearn that they all might be
saved with an everlasting salvation.

*Who overcome by faith, and are sealed by
the Holy Spirit of promise, which the Father sheds
forth upon all those who are just and true.*
DOCTRINE & COVENANTS 76:53

Those who inherit the highest glory are those who have "overcome by faith" (D&C 76:53). That is to say, through their trust in the merits and mercy and promise of Jesus Christ, they have overcome this world (John 16:33), as did their Master, and thereby prepared themselves for the glorious world to come. Alma instructed his son Helaman to teach the people "to withstand every temptation of the devil, with their faith on the Lord Jesus Christ" (Alma 37:33). To have overcome the world is to have reached the point where taint and shoddiness and vulgarity no longer appeal to us. To have overcome the world is to reach the point where we have chosen righteousness, chosen the path of the disciple, chosen to do things the Lord's way. Having thus through the years cultivated the gift of the Holy Ghost, we will eventually enjoy the ratifying seal of approval of the Holy Spirit promised to the Saints of the Most High.

They are they who are the church of the Firstborn.
DOCTRINE & COVENANTS 76:54

We enter the outward church, The Church of Jesus Christ, through receiving the first principles and ordinances of the gospel, thereby becoming a son or a daughter of the Lord Jesus Christ by adoption (Mosiah 5:7). If we then receive the covenants and ordinances of the house of the Lord and are true to them, we qualify eventually to be members of the church of the Firstborn, the inner church, or church within the veil. Through the Atonement and the ordinances of exaltation, we may be raised to inherit equally with Christ all that the Father has. We become joint heirs or co-inheritors with Christ, as though we ourselves had been the firstborn and entitled to the birthright (Romans 8:16–17). We thereby become sons and daughters of God, even the Father. "Wherefore, as it is written, they are gods, even the sons of God" (D&C 76:58; see also Psalm 82:6; John 10:34–36; D&C 132:19–20).

These are they who are just men made perfect through
Jesus the mediator of the new covenant, who wrought out this
perfect atonement through the shedding of his own blood.
DOCTRINE & COVENANTS 76:69

Ye are therefore commanded to be perfect, even as
your Father who is in heaven is perfect" (JST Matthew
5:50). Although it is hypothetically possible for a person to live a life without error, spiritual distraction, or
sin, it is, of course, highly improbable (Smith, *Lectures
on Faith* 5:2). And yet we are commanded so to do. How
do we reconcile the two sobering realities? To be perfect is to be whole, complete, fully formed, finished. As
unaided mortals, we are finite and woefully incomplete.
As we join with Christ, "the author and finisher of our
faith" (Hebrews 12:2; Moroni 6:4), by covenant we
become whole or complete, we become perfect in
Christ (Moroni 10:32). Through the infinite atonement, the Savior takes our sins upon himself and conveys to us his righteousness (2 Corinthians 5:21).
Therefore, the prophets speak of our being "made perfect" through the ransoming and redeeming power of
the perfect atonement.

*These are they who are not valiant in the
testimony of Jesus; wherefore, they obtain not
the crown over the kingdom of our God.*

DOCTRINE & COVENANTS 76:79

In this, our second estate, our mortal sojourn, those who are true to the light within them and seek to align themselves with principles of morality and decency will be led eventually to the covenant gospel, either here or hereafter (D&C 84:46–48). Individuals may be Christian in this life, having gained the testimony that Jesus is their Lord and Savior and committed themselves to a life of Christian discipleship. Valiance in that testimony would, however, entail an acceptance of the fulness of the gospel of Jesus Christ (D&C 35:12; 84:49–50). Further, even Latter-day Saints whose approach to gospel living is casual and whose adherence to the statutes and decrees of God is at best inconsistent are also not valiant in the testimony of Jesus. The issue is not where the membership records reside but rather where the heart is. Unless the flames of faith within their souls are fanned by a deeper commitment, their eternal inheritance will be a terrestrial glory.

*When he shall deliver up the kingdom, and present
it unto the Father, spotless, saying: I have overcome and have
trodden the wine-press alone, even the wine-press of the
fierceness of the wrath of Almighty God.*
DOCTRINE & COVENANTS 76:107

Christians look to the cross as the symbol of the
Atonement (1 Nephi 11:33). Jesus came into the world
that he might be lifted up upon the cross (3 Nephi
27:13–14). The Savior's suffering and agony in the
Garden were not merely fear of the hideous pain he
would experience the next day. His suffering in Gethsemane was redemptive. For the first time in his life,
Jesus was required to walk and act on his own without
the strengthening and sustaining power of the Father's
Spirit. He who had always been obedient and thus had
never been left to himself (John 8:29) now agonized
alone in the garden of the oil press. The Suffering
Servant was exposed to the wrath of God, the awful
alienation that follows in the wake of unrepented sin,
combined with the infirmities and sickness, heartache,
loneliness, despair, and feelings of inadequacy known
only too well by mortals (Alma 7:11–13). What began
in Gethsemane was completed on Calvary.

And ye cannot bear all things now; nevertheless, be of good cheer, for I will lead you along. The kingdom is yours and the blessings thereof are yours, and the riches of eternity are yours.

DOCTRINE & COVENANTS 78:18

The Savior shows us the pathway to happiness here and everlasting joy hereafter. "Be of good cheer" (John 16:33), he admonished the Saints in the meridian dispensation. Today, as then, the Great Exemplar shows us the way. He knows that we must grow line upon line in both understanding and living the gospel. "Behold, ye are little children and ye cannot bear all things now; ye must grow in grace and in the knowledge of the truth" (D&C 50:40). The Good Shepherd loves all his sheep, and he will, within the constraints imposed by human agency and divine justice and mercy, work out our rewards and punishments to the fullest blessing possible. He is the only One who can judge us honestly because He is the only One who fully understands our hearts and minds—what has shaped us, what our susceptibilities and weaknesses are, what we are capable of. He stands ready to strengthen the faithful and bless them with the riches of eternity.

My servant Jared Carter should go . . . , proclaiming glad tidings of great joy, even the everlasting gospel. And I will send upon him the Comforter, which shall teach him the truth and the way whither he shall go; and inasmuch as he is faithful, I will crown him again with sheaves.

DOCTRINE & COVENANTS 79:1–3

When we are called to Church service we are entitled to the inspiration of the Lord in our respective callings. We are to seek the guidance of the Holy Ghost to teach the truth with love and to understand how to bless others. The gospel is a message of joy and happiness. Those who live by the Spirit do not have woeful countenances or feel burdened by the "weight of glory" (2 Corinthians 4:17). And those who understand the richness of the gospel know that we need not be commanded in all things. The Lord wants us to use intelligence in making good choices. He expects us to use our faculties to go forward with faith. Clearly, he wants us to come unto him, to counsel with him, to humbly seek his inspiration in weightier matters. Having the companionship of the Holy Ghost means that we are striving to live in tune with the Spirit so that we can receive answers, direction, and solace from the Lord.

*Wherefore, go ye and preach my gospel, whether to
the north or to the south, to the east or to the west, it mattereth
not, for ye cannot go amiss. Therefore, declare the things which
ye have heard, and verily believe, and know to be true.*

DOCTRINE & COVENANTS 80:3–4

When it comes to sharing the message of salvation
with others, it matters more who we are than where
we go. Whether down the street or on the other side
of the world, we are to emulate the teachings of Christ
in our lives. Our light should shine so conspicuously
that others will inquire as to the source of our joy and
peace and want to know more. Every place in the
world is in desperate need of our light, our testimony,
our truth. But who we really are will resonate more
loudly, more convincingly, than anything we might
know or say. Members of the Church are always under
surveillance, as others watch us to see if we are prac-
ticing what we preach. We are living testimonies of the
living God, mortal, imperfect heralds of latter-day
truth.

Unto [Joseph Smith] I have given the keys of the kingdom,
which belong always unto the Presidency of the High Priesthood.
DOCTRINE & COVENANTS 81:2

The First Presidency holds the keys of the kingdom of God on earth. It is the highest council in the Church and the final authority for decisions on spiritual matters (D&C 107:78–80). Elder Marion G. Romney said: "Today the Lord is revealing his will . . . on the issues of this our day through the living prophets, with the First Presidency at the head. What they say as a presidency is what the Lord would say if he were here in person. This is the rock foundation of Mormonism. . . . So I repeat again, what the presidency say as a presidency is what the Lord would say if he were here, and it is scripture. It should be studied, understood, and followed, even as the revelations in the Doctrine and Covenants and other scriptures" (Conference Report, April 1945, 90). May God bless the great and godly men of the First Presidency, and may we follow them as we would the Savior.

Wherefore, be faithful; stand in the office which I have appointed unto you; succor the weak, lift up the hands which hang down, and strengthen the feeble knees.

DOCTRINE & COVENANTS 81:5

As followers of the Prince of Peace, we are to publish peace—proclaim the truths of salvation and witness by example that the gospel of Jesus Christ transforms people's souls. Jesus "went about doing good" (Acts 10:38). So must we. And just as the Good Shepherd went in search of the lost sheep, so we as undershepherds are called upon to do likewise. Jesus bore the burdens of all humankind. We are called upon "to bear one another's burdens," "to comfort those who stand in need of comfort," and "to stand as witnesses of God at all times" (Mosiah 18:8–9). Modern revelations attest that we are to be the "saviors of men" (D&C 103:9) in that we serve, under our blessed Master, as a lifting and liberating influence to the hungry and the hurting. As Christians we are called upon both to live in the Spirit and to walk in the Spirit (Galatians 5:25). Our walk needs to be as discernible as our talk.

For of him unto whom much is given much is required; and he who sins against the greater light shall receive the greater condemnation.

DOCTRINE & COVENANTS 82:3

Though there is one divine standard that must forevermore be held up to all mankind—the laws and commandments of Almighty God, laws and commandments by which all persons will eventually be judged—our Heavenly Father is as merciful as he is just. No one will be condemned for failing to live a law or obey an ordinance that was not available. No one will be eternally disadvantaged for failing to understand a truth or perceive a principle of which he was ignorant. On the other hand, God has grander expectations of those who have received the revealed witness and who have been blessed and prospered through receiving higher understanding. As the Savior taught, it would be better never to have known a truth than to have ignored or spurned it. Each of us is expected—no, required—to be true to the light we possess, to live a life befitting what our omniloving Lord has bestowed upon us.

And now, verily I say unto you, I, the Lord, will not lay any sin to your charge; go your ways and sin no more; but unto that soul who sinneth shall the former sins return, saith the Lord your God.

DOCTRINE & COVENANTS 82:7

Because no ones traverses life's paths without transgression, it is inevitable that some sins, particularly smaller sins, will be repeated. It would hardly be appropriate to suggest that a man who lost his temper in 1969, labored and prayed and worked to overcome that weakness for many years, and then lost his temper again in 1985 now had twice the amount of sin and guilt resting upon his shoulders. Rather, the sin has not been fully forsaken (D&C 58:42–43). Suffering and pain, guilt and remorse, relief and respite are not quantifiable factors. God does not just keep track of every deed in order to weigh the good versus the bad in our life. The gospel of Jesus Christ is intended to do more than balance the scales. It is intended to renew and rehabilitate us, to cleanse our souls, purify our desires, and empower us to become a people who have lost the inclination to repeat sin.

I, the Lord, am bound when ye do what I say;
but when ye do not what I say, ye have no promise.
DOCTRINE & COVENANTS 82:10

The Lord is "the way, the truth, and the life" (John 14:6). In him is no falsehood. He cannot lie or deceive, or he would cease to be God (Alma 42:22–25). We can have perfect confidence that what he says is true. The dying words of Joshua to ancient Israel reaffirm that God's promises are sure: "Not one thing hath failed of all the good things which the Lord your God spake concerning you" (Joshua 23:14). When we do what the Lord says, when we faithfully keep our covenants and remain steadfast and true, the Lord promises us peace here and eternal life hereafter. Though we still experience our share of adversity and heartache, we are bound to him in an everlasting promise. If we are not true to the Lord, however, we have no such promise. Our covenants, when kept, seal us to the Lord in a reassuring promise that cannot— that will not—be broken.

For Zion must increase in beauty, and in holiness; her borders must be enlarged; her stakes must be strengthened; yea, verily I say unto you, Zion must arise and put on her beautiful garments.

DOCTRINE & COVENANTS 82:14

The gospel of Jesus Christ is destined to go unto every nation, kindred, tongue, and people before the Savior comes in glory (Joseph Smith–Matthew 1:31). Eventually, "the earth shall be full of the knowledge of the Lord, as the waters cover the sea" (Isaiah 11:9). The stakes of Zion will become strongholds of strength and pillars of protection as wickedness widens and malevolence multiplies. The Prophet Joseph Smith taught: "There will be here and there a Stake [of Zion] for the gathering of the Saints. Some may have cried peace, but the Saints and the world will have little peace from henceforth. Let this not hinder us from going to the Stakes." The Prophet also taught: "The time is soon coming when no man will have any peace but in Zion and her Stakes" (*Teachings of the Prophet Joseph Smith*, 160–61). Zion puts on her strength in that she rests secure under the power and authority of the holy priesthood (D&C 113:8).

Therefore, in the ordinances thereof, the power of godliness is manifest. And without the ordinances thereof, and the authority of the priesthood, the power of godliness is not manifest unto men in the flesh; for without this no man can see the face of God, even the Father, and live.

DOCTRINE & COVENANTS 84:20–22

The word *ordinance,* as used in scripture, has a dual meaning. In its broadest sense, an ordinance is a law, a commandment, a statute: "And the keys of the mysteries of the kingdom shall not be taken from my servant Joseph Smith, Jun., through the means I have appointed, while he liveth, inasmuch as he obeyeth mine ordinances" (D&C 64:5). In addition, ordinances are rites or ceremonies (for example, baptism, confirmation, ordination to the priesthood, and so forth) performed by one holding proper authority that open the door to greater light and knowledge; they are channels of divine power. Through the administration of ordinances and obedience to them, the power of godliness is manifest. Thus, the endowments of the Spirit cannot be fully enjoyed unless the ordinances—which bring the power of godliness—are in our midst. "For without this"—the power of godliness—"no man can see the face of God, even the Father and live" (D&C 84:22).

[Moses] sought diligently to sanctify his people that they might behold the face of God; but they hardened their hearts and could not endure his presence; therefore, the Lord in his wrath . . . took Moses out of their midst, and the Holy Priesthood also.

DOCTRINE & COVENANTS 84:23–25

F ew men have lived on this earth who enjoyed the kind of direct contact and intimate association with Deity as did Moses. Indeed, the Old Testament affirms that "Moses was very meek, above all the men which were upon the face of the earth" (Numbers 12:3; Deuteronomy 34:10). In that light, it is unfortunate that the Judaeo-Christian world has often misunderstood why Moses was not allowed to enter the promised land with his people. Many point to Numbers 20:7–12, in which Moses is scolded by God for seemingly taking glory unto himself in miraculously causing water to spring forth out of the rock. Modern revelation provides us a more complete doctrinal picture: The people of Israel were not worthy of the blessings of the higher priesthood, the keys of which were held by Moses. God therefore took away the full blessings of the priesthood from Israel as a body and also the man who held the directing power of that priesthood.

The lesser priesthood . . . holdeth the key of the ministering of angels and the preparatory gospel . . . of repentance and of baptism, and the remission of sins, and the law of carnal commandments, which the Lord . . . caused to continue with the house of Aaron among the children of Israel until John.

DOCTRINE & COVENANTS 84:26–27

Wherever the holy priesthood of God is found, there is the church and kingdom of God. How much of the plan of salvation is given to a people determines the order of the priesthood that accompanies that gospel. When the fulness of the everlasting gospel, including the blessings of the temple, was taken from ancient Israel, Jehovah gave them a preparatory gospel, a law of carnal commandments, a law of performances and ordinances (Mosiah 13:30). Although such men as Elijah, Isaiah, Jeremiah, Ezekiel, Lehi, and others were ordained to the Melchizedek Priesthood in the generations from Moses to Jesus, their calls came by special dispensation (Smith, *Teachings of the Prophet Joseph Smith,* 180–81). The preparatory gospel and the Aaronic Priesthood were the priesthood of administration among the people. The lesser priesthood continued until the time of John the Baptist, who prepared the way for a full restoration at the hands of the Messiah himself.

And this is according to the oath and
covenant which belongeth to the priesthood.
DOCTRINE & COVENANTS 84:39

The covenant of the Melchizedek Priesthood is entered into specifically by those formally ordained to that sacred authority, but the duties and blessings described in Doctrine and Covenants 84 are meant for every member of the Lord's Church, both male and female. Indeed, the highest blessings of the priesthood come only to a man and a woman in the house of the Lord. We promise to magnify our callings, give diligent heed to the words of eternal life, and live by every word of God. In return, the Lord promises to sanctify, renew, and make us the elect of God and to grant unto us eternal life (D&C 84:33–44). To show the binding nature of his covenant, the Almighty swears with an oath that he will fulfill his part of the agreement, as he did anciently to Enoch and Melchizedek (JST Genesis 14:25–40), to Nephi, son of Helaman (Helaman 10:4–7), and even to the Son of Man himself (Psalm 110:4; JST Hebrews 7:3).

AUGUST

*Therefore, verily, thus saith the Lord, let
Zion rejoice, for this is Zion—THE PURE
IN HEART; therefore, let Zion rejoice,
while all the wicked shall mourn.*

DOCTRINE & COVENANTS
97:21

For the word of the Lord is truth, and whatsoever is truth is light, and whatsoever is light is Spirit, even the Spirit of Jesus Christ. . . . and the Spirit enlighteneth every man through the world, that hearkeneth to the voice of the Spirit.

DOCTRINE & COVENANTS 84:45–46

Christ is the "light which shineth in darkness" (D&C 11:11). His light, the light of Christ, is a source of revelation given of God to "every man, that he may know good from evil" (Moroni 7:16). Through the light of Christ, our conscience guides us to choose right over wrong, quickens our understanding, and gives life and light to all things (D&C 88:5–13). The light of Christ will lead those who live by it to the fulness of the gospel of Jesus Christ and the greater light of the Holy Ghost (Alma 16:16–17), whereas those who harden their hearts and reject the Light of Truth will be filled with the darkness of sin and unbelief. Light comes from God and his truth: "God is light, and in him is no darkness at all" (1 John 1:5). Through this light, which emanates from God and fills the immensity of space, members of the Godhead are omnipresent.

They shall remain under this condemnation until they repent and remember the new covenant, even the Book of Mormon and the former commandments which I have given them, not only to say, but to do according to that which I have written.

DOCTRINE & COVENANTS 84:57

We have been richly blessed with scripture: the mind and will of God preserved for us and our generations. The Book of Mormon and the Doctrine and Covenants were written for our day and given to us by a loving God through his prophets. "Do we, as Saints of the Most High God, treasure the word He has preserved for us at so great a cost?" asked President Ezra Taft Benson. "Are we using these books of latter-day revelation to bless our lives and resist the powers of the evil one? This is the purpose for which they were given. How can we not stand condemned before the Lord if we treat them lightly by letting them do no more than gather dust on our shelves?" (*A Witness and a Warning,* 28). These scriptures—if sincerely feasted and pondered upon—will help us keep the commandments. They will bring the Spirit into our hearts and homes. They will strengthen our resolve to live the gospel.

Neither take ye thought beforehand what ye shall say;
but treasure up in your minds continually the words of life,
and it shall be given you in the very hour that portion
that shall be meted unto every man.

DOCTRINE & COVENANTS 84:85

Spiritual work must be accomplished through spiritual means. We are called as agents of God, who is our Principal, and we are expected to do his work the way he wants it done (D&C 64:29). His message thus becomes our message, and his words should thus become our words. We are not converted to the truth because of smooth or spectacular rhetoric, nor do we come unto Christ or his restored gospel through physical evidence alone. The heralds of divine truth are expected to align their lives to the will of the Almighty so that they, as spokespersons, may deliver the distinctive message that should be delivered at that very moment. In short, they are to speak by the power of the Holy Ghost. In so doing, they speak with "the tongue of angels," for they speak "the words of Christ" (2 Nephi 32:2–3), and thereby become a means whereby God's Spirit communicates directly to the spirits of others.

Let every man stand in his own office, and labor in his own calling. . . . Also the body hath need of every member, that all may be edified together, that the system may be kept perfect.

DOCTRINE & COVENANTS 84:109–10

Priesthood correlation is that divinely instituted system of Church government in which all of the programs and all of the members of the Church are brought together under one head and where all tasks are accomplished under the direction of the holy priesthood. Because there must be order in the Lord's house (D&C 132:8), we must coordinate our efforts and share our talents so that the Church, the body of Christ, will operate most effectively and efficiently. Faithful Saints do not step beyond their bounds and assume the duties of another; rather, they stand in their own office and labor in their own calling, knowing that every part of the ecclesiastical machinery is vital to the proper organization and function of the kingdom. In the end, as we do the Lord's work in the Lord's way—under the revealed plan of priesthood correlation—the Saints are edified and the work goes forward as the Master intended.

Let him trust in me and he shall not be confounded;
and a hair of his head shall not fall to the ground unnoticed.
DOCTRINE & COVENANTS 84:116

Life in an imperfect world is, by nature, unpredictable. Everything is changing, life is perplexing, and we feel at times that our lives are continuous confusion and commotion. Stability is only found by anchoring our faith on the unchanging Lord and trusting him whose love is all encompassing. When others let us down or disappoint, there is One in whom we can have perfect trust. When it seems like nothing and no one can be counted on, there is One in whom we can have complete confidence. We must "trust in the name of the Lord" (Isaiah 50:10). Our hope can be as steady as the sunrise, even when the events around us are moving from wonderful to tragic. We have the comforting assurance that the Lord will accompany us as we sojourn through life, if we trust him, believe him, love him, and seek to do his will. His peace is there for those who choose him, for those who trust him.

Yea, thus saith the still, small voice, which whispereth through and pierceth all things, and often times it maketh my bones to quake while it maketh manifest.
DOCTRINE & COVENANTS 85:6

God will choose what means he will employ when he addresses himself to his living oracles. President Gordon B. Hinckley pointed out: "There is a tremendous history behind this church, a history of prophecy, a history of revelation, and a backlog of decisions which set the pattern of the Church so that there aren't constant recurring problems that require any special dispensation. But there are occasionally things that arise where the will of the Lord is sought, and in those circumstances I think the best way I could describe the process is to liken it to the experience of Elijah. After Elijah had encountered a wind, an earthquake, and a fire, he heard 'a still, small voice,' which I describe as the whisperings of the Spirit. . . . [O]ne must have and seek and cultivate that Spirit, and there comes understanding and it is real. I can give testimony of that" (in Dew, *Go Forward with Faith*, 585–86).

Verily, thus saith the Lord unto you my servants,
concerning the parable of the wheat and of the tares.
DOCTRINE & COVENANTS 86:1

The Latter-day Saints, like the Former-day Saints, need to understand the principle taught by the parable of the wheat and the tares: While the kingdom grows in strength and numbers, it is inevitable that untoward individuals or distracting influences will come into the Church. In some cases, they will be difficult to recognize, for in their early stages of development they appear to be very much like the member who is in good standing and who is walking in strait paths. As time passes, however, the deeper differences—doctrinal or behavioral—between the wheat (the faithful) and the tares (the mischievous or the imposters) begin to emerge. If the latter's offenses are not such that the leaders of the Church feel directed to impose Church discipline, the tares gradually lose the influence of the Spirit of God and begin to disfellowship themselves. In the end, "the hypocrites shall be detected and shall be cut off, either in life or in death" (D&C 50:8).

Thus saith the Lord concerning the wars that will
shortly come to pass, beginning at the rebellion of South
Carolina, which will eventually terminate in the death and
misery of many souls; and the time will come that war will be
poured out upon all nations, beginning at this place.
DOCTRINE & COVENANTS 87:1–2

Doctrine and Covenants 87 is a remarkable
prophecy that stands as one more evidence of Joseph
Smith's prophetic powers. The revelation was given
on Christmas Day 1832, some twenty-nine years
before the first shot was fired in the American Civil
War. That war began in South Carolina (v. 1), the divi-
sion was between North and South (v. 3), the Con-
federacy called on Great Britain for help (v. 3), and
Southern slaves rebelled against their masters (v. 4).
But Section 87 has a broader application. This
prophecy reveals that a new era of warfare and bloodshed would come as an outgrowth of the Civil War.
From the War between the States until today, millions
have suffered and died in regional and world wars. It
seems that conflict and the technology of war acceler-
ate all about us. This revelation testifies of Joseph
Smith's prophetic calling as it prepares the Saints for
the turmoil ahead.

Stand ye in holy places, and be not moved, until the day of the Lord come; for behold, it cometh quickly, saith the Lord. Amen.
DOCTRINE & COVENANTS 87:8

In the midst of conflict and turmoil, we are to stand in holy places, apart from the wickedness of the world (D&C 45:32). By doing so, the faithful will be blessed "amid the encircling gloom" of latter-day tribulations (D&C 63:34; 115:6; *Hymns,* no. 97). Holy places are the home and family, the place where covenants are kept in daily interaction with others. Holy places are the temple, where covenants are made that lead to eternal joy and everlasting life. Holy places are the chapel, where we partake of the sacrament and serve one another in humility and love. A holy place is any place where we hold back the world, cleave unto light, and grow in righteousness. As Saints we gather to holy places, where we are buoyed up in our faith and strengthened in our desire to live the gospel more fully. Those who stand apart from the world in holy places look forward to the coming day of the Lord.

Wherefore, I now send upon you another Comforter,
even upon you my friends, that it may abide in your hearts,
even the Holy Spirit of promise; which other Comforter
is the same that I promised unto my disciples, as is
recorded in the testimony of John.

DOCTRINE & COVENANTS 88:3

For three years Jesus had taught his disciples as their Tutor and their Comforter. "If ye love me," he taught them, "keep my commandments. And I will pray the Father, and *he shall give you another Comforter,* that he may abide with you forever; even the Spirit of truth" (John 14:15–17; emphasis added). The word *another* means "someone of the same kind," that is, someone like Jesus himself who would take his place and do his work. Other translations of the Bible render the passage in John 14 as "another Helper" (New King James Version), "another Counselor" (New International Version), and even "another Advocate" (New Revised Standard Version). Although ultimately Christ is our Advocate with the Father (D&C 45:3–5), the Savior has sent his Holy Spirit to convict us of sin, convince us of the truth, and direct us toward righteousness (John 16:8–11). The Holy Ghost, one called to help, is the member of the Godhead who encourages and exhorts the Saints.

*Truth shineth. This is the light of Christ. As also he
is in the sun, and the light of the sun, and the power thereof
by which it was made. As also he . . . is the light of the
moon . . . ; as also the light of the stars.*

DOCTRINE & COVENANTS 88:7–9

The light of Christ or the Spirit of Christ is law and
light and life. It has both natural and redemptive functions. Like our Heavenly Father, the Holy Ghost can
be in only one place at a time, so he draws upon the
light of Christ to communicate sacred truths and dis-
pense spiritual gifts to myriads of beings separated in
time and space (Moroni 10:17; McConkie, *New Witness,*
70, 258). Thus, the same power that makes it possible
for us to see with our physical eyes also makes it possible for us to see with spiritual eyes (D&C 88:6–13).
Discernment—the innate capacity to distinguish good
from evil, the relevant from the irrelevant—also comes
through this Spirit (Moroni 7:12–19). Further, those
who are true to this light within them will be led,
whether in this life or the next, to the higher light of
the Holy Ghost that comes through the covenant
gospel (D&C 84:44–53).

*The spirit and the body are the soul of man. And the
resurrection from the dead is the redemption of the soul. And
the redemption of the soul is through him that quickeneth all
things, in whose bosom it is decreed that the poor and
the meek of the earth shall inherit it.*

DOCTRINE & COVENANTS 88:15–17

Almost always, when the prophets use the word *soul*,
they are speaking of the spirit of man. Alma explained
that "the soul shall be restored to the body, and the
body to the soul" (Alma 40:23). Jesus likewise counseled his disciples not to fear those who can do harm
to the body but rather "fear him which is able to
destroy both soul and body in hell" (Matthew 10:28;
see also Job 14:22; Psalm 16:10). Doctrine and
Covenants 88:15–17 represents the strictest definition
of the soul, namely, the spirit united with the body. As
mortals we are souls in the sense that we have a spirit
and a body, but after the resurrection we will experience "the redemption of the soul," in that spirit and
body will be inseparably united, never again to be
divided, and we will be clothed upon with glory and
honor everlasting. We will then experience a fulness
of joy (D&C 93:33).

*After it [Earth] hath filled the measure of its creation,
it shall be crowned with glory, even with the presence of God the
Father; that bodies who are of the celestial kingdom may possess
it forever and ever; for, for this intent was it made and
created, and for this intent are they sanctified.*

DOCTRINE & COVENANTS 88:19–20

As a living entity, the earth has gone through stages of development. When Adam and Eve were placed in the Garden of Eden, the earth was in a terrestrial, paradisiacal condition. As a result of the Fall, our planet descended to a telestial level. When the Son of Man returns in glory, the end of the world—meaning the end of worldliness, or "the destruction of the wicked" (Joseph Smith–Matthew 1:4)—will occur. The earth and its inhabitants will be transfigured, lifted to a higher (terrestrial) plane, and for a thousand years Satan and his hosts will be removed from the paradisiacal earth and bound. At the end of the thousand years, a final great battle will be fought between the forces of good and evil, and Satan and his followers will be cast out forever. The earth will then undergo its final change—it will be made celestial and become the permanent abode of its inhabitants who inherit the highest degree of glory.

*Ye who are quickened by a portion of the celestial
glory shall then receive of the same, even a fulness. And they
who are quickened by a portion of the terrestrial glory shall
then receive of the same. . . . And also they who are
quickened by a portion of the telestial glory.*

DOCTRINE & COVENANTS 88:29–31

Alma taught the law of restoration: We cannot be transformed from waywardness in this life to spirituality in the life to come (Alma 41). Paul similarly taught the Galatian Saints the law of the harvest: "Be not deceived; God is not mocked: for whatsoever a man soweth, that shall he also reap" (Galatians 6:7). Those who live the law of the celestial kingdom in this life, who endure faithfully to the end in observing their covenants, and who are thus quickened by the Spirit (a portion of celestial glory) will, in the resurrection, receive what the scriptures call the fulness of the glory of the Father (D&C 76:56; 93:16, 19). The same is true for those who live a terrestrial law or a telestial law and are thus quickened by a portion of the glory associated with those kingdoms—they will receive there what they have become acclimated to here. Truly, "this life is the time for men to prepare to meet God" (Alma 34:32).

Draw near unto me and I will draw near unto you;
seek me diligently and ye shall find me; ask, and ye shall
receive; knock, and it shall be opened unto you.

DOCTRINE & COVENANTS 88:63

We live in a time when drawing upon the powers of heaven through prayer is needed more than ever. So much about our lives can fill our days with worry and keep us awake at night—health and family challenges, financial concerns, daily difficulties, fear about the future. Elder Boyd K. Packer said: "If you need a transfusion of spiritual strength, then just ask for it. We call that prayer. Prayer is powerful spiritual medicine" (*Memorable Stories with a Message*, 126). Prayer can help see us through to the other side of sorrow; it can strengthen us when we feel like giving up, it can prompt us with inspiration about what to do and how to do it. The apostle Paul urged us to "pray without ceasing" and "by prayer and supplication with thanksgiving let [our] requests be made known unto God" (1 Thessalonians 5:17; Philippians 4:6). The Lord will draw near unto us if we come before him diligently and with a humble heart.

Behold, that which you hear is as the voice of one crying in the wilderness—in the wilderness, because you cannot see him—my voice, because my voice is Spirit; my Spirit is truth; truth abideth and hath no end; and if it be in you it shall abound.

DOCTRINE & COVENANTS 88:66

We often observe that we "hear" the word of the Lord. That word may come through words spoken by living apostles and prophets (D&C 1:38; 21:5). It may come through hearing the scriptures read and recognizing the relevance of holy writ (D&C 18:34–36). It may come through vision or appearance or an audible voice or a strong feeling or impression. In other words, the voice of the Lord sounds and is received in varied ways. In general, it is perfectly appropriate to say that we have "heard" the word of the Lord on a matter when we have felt an outpouring of the Holy Spirit. Surely, God's voice is his Spirit, and when we encounter that Spirit, we feel his involvement in our lives, sense his approbation, and delight to bask in his lifting influence. In short, we hear his voice.

And if your eye be single to my glory, your whole bodies shall be filled with light, and there shall be no darkness in you; and that body which is filled with light comprehendeth all things.
DOCTRINE & COVENANTS 88:67

The distinct distillation of God's purpose and plan is as follows: "For behold, this is my work and my glory—to bring to pass the immortality and eternal life of man" (Moses 1:39). In short, God is in the business of people; his joy and his delight come through the redemption and exaltation of his children. To have our eye single to the glory of God is to have our heart and mind directed by that divine mandate. It is to share with the Almighty the undergirding and overarching mission to lead souls to Christ and thereby help them to gain peace here and acquire eternal reward hereafter. When our eye is single to the glory of God, we have no private agenda, no hidden purpose, no double mindedness, no distraction that would cause us to treat the work of the Lord as secondary. Rather, we are set on doing things the Lord's way and thus assisting to accomplish his consummate purposes.

*I give unto you a commandment that you shall teach
one another the doctrine of the kingdom. Teach ye diligently and
my grace shall attend you, that you may be instructed more
perfectly . . . in all things that pertain unto the kingdom
of God, that are expedient for you to understand.*

DOCTRINE & COVENANTS 88:77–78

Alma explained that God gave the ancients commandments *after* he had taught them the plan of redemption (Alma 12:32). Doctrine and Covenants 88:77–78 sets forth a similar concept: Teach doctrine first, and then upon that doctrinal foundation teach behavior. Once people know the doctrine, the plan of salvation, then they understand why they are to do certain things and refrain from doing other things. Some wanderers are reclaimed only through hearing the pure testimony of sound doctrine (Alma 4:19). "True doctrine, understood, changes attitudes and behavior," Elder Boyd K. Packer explained. "The study of the doctrines of the gospel will improve behavior quicker than a study of behavior will improve behavior. . . . That is why we stress so forcefully the study of the doctrines of the gospel" (*Ensign,* November 1986, 17). In short, doctrine explains why. In some cases, it teaches how. Sound doctrine enlightens the mind and settles the heart.

And as all have not faith, seek ye diligently and teach one
another words of wisdom; yea, seek ye out of the best books words
of wisdom; seek learning, even by study and also by faith.
DOCTRINE & COVENANTS 88:118

All of us have seasons of life when our reservoir of spiritual strength is low. We wonder how we can build up our faith to reach new heights of spiritual development. Faith is a gift of God given to those who diligently seek him. Alma admonished us to "awake and arouse your faculties, even to an experiment upon my words, and exercise a particle of faith" (Alma 32:27). We are strengthened in our faith and testimony by study and pondering, by consistently exercising our faith. By seeking diligently the everlasting things, by sincerely feasting upon the words of eternal life, by becoming anxiously engaged in good causes, we will grow strong in our faith. We are not built up in our faith by reading just any book. There is a hierarchy of "best books"—some provide good entertainment but are not treasures of truth; some provide wisdom but do not spiritually strengthen. The best books are those that lead us to God and his truth.

Above all things, clothe yourselves with the bond of charity,
as with a mantle, which is the bond of perfectness and peace.
DOCTRINE & COVENANTS 88:125

Charity is the pure love of Christ, and it endureth
forever" (Moroni 7:47). But how do we make charity *live*
in our hearts? Elder Marvin J. Ashton observed:
"Perhaps the greatest charity comes when we are kind
to each other, when we don't judge or categorize someone else, when we simply give each other the benefit of
the doubt or remain quiet. Charity is accepting someone's differences, weaknesses, and shortcomings; having
patience with someone who has let us down; or resist-
ing the impulse to become offended when someone
doesn't handle something the way we might have hoped.
Charity is refusing to take advantage of another's weakness and being willing to forgive someone who has hurt
us. Charity is expecting the best of each other" (*Ensign,*
May 1992, 19). We exercise charity as we come to know
another's heart, as we reach out in kindness, as we do
small things with great love. Charity is our love for the
Lord, shown through our love for others.

And all saints who remember to keep and do these sayings,
walking in obedience to the commandments, shall receive health in
their navel and marrow to their bones; and shall find wisdom
and great treasures of knowledge, even hidden treasures.
DOCTRINE & COVENANTS 89:18–19

Blessings are connected to laws, "and when we obtain any blessing from God, it is by obedience to that law upon which it is predicated" (D&C 130:21). Saints who obey the Word of Wisdom are promised health, strength, wisdom, and both great and hidden treasures of knowledge. That does not mean, of course, that obedient Saints will not have illness or pain or be instantly more sagacious than others. But it does mean that they will have the peace that comes from willing obedience, the wisdom that comes from understanding principles and promises, and the treasures of knowledge that come to those who follow the Lord's commands. In 1833 when the revelation was given, people did not fully understand its reasons or expectations. Even today, with an abundance of supportive scientific information, we still do not understand all things related to the Word of Wisdom. But we know that this "principle with promise" (D&C 89:3) is given in love and for our well-being.

And [they] shall run and not be weary, and shall
walk and not faint. And I, the Lord, give unto them a promise,
that the destroying angel shall pass by them, as the children
of Israel, and not slay them. Amen.
DOCTRINE & COVENANTS 89:20–21

The Word of Wisdom is a "principle with promise" (D&C 89:3) that will shield and protect us in these latter days. We are bombarded daily with enticements to eat and drink that which is improper. We are assaulted with allurements to partake of that which would only harm, enslave, and separate us from the Spirit of the Lord. The adversary knows that if we sample the things of this world and become addicted to harmful and unhealthy substances, we will have little reason to "seek for the things of a better" world (D&C 25:10). The Word of Wisdom contains proscriptions, prescriptions, and promises. If we follow the Word of Wisdom, we receive the Passover promise of ancient Israel that the destroying angel will pass us by, and we will be blessed with both physical and spiritual strength. We will not falter or die spiritually. We'll go forward in the confidence of the Lord, knowing that we have kept his word and followed his commandments.

All they who receive the oracles of God, let them beware
how they hold them lest they are accounted as a light thing, and
are brought under condemnation thereby, and stumble and
fall when the storms descend, and the winds blow and
the rains descend, and beat upon their house.

DOCTRINE & COVENANTS 90:5

Each of us builds a house of faith. As every builder knows, a house is only as good as its foundation. Foolish people build upon the footings of fame, the shifting sands of secularism, and the marshlands of materialism. All of these will inevitably disappoint and ultimately fail. Enduring faithfulness—and safety from the adversary of righteousness—never comes from fleeting falsehood or the emptiness of immediate gratification. With an eternal perspective, the wise build upon the rock of revelation, giving careful attention to the living oracles of God. Their chief cornerstone is the Savior, and their hearts are riveted upon the things of the Spirit, those internal realities that provide meaning, perspective, and sustenance for all that matters in life. All that we do as Saints must be built upon a foundation of faith and truth and testimony and conversion. Christian disciples build their house of faith on the solid bedrock of the gospel as they center their lives on Jesus Christ.

It is not needful that the Apocrypha should be translated. Therefore, whoso readeth it, let him understand, for the Spirit manifesteth truth; and whoso is enlightened by the Spirit shall obtain benefit therefrom; and whoso receiveth not by the Spirit, cannot be benefited.

DOCTRINE & COVENANTS 91:3–6

When the Prophet Joseph inquired of the Lord concerning the ancient writings called the Apocrypha, he was told: "There are many things contained therein that are true, and it is mostly translated correctly; there are many things contained therein that are not true, which are interpolations by the hands of men" (D&C 91:1–2). We find out the truth of all things by personal revelation, by studying a matter and then seeking a spiritual witness by the power of the Holy Ghost, who manifests truth to the humble seeker. The Lord also taught his prophet that the contents of the Apocrypha, although interesting, are not essential to our salvation. The Prophet's time was limited and valuable. It was absolutely crucial that he spend it on things of greatest worth. So it is with us. With pressing demands and inadequate time for all we might want to do, we must focus our hearts and minds on scriptural truth that is of greatest value and everlasting worth.

*I say unto you my servant Frederick G. Williams,
you shall be a lively member in this order.*
DOCTRINE & COVENANTS 92:2

Frederick G. Williams had recently been appointed as counselor to Joseph Smith in the First Presidency and was a member of the united order (D&C 92:1). Consequently, he was directed by the Lord to "be a lively member in this order" (D&C 92:2). To be lively means to be active, involved, anxiously engaged, diligent, energetic. These are qualities we can each take into our respective Church callings and stewardship responsibilities. We cannot be bystanders in the important and continuing work of the kingdom (D&C 58:27–28). To continue to grow spiritually as individuals and families, we must "put [our] shoulder to the wheel" (*Hymns,* no. 252) and do our part to contribute to the whole. The Church needs our contribution and conscientiousness in stewardships. The work of the Lord is done by those who magnify their callings and let their light shine with love and dedication (D&C 84:33; Matthew 5:16). Diligent activity is the seedbed of spirituality.

I, John, saw that he received not of the fulness at the first, but received grace for grace; and he received not of the fulness at first, but continued from grace to grace, until he received a fulness.
DOCTRINE & COVENANTS 93:12–13

John the Baptist attests that Jesus of Nazareth received "grace for grace" (D&C 93:12). Grace is unmerited divine favor, unearned divine assistance, supernal enabling power. Thus, as the Master gave of himself in service to those about him (as he extended grace), God the Father endowed his Beloved Son with even deeper and more profound spiritual outpourings (he received grace). Furthermore, because Jesus was born not only the son of Elohim but also the son of Mary, a mortal woman, his spiritual development took place as does ours—line upon line and precept upon precept. His was not a progression from gracelessness to grace but rather from grace to grace, from one spiritual height to a greater. Finally, in the resurrection Jesus received a fulness of the glory and power of the Father and thus stated: "All power is given unto me in heaven and in earth" (Matthew 28:18).

I give unto you these sayings that you may understand and know
how to worship, and know what you worship, that you may come
unto the Father in my name, and in due time receive of his fulness.

DOCTRINE & COVENANTS 93:19

Understanding how the Son of Man gave and received during his mortal life enables us to understand how we are to do likewise. As we give to others, our cruse of oil is refilled—we receive grace for grace. As we continually strive to bring our desires and hopes and dreams into harmony with heaven's purposes, we climb the spiritual ladder—we continue from grace to grace. Such a knowledge enables us to worship the Master in the highest way—to emulate him. These principles thus teach us both who we worship and how to worship him. It is the imitation of Christ, the quest to become like the Prototype of all saved beings, that motivates and moves us toward eternal life.

And now, verily I say unto you, I was in the beginning with the Father, and am the Firstborn.... Ye were also in the beginning with the Father; that which is Spirit, even the Spirit of truth.

DOCTRINE & COVENANTS 93:21–23

In the beginning was the Word, and the Word was with God, and the Word was God. The same was in the beginning with God" (John 1:1–2). Jehovah, who is Jesus Christ, is the Word, the "messenger of salvation" (D&C 93:8). In the beginning, meaning in the pre-mortal existence, Jehovah was with Elohim, the Father. Elohim was God, and so was Jehovah. Through the eons of time following his spiritual birth (Jehovah was the firstborn in the spirit), Jehovah grew and progressed to the point that he was "like unto God" (Abraham 3:24). One of the transcendent truths of the Restoration is the soul-settling statement that man also was in the beginning with God, that he lived as a spirit, or organized intelligence, before his mortal birth. This knowledge goes a long way toward explaining many of the mysteries of life and bringing an elevated perspective to much of our pain and distress. It is a singular and sanctifying doctrine.

Truth is knowledge of things as they are,
and as they were, and as they are to come.
DOCTRINE & COVENANTS 93:24

A religious leader commented a few years ago that for centuries the scripture quoted most often throughout the Christian world was "God so loved the world, that he gave his only begotten Son . . ." (John 3:16). This leader had noticed that in recent decades, however, this passage had begun to fade in favor of another one that seemed particularly appealing to college students caught up in a postmodern worldview, principally because they did not know or understand its true meaning: "Judge not, that ye be not judged" (Matthew 7:1). For him, the cultural shift was frightening, bespeaking excessive tolerance that was really ethical relativism. Many in today's world have become so tolerant of falsehood that they no longer discern the truth. The Restoration affirms that some truths are absolute, just as there is a God who possesses all power, all might, all knowledge, and all dominion. Some things just are. Such truths cannot be altered in the eternal scheme of things by social consensus.

*The glory of God is intelligence, or, in other words,
light and truth. Light and truth forsake that evil one.*
DOCTRINE & COVENANTS 93:36–37

Intelligence is light and truth, not mere knowledge
or information. Satan knows many things: that God
lives, that Jesus is the Christ, that God has a living
prophet upon the earth. But that knowledge does him
no good. He has no intelligence (light and truth), or
he would humble himself and obey the principles of
the gospel. All the knowledge in the world will do
nothing for us if it does not bring us into communion
with the Infinite. "To be learned is good if they
hearken unto the counsels of God" (2 Nephi 9:29).
We must not just *know truth* but *live truth.* Living truthfully means living in the light of the Lord and his
gospel. Living truthfully means being humble and
teachable, willing to obey the Lord and seeking to do
his will. Satan wants only to destroy our souls—to take
us from light and truth and leave us in spiritual darkness. Intelligence is the light and truth that lead to salvation.

*Verily I say unto Joseph Smith, Jun.—You have not
kept the commandments, and must needs stand rebuked before
the Lord; your family must needs repent and forsake some
things, and give more earnest heed unto your sayings,
or be removed out of their place.*

DOCTRINE & COVENANTS 93:47–48

President Boyd K. Packer explained that the only
time the Lord used the word *rebuke* to chasten Joseph
Smith was when he failed to teach his children (*Ensign*,
November 1998, 22). Even with all his weighty responsibilities as head of the dispensation of the fulness of
times, the Prophet was still expected to teach his children the gospel, to bring them up "in light and truth"
(D&C 93:40). We are to do the same. Whatever our
stewardship in the kingdom may be, our family should
not suffer or fall into disbelief because of our busyness—even if that busyness is for worthwhile purposes.
We are here to learn to put first things first. Our marriages and family relationships can continue beyond the
grave and are worthy of our best and most diligent
efforts. As the First Presidency emphasized, "As we
strengthen families, we will strengthen the entire
Church" (First Presidency letter, 11 February 1999).
The Church is only as strong as its families.

SEPTEMBER

Wherefore, now let every man learn his
duty, and to act in the office in which he
is appointed, in all diligence. He that is
slothful shall not be counted worthy to
stand, and he that learns not his duty
and shows himself not approved shall
not be counted worthy to stand.

DOCTRINE & COVENANTS
107:99–100

*And again, verily I say unto you, my friends, a
commandment I give unto you, that ye shall commence a
work of laying out and preparing a beginning and
foundation of the city of the stake of Zion.*
DOCTRINE & COVENANTS 94:1

In 1833 the young Church was growing, and facilities
were necessary to help carry out the expanding work
of the Church. In revelation the Lord speaks of the
temple as "my house" (D&C 94:1). In connection with
the building for the First Presidency, the Lord says, "It
shall be wholly dedicated unto the Lord for the work
of the presidency," and "my glory . . . and my presence
shall be there" (D&C 94:7–8). The Lord speaks of the
printing building as "a house unto me" (D&C 94:10).
And the building committee is responsible "to build
mine houses" (D&C 94:15). Then, as now, the Lord
has a building program and is concerned about the
physical facilities of his Church. These buildings are
the Lord's buildings. We ought to view them as the
Lord's sacred houses and willingly assist in their care
and upkeep.

*Verily I say unto you, that there are many who have been
ordained among you, whom I have called but few of them are
chosen. They who are not chosen have sinned a very grievous
sin, in that they are walking in darkness at noon-day.*

DOCTRINE & COVENANTS 95:5–6

We learn from the Prophet Joseph's writings in the
Liberty Jail that many are called but few are chosen
"because their hearts are set so much upon the things
of this world" (D&C 121:34–35). In Doctrine and
Covenants 95 we learn an accompanying truth that
many are called but few are chosen because they have
chosen instead to walk in darkness at noonday. In
encouraging a congregation to feel a deeper sense of
appreciation for the marvelous flood of light that had
come through the Restoration, one Latter-day Saint
observed that the Saints are often like fish that discover
water last. We are immersed in a dispensation of revelation. It is all about us, and yet sometimes, either
through sin, distraction, or preoccupation, we do not
open ourselves to that divine light. How could a person walk in darkness at noonday? Doctrine and
Covenants 95 is a call for the Saints to lift up their eyes,
open their ears, and attune their hearts to the Infinite.

*Verily I say unto you, I gave unto you a commandment
that you should build a house, in the which house I design to
endow those whom I have chosen with power from on high.*
DOCTRINE & COVENANTS 95:8

We live in a time of unprecedented temple building, a time when the supernal blessings of the temple
are being brought within the reach of more people
than at any other time in earth's history. Elder Joseph B.
Wirthlin said: "The ideals of faith, hope, and charity
are most evident in the holy temples. There we learn
the purpose of life, strengthen our commitment as
disciples of Christ by entering into sacred covenants
with Him, and seal our families together for eternity
across generations. . . . In the house of the Lord, faithful Church members can be endowed 'with power
from on high,' power that will enable us to resist
temptation, honor covenants, obey the Lord's commandments, and bear fervent, fearless testimony of
the gospel to family, friends, and neighbors" (*Ensign,*
November 1998, 27). How marvelous that the eternal
blessings of the temple are spreading across the land
in preparation for the Lord's triumphant return.

*If you keep not my commandments,
the love of the Father shall not continue with you,
therefore you shall walk in darkness.*
DOCTRINE & COVENANTS 95:12

Passages such as Doctrine and Covenants 95:12 occasionally lead individuals who have been guilty of serious sin to feel helpless and to conclude that they are no longer loved by God. In truth, however, God loves all his children, even those who are guilty of major transgression. To say that the love of the Father does not continue with such individuals is to say that they do not enjoy the love of God in their life, that they are devoid of the Spirit and unable to feel the perfect and infinite love of a tender Parent. Nephi taught: "Behold, the Lord esteemeth all flesh in one; he that is righteous is favored of God" (1 Nephi 17:35). These passages of scripture teach us not that God loves one child more than another but rather that one who keeps the commandments places oneself in a position to receive and enjoy the blessings of the Almighty.

*Behold, I say unto you, here is wisdom, whereby
ye may know how to act concerning this matter, for it is
expedient in me that this stake that I have set for the
strength of Zion should be made strong.*
DOCTRINE & COVENANTS 96:1

Each stake of Zion must be a place of spiritual
strength. It is the place where we work to benefit and
bless those who are earnestly seeking a celestial inheritance (D&C 96:3). It is a place where the gospel is
taught by example and precept, a place from whence
missionaries are sent to preach the truth to a darkening world in desperate need of gospel light (D&C
96:4). It is a place where our hearts are humbled and
our spirits subdued as we mature in the gospel and
willingly serve in the kingdom (D&C 96:5). Great
strength is found in the stakes of Zion. Yet, the
strength of any stake or ward wholly depends on the
personal righteousness of individual members. Zion
can be found in any part of the world—north or south,
east or west. We contribute our part to the whole as
we learn and live truth, serve others, and come unto
the Lord with full purpose of heart.

Verily I say unto you, all among them who know their hearts are honest, and are broken, and their spirits contrite, and are willing to observe their covenants by sacrifice—yea, every sacrifice which I, the Lord, shall command—they are accepted of me.

DOCTRINE & COVENANTS 97:8

President David O. McKay taught that "spirituality is the consciousness of victory over self, and of communion with the Infinite" (*Gospel Ideals,* 390). It is not just that individuals become masters of themselves—their desires, appetites, and passions—but, in addition, they are aware, or conscious, of such mastery. From this mastery comes a quiet and solid confidence, a peace that certifies God's approval. The Prophet Joseph Smith taught that "a religion that does not require the sacrifice of all things never has power sufficient to produce the faith necessary unto life and salvation" (*Lectures on Faith,* 6:7). An individual who is willing to give his all in sacrifice, not even withholding his own life if called upon to lay it down, gains the knowledge that the course of life he is pursuing is according to the will of God. Such an assurance, such a hope, provides an anchor to the soul, a steadying influence in a day of turmoil.

*And inasmuch as my people build a house unto me in
the name of the Lord, and do not suffer any unclean thing to
come into it, that it be not defiled, my glory shall rest upon it; yea,
and my presence shall be there, for I will come into it, and all
the pure in heart that shall come into it shall see God.*

DOCTRINE & COVENANTS 97:15–16

Who shall ascend into the hill of the Lord? or who shall stand in his holy place? He that hath clean hands, and a pure heart" (Psalm 24:3–4). When we enter the house of the Lord, we are expected to do so with clean hands (actions) and pure hearts (desires or motives). Individuals who are unholy, stained with serious unrepented sin, cannot feel the lifting and sanctifying influences that flow freely to others who are striving to keep their covenants. Members of the Church have been called to be a temple-loving and a temple-attending people. Temple worship enables us to render a vicarious service in behalf of those who have gone before and to ensure that our life is in order, that we are striving to the best of our ability to resist evil and keep our covenants with fidelity and devotion. Those who do so come to see God.

Therefore, verily, thus saith the Lord, let Zion rejoice,
for this is Zion—THE PURE IN HEART; therefore,
let Zion rejoice, while all the wicked shall mourn.

DOCTRINE & COVENANTS 97:21

Early in the history of the restored Church, the Saints were asked to gather to Zion, the location where the Saints could form a strong nucleus, combine their talents and resources, and provide a central spot from which missionaries would be sent out. When a strong and stable base had been established by the turn of the twentieth century, the leaders of the Church began to emphasize what the Savior had also taught years earlier in the revelations—that Zion was not only a location or gathering place but also a state of being, a state of mind. Of Enoch's Zion the scripture attests: "And the Lord called his people ZION, because they were of one heart and one mind, and dwelt in righteousness; and there was no poor among them" (Moses 7:18). Zion is a people, and Zion is the place where such a people dwells.

That law of the land which is constitutional, supporting that principle of freedom in maintaining rights and privileges, belongs to all mankind, and is justifiable before me. . . . as pertaining to law of man, whatsoever is more or less than this, cometh of evil.

DOCTRINE & COVENANTS 98:5–7

Nephi saw that it was by the power of the Almighty, the power of divine deliverance, that the American colonists were able to break their tie with Great Britain (1 Nephi 13:17–19). But once this choice land was discovered, settled, and fought for, it was needful that God raise up wise men to prepare the document upon which its laws and statutes were founded—the Constitution of the United States (D&C 101:80). The principles of freedom, justice, and equity set forth in the Constitution pertain to all nations. Although we are not yet under the direct dictation of the Almighty in things civil, "that law of the land which is constitutional . . . is justifiable" before God (D&C 95:5), and he "has suffered [it] to be established, and [it] should be maintained for the rights and protection of all flesh, according to just and holy principles" (D&C 101:77).

*And I give unto you a commandment, that ye shall
forsake all evil and cleave unto all good, that ye shall live by every
word which proceedeth forth out of the mouth of God.*
DOCTRINE & COVENANTS 98:11

So many important things compete for our attention
in mortality. Time cannot be wasted on slothfulness
and sinfulness. We must obtain essential ordinances
and keep sacred covenants. We must love and serve
one another. We must live by all the words that come
from the apostles and prophets of the latter day. Our
inspired leaders help us to forsake evil and seek for
that which is good. Their only desire is our eternal
well-being. A test of our conversion is how we
respond to the words of God given to us through mortal men. Yes, they are mortal; they have shortcomings,
as do we all; but acting in their office and as inspired
by the Holy Ghost, they give us the words of everlasting life. Inspired sisters, acting as directed by proper
priesthood authority, also give us the word of God as
they speak by the Spirit. How grateful we feel for
faithful Saints who both live and teach the word of
God.

*Therefore, be not afraid of your enemies, for I have
decreed in my heart, saith the Lord, that I will prove you
in all things, whether you will abide in my covenant,
even unto death, that you may be found worthy.*

DOCTRINE & COVENANTS 98:14

Life is difficult. There will be trials and disappointments, dashed dreams and painful events. How we respond to all these difficulties will turn out to be the real measure of our salvation. The Lord provides each of us customized challenges to give us the opportunity to grow, to learn, to develop into the kind of faithful Saints who are determined to follow God regardless of the circumstance. During the storms of winter, will we keep the covenants we enter into during summer's warmth? Will we retreat from the enemies of righteousness when life's battles seem overwhelming? We find out the strength of an enemy when we stand up to it. Stand strong against the enemies of righteousness; remain faithful even when faced with the vicissitudes of life; be believing despite the powers of negativism. A glorious and joyful crown of righteousness awaits those who stand strong in the faith and abide in their covenants with the Lord.

*Therefore, renounce war and proclaim peace, and seek diligently
to turn the hearts of the children to their fathers, and the hearts of
the fathers to the children; . . . lest I come and smite the whole
earth with a curse, and all flesh be consumed before me.*
DOCTRINE & COVENANTS 98:16–17

Earth has had few seasons of complete peace,
particularly since the time of the American Civil War,
which marked the beginning of uninterrupted warfare
somewhere on the earth (D&C 87). When the Saints
are commissioned to "renounce war and proclaim
peace," they are not commissioned to be pacifists, for
there are those unfortunate times when we must
defend our families or our homes, even unto bloodshed
(Alma 43–47; 48:14). We should strive for peace, we
should pray for the leaders of nations, and we should
do everything possible in our immediate surroundings
to create a peaceful atmosphere. Most important, we
are called to teach the gospel of Jesus Christ, which in
the end is the world's only hope. Only the gospel can
bring peace of mind, build and strengthen interper-
sonal relationships, bind and seal families everlastingly,
chase darkness from our midst, and banish pride and
arrogance from the hearts of those hungry for power.

*And whoso receiveth you receiveth me; and you shall
have power to declare my word in the demonstration of my Holy
Spirit. And who receiveth you as a little child, receiveth my
kingdom; and blessed are they, for they shall obtain mercy.*

DOCTRINE & COVENANTS 99:2–3

Missionaries are sent forth to proclaim the new and everlasting gospel "from house to house . . . and from city to city" (D&C 99:1). They are called to serve as the Lord's representatives and function as his agents in the work of the kingdom. The Lord has always worked through his authorized representatives, stating "whether by mine own voice or by the voice of my servants, it is the same" (D&C 1:38). We, too, are called to share gospel truth with others, by example and precept. When the humble and honest in heart embrace the message of the Restoration, as presented by representatives of the Lord, and enter into a covenant relationship with Christ, they are blessed beyond measure. The converse is also true: "Whoso rejecteth [the Lord's representatives] shall be rejected of my Father and his house" (D&C 99:4). Both full-time missionaries and member-missionaries will be given power and inspiration as they share the gospel with others.

Lift up your voices unto this people; speak the thoughts that I shall put into your hearts, and you shall not be confounded before men; for it shall be given you in the very hour, yea, in the very moment, what ye shall say.

DOCTRINE & COVENANTS 100:5–6

We cannot teach with spiritual power unless we have the influence of the Spirit (D&C 42:14). We may impart information, but real teaching is done only by the Spirit—when heart speaks to heart and the confirming whisperings of the Holy Ghost touch the soul. If we are worthy and in tune with divine inspiration, the Lord will bless us with impressions, thoughts, and promptings as to exactly what is needed at a given time and place. The Lord promises: "Ye shall declare whatsoever thing ye declare in my name, in solemnity of heart, in the spirit of meekness, in all things. And I give unto you this promise, that inasmuch as ye do this the Holy Ghost shall be shed forth in bearing record unto all things whatsoever ye shall say" (D&C 100:7–8). The responsibility is ours; the obligation serious. The Lord will be with us every step of the way as we humbly seek him with full purpose of heart.

In the day of their peace they esteemed lightly my counsel;
but, in the day of their trouble, of necessity they feel after me.
DOCTRINE & COVENANTS 101:8

It seems natural to petition the heavens in times of turmoil or stress. We feel impelled to seek divine guidance and miraculous assistance when we find there is little we can do on our own. But what is the nature of our prayers during times of prosperity, seasons of peace and goodwill, days when everything seems to be in place? How earnestly do we come boldly to the throne of grace when life is treating us well? How often do we find ourselves pouring out our souls in gratitude, asking for little but acknowledging much? Doctrine and Covenants 101:8 is a haunting passage of scripture, reminding us that our marriage to the Bridegroom requires that we be true to him and communicate with him in times of joy or sorrow or sickness or health, whether we are rich or poor.

Therefore, let your hearts be comforted concerning Zion;
for all flesh is in mine hands; be still and know that I am God.
DOCTRINE & COVENANTS 101:16

There is a tremendous need for the Latter-day Saints to simplify and reduce. Of course, we need to do the work of the Lord as efficiently and as effectively as we can, for his is "a house of order" (D&C 132:8). In addition, we must find ways to escape the myriad voices in the world, the noises and distractions that turn our attention and our hearts away from things sacred. Although mundane tasks must always be attended to, the wisest among us seek out and take advantage of opportunities to be alone, to listen to the quiet, and to reflect on things that matter most. Revelation does not come to us when our souls are filled with noise. The still, small voice cannot be heard or felt while the loud janglings of today's busy world sound at every turn. When we are still, we come to know that our God lives, and we come to sense his mind and will for us.

Wherefore, fear not even unto death; for in this world your joy is not full, but in me your joy is full.
DOCTRINE & COVENANTS 101:36

The beauties and wonder of nature, the innocence of little children, kindly deeds—these are some of the many scenes that make us grateful for life. There is much pleasure to be had in today's world, so much that pleases the eye, gladdens the heart, strengthens the body, and enlivens the soul (D&C 59:18–19). But the fulness of joy, the peace that passes all understanding (Philippians 4:7), comes only through Jesus Christ. Through him we are reborn, renewed, reconciled, and redeemed. To paraphrase C. S. Lewis, we believe in Christ as we believe that the sun has risen, not just because we can see it, but also that through it we're able to see all other things more clearly (*Weight of Glory,* 106). It is by our Savior and his marvelous light that we are enabled to see things as they really are and to find not only deeper delight in this life but a fulness of joy in the life to come.

When men are called unto mine everlasting gospel, and covenant with an everlasting covenant, they are accounted as the salt of the earth and the savor of men; . . . therefore, if that salt of the earth lose its savor, behold, it is thenceforth good for nothing.

DOCTRINE & COVENANTS 101:39–40

Doctrine and Covenants 101:39–40 attest that the people of the covenant—those who have come out of the world into the marvelous light of Christ, who have accepted his gospel and participated in the saving ordinances—are under sacred obligation to be as the salt of the earth. Salt does not lose its savor with age; rather, it loses its savor, its distinctive influence, through mixture and contamination. The people of the covenant are called to live in the world but to avoid worldliness, to participate in daily living without partaking of the forbidden. The world ought to be different—better—because the Saints are in it. As salt improves flavor, so the people of the covenant ought to bring out the best in others. As salt preserves, so the people of the covenant ought to do all in their power to preserve the earth they are put onto, as well as preserve and hold tenaciously to absolute values and time-honored teachings.

SEPTEMBER 19

*That every man may act in doctrine and principle
pertaining to futurity, according to the moral agency which
I have given unto him, that every man may be accountable
for his own sins in the day of judgment.*

DOCTRINE & COVENANTS 101:78

The Lord wants us to use our agency to choose to
obey him. The devil cannot compel us to sin, and the
Lord will not force us to righteousness; otherwise,
what could our choices mean? We are in mortality to
show by our choices whether we want to be part of the
kingdom of God more than anything else. "If you
question everything you are asked to do, or dig in your
heels at every unpleasant challenge, you make it harder
for the Lord to bless you," said Elder Richard G. Scott.
"Your agency, the right to make choices, is not given
so that you can get what you want. This divine gift is
provided so that you will choose what your Father in
Heaven wants for you. That way He can lead you to
become all that He intends you to be. That path leads
to glorious joy and happiness" (*Ensign,* May 1996, 25).
We are here on probation. May we freely choose righteousness.

*The high council was appointed by revelation for the purpose
of settling important difficulties which might arise in the church.*

DOCTRINE & COVENANTS 102:2

The Lord's house is a house of order. It can be challenging to sit in judgment in the Church, but those called to do so, inspired of the Lord and desiring the welfare of Church members, seek humbly to know and do the will of the Lord in whatever matters come before them. Church disciplinary councils have sometimes been called "councils of love." Their purpose is to help people come back into the faithful fold of Christ. These councils also protect the Church and its members from false teachers and those who engage in conduct unbecoming a Saint. All who participate in a priesthood council sincerely desire to lovingly assist transgressors in the process of repentance. Their earnest purpose is to protect the integrity of the institution of the Church and those within their stewardship. The Lord has provided the means whereby individuals can repent and be brought back into full fellowship in the Church.

Let no man be afraid to lay down his life for my sake; for whoso layeth down his life for my sake shall find it again. And whoso is not willing to lay down his life for my sake is not my disciple.

DOCTRINE & COVENANTS 103:27–28

Zion's Camp consisted of more than two hundred men who marched a thousand miles from Kirtland, Ohio, to redeem Zion (Jackson County, Missouri) by rescuing the Saints and restoring property taken by mobs. It was led by Joseph Smith, whom the Lord refers to as "a man, who shall lead them like as Moses led the children of Israel" (D&C 103:16). Then, as now, the Lord needed faithful disciples willing to lay down their lives for Zion. The Camp was a learning experience as its members daily walked with the Prophet and were taught by him. It was also a severe trial of faith for participants and a proving ground that separated the faithful from the murmurers. Upon arriving in Missouri, the Prophet received a revelation (D&C 105) disbanding Zion's Camp, explaining that because of the transgressions of the people, Zion was not to be redeemed at that time. Nevertheless, this crucible experience prepared Brigham Young and others for the great pioneer exodus of 1847.

*Organize yourselves and appoint every man his stewardship;
that every man may give an account unto me of the stewardship
which is appointed unto him. For it is expedient that I, the Lord,
should make every man accountable, as a steward over
earthly blessings, which I have made and prepared.*

DOCTRINE & COVENANTS 104:11–13

The united order, a group of Church leaders organized in 1832 to assist the bishop in managing the law of consecration, was dissolved in 1834 (D&C 104). The members were called to hold property jointly and organize a storehouse for the benefit of the poor (D&C 78:3–4; 82:11–12). Then, as now, we are each given a stewardship responsibility. In our homes and Church units we have sacred responsibilities for which we are accountable. The Lord cares a great deal about how seriously we take our appointed stewardships. Do we put first things first in marriage and family relationships? Do we magnify our callings and willingly serve others? Do we worthily exercise our priesthood in blessing those both inside and outside our families? Do we consecrate our time and energies in building the kingdom? Doctrine and Covenants 104 teaches us to be wise and diligent stewards of all that God has given us.

For the earth is full, and there is enough and to spare. . . .
Therefore, if any man shall take of the abundance which I have
made, and impart not his portion . . . unto the poor and the needy,
he shall, with the wicked, lift up his eyes in hell, being in torment.

DOCTRINE & COVENANTS 104:17–18

The Lord created the heavens and the earth and
everything in them (3 Nephi 9:15). He who knows all
things from beginning to end and everything in
between knows each of us and also how many people
will live upon the earth. He has provided sufficient
resources whereby all our physical needs can be met if
we use those resources properly. That does not mean
we can waste the earth's fulness and disregard the
Lord's command to be wise stewards (D&C
104:12–13). We are to enjoy the abundance of life that
the Lord has provided, and we are to share our bounty
with others. Besides, we cannot take any of earth's fulness with us into the next life. We take only our heart
and soul—our charity, our wisdom, our nature, and
willingness to share with others. All of us on this beautiful planet partake of the Lord's abundance. Life itself
is a gift. But we must give back freely, willingly, and
abundantly.

Verily I say unto you, concerning your debts—behold it
is my will that you shall pay all your debts. And it is my will that
you shall humble yourselves before me, and obtain this blessing
by your diligence and humility and the prayer of faith.

DOCTRINE & COVENANTS 104:78–79

Latter-day prophets have always counseled the Saints regarding debt. President Gordon B. Hinckley said: "Many of our people are heavily in debt for things that are not entirely necessary. . . . I urge you as members of this Church to get free of debt where possible and to have a little laid aside against a rainy day" (*Ensign,* November 2001, 73). Decades earlier, President Heber J. Grant said: "If there is any one thing that will bring peace and contentment into the human heart, and into the family, it is to live within our means. And if there is any one thing that is grinding and discouraging and disheartening, it is to have debts and obligations that one cannot meet" (*Gospel Standards,* 111). To get out of debt and stay out requires humility, diligence, and mighty prayer. We can begin where we are, little by little, to live within our means so we can enjoy the peace and contentment such freedom brings.

But behold, they have not learned to be obedient
to the things which I required at their hands, but are full of
all manner of evil, and do not impart of their substance, as
becometh saints, to the poor and afflicted among them.
DOCTRINE & COVENANTS 105:3

True Saints manifest their covenant commitment to Christ by freely sharing their substance with others. Elder Joe J. Christensen said: "The more our hearts and minds are turned to assisting others less fortunate than we, the more we will avoid the spiritually cankering effects that result from greed, selfishness, and overindulgence. Our resources are a stewardship, not our possessions. I am confident that we will literally be called upon to make an accounting before God concerning how we have used them to bless lives and build the kingdom" (*Ensign,* May 1999, 10). Nothing scourges the soul like the self-interested scarcity mentality of selfishness. One of the sure measures of our devotion to Christ is our willingness to abundantly reach out to others in love. Substance implies more than money, however. Substance is also time—a desire to listen and give of self, a yearning to serve and lift another. The righteous freely impart of their substance.

Zion cannot be built up unless it is by the principles of the law of the celestial kingdom; otherwise I cannot receive her unto myself. And my people must needs be chastened until they learn obedience, if it must needs be, by the things which they suffer.

DOCTRINE & COVENANTS 105:5–6

Zion is built on the law of the celestial kingdom, which is that we learn obedience and submission by seeking with all our heart to become more like the Lord. The Lord chastens those whom he loves (D&C 95:1). He knows that if we are to develop the attributes of godliness, we must learn obedience, we must become softened, we must follow the Savior and exercise our agency in suffering (Hebrews 5:8). The chastening continuum varies with each of us. As parents of more than one child know, each child is different; each child needs a different amount and method of chastening or correction. Some need more; others need very little. But we all must be chastened by the Lord. That's how we learn and grow, become sanctified before the Lord, and mature in the qualities of divinity. Zion is built person by person, in quiet and steady ways, as we turn our hearts to heaven in willing obedience and humble submission.

*There has been a day of calling, but the time has come
for a day of choosing; and let those be chosen that are worthy.
And it shall be manifest unto my servant, by the voice of the
Spirit, those that are chosen; and they shall be sanctified.*

DOCTRINE & COVENANTS 105:35–36

Some who join the true Church, covenant with the Savior to abide by the statutes of his earthly kingdom, and agree to a life of dedicated discipleship do not realize what it will require to remain on the strait path that leads to the highest of eternal rewards. Elder Bruce R. McConkie taught: "Many are called to the Lord's work, but few are chosen for eternal life. So that those who are chosen may be sealed up unto eternal life, the scripture says: 'It shall be manifest unto my servant, by the voice of the Spirit, those that are chosen; and they shall be sanctified.' (D&C 105:36.) They are chosen by the Lord, but the announcement of their calling and election is delivered by the Spirit" (*New Witness*, 270). Those who receive such an assurance from the Lord are the worthy—not the perfect. They are the steadfast and immovable—not the ones who never misstep. They are those whose hearts have been surrendered to the Master.

And again, verily I say unto you, the coming of the Lord draweth nigh, and it overtaketh the world as a thief in the night— therefore, gird up your loins, that you may be the children of light, and that day shall not overtake you as a thief.

DOCTRINE & COVENANTS 106:4–5

The scriptures speak of the Master returning as "a thief in the night" (1 Thessalonians 5:2; 2 Peter 3:10). It is true that no mortal will know the precise day of the Lord's second advent. On the other hand, the Saints are promised that if they are in tune with the Spirit, they can recognize the season. The apostle Paul chose the descriptive analogy of a pregnant woman about to deliver. She may not know the exact hour or day when the birth is to take place, but one thing she knows for sure: it will be soon. It *must* be soon! The impressions and feelings and signs within her own body so testify. In a similar way, those who give heed to the words of scripture and especially to the living oracles will stand as the "children of light, and the children of the day," those who "are not of the night, nor of darkness" (1 Thessalonians 5:5).

Therefore, blessed is my servant Warren, for I will have mercy on him; and, notwithstanding the vanity of his heart, I will lift him up inasmuch as he will humble himself before me.

DOCTRINE & COVENANTS 106:7

It is unfortunate that Warren Cowdery, older brother of Oliver Cowdery, failed to follow Joseph Smith's example, as described by the Prophet before receiving the revelation for Warren: "No month ever found me more busily engaged than November; but as my life consisted of activity and unyielding exertions, I made this my rule: *When the Lord commands, do it*" (*History of the Church*, 2:170). Warren Cowdery joined the Church in 1831 and left in 1838. He did not return when his brother was reunited with the Church in 1848. This revelation tells us much about the Lord—and about us. The Lord knows us perfectly. He knows our weaknesses and foibles, but even so, he loves us and desires to bless us with a crown of righteousness, if we will humble ourselves and stay faithful (D&C 106:8). The heavens rejoice when we forsake worldliness and come to the Lord (D&C 106:6). Our joy will be everlasting if we remain faithful to the end.

*There are, in the church, two priesthoods, namely, the
Melchizedek and Aaronic, including the Levitical Priesthood.*
DOCTRINE & COVENANTS 107:1

All priesthood comes from God. It is the power and
authority of God delegated to man to bless people and
save souls. There is one priesthood with two functions
or divisions: Melchizedek and Aaronic (D&C
107:5–6). Joseph Smith explained: "The Melchizedek
Priesthood comprehends the Aaronic or Levitical
Priesthood, and is the grand head, and holds the highest authority which pertains to the priesthood, and the
keys of the Kingdom of God in all ages of the world
to the latest posterity on the earth; and is the channel
through which all knowledge, doctrine, the plan of salvation and every important matter is revealed from
heaven" (*Teachings of the Prophet Joseph Smith*, 166–67).
With priesthood power, we are able to receive the fulness of the Lord's blessings, here and hereafter.
Without priesthood power, we are forever lost and
without hope. Thanks be to God for the power and
authority to represent him and act in his name.

OCTOBER

How long can rolling waters remain impure?
What power shall stay the heavens? As well
might man stretch forth his puny arm to stop
the Missouri river in its decreed course, or to
turn it up stream, as to hinder the Almighty
from pouring down knowledge from heaven
upon the heads of the Latter-day Saints.

DOCTRINE & COVENANTS
121:33

Why the first is called the Melchizedek Priesthood is because
Melchizedek was such a great high priest. Before his day it was called
the Holy Priesthood, after the Order of the Son of God.
DOCTRINE & COVENANTS 107:2–3

In the revelation on priesthood and church government
(D&C 107), the Lord revealed the complete and sacred
name of the higher priesthood and why the name was
changed. Melchizedek, a type and shadow of the Savior
to come, was called in his day "the prince of peace" and
the "king of Salem" (Alma 13:18). He was a righteous
king and high priest who preached repentance to his
people and established peace in the land. Abraham, the
father of nations, paid tithes to Melchizedek. As pertaining to righteous leadership, none have been greater
(Alma 13:14–19). The Lord honored the name of
Melchizedek: "Out of respect or reverence to the name
of the Supreme Being, to avoid the too frequent repetition of his name, they, the church, in ancient days, called
that priesthood after Melchizedek" (D&C 107:4). All
who hold this holy power and authority ought to feel
humbly grateful for the Lord, from whom all priesthood
comes, and for the Lord's righteous servant Melchizedek.

*The Melchizedek Priesthood holds the right of presidency,
and has power and authority over all the offices in the church in
all ages of the world, to administer in spiritual things.*
DOCTRINE & COVENANTS 107:8

In 1829 Peter, James, and John conferred upon Joseph
Smith and Oliver Cowdery the holy apostleship and the
keys of the higher priesthood. Keys are the right of
presidency, the directing power. Those who hold keys
(quorum presidents, bishops, stake presidents, mission
presidents, general authorities) hold the right to regulate the affairs of the Church within their area of
responsibility, including the proper performance of the
ordinances of salvation. A righteous father may have the
priesthood authority to baptize his eight-year-old
daughter, but he may do so only under the directing
power of the one in the ward who holds the keys,
namely, the bishop. Order in the house of the Lord is
thus maintained. The Great Apostasy came about not
only because the priesthood was lost but also because
the keys of the priesthood, the directing power that
empowers priesthood bearers to transmit to others the
same authority, were also taken from the earth.

*The power and authority of the higher, or Melchizedek
Priesthood, is to hold the keys of all the spiritual blessings of the
church—to . . . enjoy the communion and presence of God
the Father, and Jesus the mediator of the new covenant.*

DOCTRINE & COVENANTS 107:18–19

We as a people have not yet begun to grasp, much less to enjoy, the spiritual privileges associated with the Melchizedek Priesthood. This priesthood is God's own power, the power by which worlds came into being and were peopled, the power by which the sons and daughters of God are healed, renewed, redeemed, resurrected, and glorified hereafter. The priesthood is a sacred power, the power and authority of God delegated to man on earth to act in all things pertaining to the salvation of humankind. It is, in a very real sense, an investiture of authority, an illustration of divine trust whereby Deity delegates and empowers his servants on earth.

*Of the Melchizedek Priesthood, three Presiding High
Priests, chosen by the body, appointed and ordained to that office,
and upheld by the confidence, faith, and prayer of the church,
form a quorum of the Presidency of the Church.*
DOCTRINE & COVENANTS 107:22

Although a member of the First Presidency need
not hold the office of apostle, as an administrator in
the highest council of the Church, he must be a high
priest (Smith, *Gospel Doctrine,* 173–74). The president
of the Church, who is the prophet, seer, and revelator
for the entire Church, the president of the high priesthood of the Church (D&C 107:65), is assisted in his
weighty responsibilities by two men who are called to
hold the keys of the kingdom jointly with the president (D&C 90:6). These three men are chosen and
approved "by the body," meaning the Quorum of the
Twelve Apostles (Lee, Conference Report, October
1972, 17) and are upheld by the confidence, faith, and
prayers of the Saints throughout the world. The
Almighty honors and sustains those whom he chooses,
and that same God honors the fervent prayers of the
household of faith (James 5:16) in behalf of his living
oracles.

The twelve traveling councilors are called to be the Twelve Apostles, or special witnesses of the name of Christ in all the world—thus differing from other officers in the church in the duties of their calling. And they form a quorum, equal in authority and power to the three presidents.

DOCTRINE & COVENANTS 107:23–24

Apostles are "special witnesses of the name of Christ in all the world" (D&C 107:23). As seers and revelators, theirs is the spirit of prophecy, the testimony of Jesus (Revelation 19:10)—the sure knowledge of who he was, who he is, what he has done for the benefit of all humankind. The statement that "they form a quorum, equal in authority and power" to the First Presidency is an allusion to the principle of apostolic succession (D&C 107:24). The Prophet Joseph taught that "the Twelve are not subject to any other than the First Presidency, . . . and where I am not, there is no First Presidency over the Twelve" (*Teachings of the Prophet Joseph Smith,* 105–6). At the death of the president of the Church, the First Presidency is dissolved, the counselors to the president take their place in seniority among the Twelve, and the Twelve then become the presiding council, with the senior apostle at their head.

*The Seventy are also called to preach the gospel,
and to be especial witnesses unto the Gentiles and in all the
world—thus differing from other officers in the church
in the duties of their calling.*

DOCTRINE & COVENANTS 107:25

As in New Testament times (Luke 10:1), the Seventy are also called to be special witnesses of the name of Christ and to labor under the direction of the Twelve to build up the kingdom of God and regulate the affairs of the Lord's earthly Church in all the world (D&C 107:34). President Gordon B. Hinckley explained that the office of Seventy "carries with it the responsibility of bearing apostolic witness of the name of Christ" (Conference Report, April 1984, 73). "The seventies are called to be assistants to the twelve apostles, indeed, they are apostles of the Lord Jesus Christ, subject to the direction of the Twelve, . . . to preach the gospel to every creature, to every tongue and people under the heavens, to whom they may be sent" (Smith, *Gospel Doctrine,* 183).

*The duty of the president of the office of the High
Priesthood is to preside over the whole church, and to be like unto
Moses—behold, here is wisdom; yea, to be a seer, a revelator, a
translator, and a prophet, having all the gifts of God.*
DOCTRINE & COVENANTS 107:91–92

The living prophet is as Moses for our day: He leads modern Israel out of the bondage of sin and into the promised land of righteousness; he receives revelation to guide the Church today; he holds and exercises the keys of the priesthood to bless the Saints. The president of the Church presides over all of its members and over all of the gifts given the faithful Saints of God to aid in the building of his earthly kingdom (D&C 46:29). Under his direction, calls are made to use those gifts of the Spirit in sharing the gospel with the peoples of the earth and in teaching and strengthening those already in the Church. As in ancient days, the living prophet's sacred stewardship is to testify boldly as a special witness of the Lord and build up the Church in faith and testimony. Moses is the example and pattern followed by the man who stands as the earthly head of the Church.

*Let every man learn his duty, and to act in the office in which
he is appointed, in all diligence. He that is slothful shall not be
counted worthy to stand, and he that learns not his duty and shows
himself not approved shall not be counted worthy to stand.*

DOCTRINE & COVENANTS 107:99–100

The Lord admonished every priesthood holder to learn his duty and to act diligently in the office to which he is appointed. The power of God is no trifling matter. Those who bear the priesthood are expected to exercise this sacred authority for righteous purposes, as they represent the Lord in thought, word, and deed. As they willingly serve in callings and reach out to others in love and righteousness, they grow and develop in the attributes of godliness. As priesthood bearers, they are willing to be inconvenienced to act in the name of God and to live in such a way that the Spirit of the Lord can attend them at all times and places. They never know when they will be called upon to bless another—whether formally with hands laid on the head, or informally in families, wards, and communities. Priesthood bearers must strive ever to live so that the Lord's influence will be with them as they seek to bless others.

Strengthen your brethren in all your conversation, in all your prayers, in all your exhortations, and in all your doings. And behold, and lo, I am with you to bless you and deliver you forever.

DOCTRINE & COVENANTS 108:7–8

Covenant followers of Christ are "willing to mourn with those that mourn; yea, and comfort those that stand in need of comfort, and to stand as witnesses of God at all times and in all things, and in all places" (Mosiah 18:9). Authentic Christian living requires that we do more than *speak* kindly—we must *be* kind. Paul refers to "conversation" as conduct (Galatians 1:13). So, our *talk* must match our *walk:* That is the difference between those who have truly taken upon them the name of Christ. Like dye, it seeps through to their very soul, rather than being a veneer that thinly covers the surface. Of course, no one is perfect; we all fall short of the best within us. But the Lord will bless us in our efforts to be "an example of the believers, in word, in conversation, in charity" (1 Timothy 4:12). Our conduct must reflect an inner commitment to Christ and a humble desire to bless and lift another.

And when thy people transgress, any of them, they may
speedily repent and return unto thee, and find favor in thy sight,
and be restored to the blessings which thou hast ordained to be
poured out upon those who shall reverence thee in thy house.
DOCTRINE & COVENANTS 109:21

Each one of us knows of noble men and women who
have given their lives to the Redeemer, have suffered
all manner of insult and injury for his sake, and have
endured faithful to their covenants to the end of their
mortal existence. They have died firm in the faith and
valiant in the testimony of Jesus, but they were not
perfect. They surely had been born of the Spirit,
changed from a carnal and fallen state to a state of
righteousness (Mosiah 27:25), but it could never be
said that they were completely flawless or that they
had never made a mistake. Rather, "Whosoever is
born of God *doth not continue* in sin" (JST 1 John 3:9;
emphasis added). Having walked in the light, the
God-fearing cannot remain long in darkness; they
repent quickly and return to that light which brings
comfort and peace and assurance.

Put upon thy servants the testimony of the
covenant, that when they go out and proclaim thy word
they may seal up the law, and prepare the hearts of thy saints
for all those judgments thou art about to send, ... that thy
people may not faint in the day of trouble.

DOCTRINE & COVENANTS 109:38

We are children of the covenant, descendants of Abraham, Isaac, and Jacob, heirs to the blessings and responsibilities that attend such a birthright. The scriptures remind us soberly that "they are not all Israel, which are of Israel" (Romans 9:6). Rather, "as many of you as have been baptized unto Christ have put on Christ. . . . And if ye be Christ's, then are ye Abraham's seed, and heirs according to the promise" (Galatians 3:27–29; compare 2 Nephi 30:1–2). As we cultivate the influence of the Holy Spirit in our lives, we begin to sense who we are and Whose we are: We are the spirit sons and daughters of God the Father and the children of Christ by adoption into his everlasting covenant (Mosiah 5:7). Further, we are the posterity of the faithful ancients and are expected to "be loyal to the royal within" us (Lee, *Teachings*, 625). The command is for us to "go ye, therefore, and do the works of Abraham" (D&C 132:32).

But thy word must be fulfilled. Help thy servants to say, with thy grace assisting them: Thy will be done, O Lord, and not ours.
DOCTRINE & COVENANTS 109:44

Each of us knows, deep down, that eventually we must surrender to the Lord and open ourselves to his will. But not today. Not now. As C. S. Lewis soberly observed, there are really only two kinds of people: those who in this life say to God "Thy will be done" and those to whom God says, in the end, "*Thy* will be done" (*Great Divorce,* 72; emphasis added). If we in time seek God first, he will in eternity grant unto us whatsoever we ask, for our desires will have been educated and our hearts purified of selfishness. If we here submit, we will hereafter inherit. "Thy will be done" thus represents our petition that the Almighty work his wonders through us, that he soften our hearts to new ideas, bring to our minds new avenues of understanding, and open to us new paths of opportunity when it is best for us to move in another direction.

O Lord God Almighty, hear us in these our petitions,
and answer us from heaven, thy holy habitation, where thou
sittest enthroned, with glory, honor, power, majesty, might,
dominion, truth, justice, judgment, mercy, and an infinity
of fulness, from everlasting to everlasting.
DOCTRINE & COVENANTS 109:77

Because we as Latter-day Saints believe that our Heavenly Father is indeed a glorified, exalted Man of Holiness (Moses 6:57), some fear that we have inappropriately sought to bridge the chasm between the Creator and the creature. Although we do believe that man is of the same species as God and that through the Atonement we may, in process of time, become more and more like our Savior (Matthew 5:49; Romans 8:17; 2 Peter 1:4; 1 John 3:1–3), we also acknowledge the immense distance between finite and infinite, between imperfection and perfection, between humanity and divinity. Joseph Smith said: "God is the only supreme governor and independent being in whom all fullness and perfection dwell; who is omnipotent, omnipresent, and omniscient; . . . in him every good gift and every good principle dwell; . . . he is the object in whom the faith of all other rational and accountable beings center for life and salvation" (*Lectures on Faith,* 2:2). In short, our God is God!

*Help us by the power of thy Spirit, that we may
mingle our voices with those bright, shining seraphs around thy
throne, with acclamations of praise, singing Hosanna to God
and the Lamb! And let these, thine anointed ones, be clothed
with salvation, and thy saints shout aloud for joy.*

DOCTRINE & COVENANTS 109:79–80

As part of every temple dedication, we stand and three
times joyously shout, "Hosanna, Hosanna, Hosanna, to
God and the Lamb! Amen, Amen, and Amen." We also
sing these same words in the beloved hymn by W. W.
Phelps, "The Spirit of God," which was written for the
dedication of the Kirtland Temple (*Hymns,* no. 2).
Hosanna is Hebrew for "save, we pray." The acclamation
was accompanied anciently with the waving of branches,
as today we wave white cloths. Two thousand years ago a
crowd of believers gathered to give Jesus a royal welcome
the Sunday before his crucifixion and resurrection. As he
descended the Mount of Olives and entered Jerusalem,
they laid cloths on the ground and waved palm branches,
calling out "Hosanna" (John 12:12–13; Mark 11:8–10).
Interestingly, the Kirtland Temple was dedicated on
Sunday, 27 March 1836, the very day Christians around
the world celebrated Palm Sunday. Then, too, we joyously
shouted, "Hosanna to God and the Lamb!"

Yea the hearts of thousands and tens of thousands
shall greatly rejoice in consequence of the blessings which
shall be poured out, and the endowment with which my
servants have been endowed in this house.
DOCTRINE & COVENANTS 110:9

The building of the Kirtland Temple was of monumental significance in the continuing work of the
Restoration. God commanded the early Saints to
build a temple, and he promised them, as he had
promised the ancients, that they would there be
"endowed with power from on high" (D&C 38:32;
Luke 24:49). They were told that sacrifice would bring
forth the blessings of heaven. The Almighty was true
to his word, for the season of pentecostal outpouring
that took place during the weeks close to the dedication of the temple edified and uplifted our forebears
and confirmed their faith that "signs follow those that
believe" (D&C 63:9). Although only a "partial endowment" was delivered in the Kirtland Temple, the
covenants and ordinances and teachings presented by
the Prophet and his associates laid the foundation for
the more complete endowment that would be vouchsafed by a gracious Lord to the Saints in Nauvoo.

After this vision closed, the heavens were again opened unto us; and Moses appeared before us, and committed unto us the keys of the gathering of Israel from the four parts of the earth, and the leading of the ten tribes from the land of the north.

DOCTRINE & COVENANTS 110:11

Moses bestowed "the keys of the gathering of Israel" (D&C 110:11) upon Joseph Smith and Oliver Cowdery on 3 April 1836. Since that time, missionaries have carried the gospel across the earth, and the receptive descendants of Israel have gathered into stakes of Zion in the Lord's true Church. All who gather into the kingdom of God are recipients of the blessings that have resulted from the restoration of keys in the Kirtland Temple. Today the Church is growing at an ever-increasing rate, as was foretold anciently: "I will take you one of a city, and two of a family, and I will bring you to Zion" (Jeremiah 3:14). The gospel fold enlarges as individuals and families come into the Church. We are not baptized as a congregation or given the gift of the Holy Ghost as a group. One by one we make a choice for Christ and his restoration of priesthood keys and power.

*After this, Elias appeared, and committed the
dispensation of the gospel of Abraham, saying that in us
and our seed all generations after us should be blessed.*

DOCTRINE & COVENANTS 110:12

W e are not told the name of the heavenly messenger
identified in Doctrine and Covenants 110:12 as Elias.
More important is what he brought. Simply stated, Elias
restored celestial marriage, what we know as the patriar-
chal order, the new and everlasting covenant of marriage.
God had promised Abraham, the father of the faithful,
that through him and his seed all generations after him
would be blessed (Genesis 13; 15; 17). Elias brought the
power to make of Joseph Smith a modern Abraham
(D&C 124:58; 132:31–32), such that through the keys and
powers delivered through the Prophet and through the
blessings associated with the endowment and temple
marriage, all generations after Brother Joseph would be
blessed. Moses restored the keys of gathering, the keys
associated with bringing people into the kingdom, and
Elias restored the keys to form those Church members
into eternal family units through celestial marriage and
through continued faithfulness to their covenants.

*After this vision had closed, another great and
glorious vision burst upon us; for Elijah the prophet, who was
taken to heaven without tasting death, stood before us.*

DOCTRINE & COVENANTS 110:13

Elijah restored the keys associated with the sealing power, that binding power which cements families for eternity. Elijah also restored what we know as the fulness of the Melchizedek Priesthood, the power to make of men kings and of women queens in the kingdom of God. "Then what you seal on earth, by the keys of Elijah, is sealed in heaven; and this is the power of Elijah, and this is the difference between the spirit and power of Elias and Elijah; for while the spirit of Elias is a forerunner, the power of Elijah is sufficient to make our calling and election sure" (Smith, *Teachings of the Prophet Joseph Smith,* 338; see also 322). Each heavenly messenger who came to the Kirtland Temple brought significant powers and authority: Moses brought the power to gather people into the Church and kingdom; Elias brought the power to form them into eternal family units through celestial marriage; and Elijah brought the power to bind those families everlastingly.

I, the Lord your God, am not displeased with your coming this journey, notwithstanding your follies. . . . For there are more treasures than one for you in this city. Therefore, be ye as wise as serpents and yet without sin; and I will order all things for your good.

DOCTRINE & COVENANTS 111:1–11

In 1836, having just completed the Kirtland Temple, the Church was under great pressure of indebtedness. Receiving word of a large amount of unclaimed money in Salem, Massachusetts, the Prophet Joseph took several brethren to that city to secure the money. It turned out to be a folly—an honest mistake, an unwise decision—to make the journey. Knowing the brethren had gone to Salem with a sincere desire to help the Church, the Lord taught his young prophet that the most valuable treasure on earth is the soul of a person. The brethren who made the journey had shared the gospel along the way. They had learned to make the best of a bad situation. They also learned to exercise more wisdom in seeking the will of the Lord. Often, if we are teachable and honest in heart, when one door closes, another opens, and good can come from an error.

*Be thou humble; and the Lord thy God shall lead
thee by the hand, and give thee answer to thy prayers.*
DOCTRINE & COVENANTS 112:10

The Lord will be our leader and our strength, if we in humility will follow him. To follow the Good Shepherd means that we take his hand, recognizing that without him we are as lost sheep, weak and powerless to rescue ourselves, unable to find our way home again. He knows everything about us—our strengths and weaknesses, our abilities and our deficiencies. We need never be ashamed or embarrassed to acknowledge our weakness. Indeed, "the Lord God showeth us our weakness that we may know that it is by his grace, and his great condescensions unto the children of men, that we have power" (Jacob 4:7; Ether 12:27). Some answers to prayer come soon, some come later, but they surely come to those who draw near to the Lord in sincere prayer. It matters not how simple the words may be. If we come before the Lord with a humble heart, he will lead us by the hand.

Whosoever receiveth my word receiveth me, and whosoever receiveth me, receiveth those, the First Presidency, whom I have sent, whom I have made counselors for my name's sake unto you.

DOCTRINE & COVENANTS 112:20

The Church of Jesus Christ of Latter-day Saints administers the gospel of Jesus Christ and extends the ordinances and covenants of salvation to the people of the earth. Though it is true that the power of life and salvation is centered in Christ the Person, such powers are only accessed through the divine program we know as the kingdom of God on earth. Further, loyalty to the Lord's anointed servants is prerequisite to loyalty to the Lord himself. The extended list of Beatitudes the Risen Lord gave to the Nephites begins with "Blessed are ye if ye shall give heed unto the words of these twelve whom I have chosen from among you to minister unto you, and to be your servants" (3 Nephi 12:1). Loyalty and love for the First Presidency, the highest council of the Church and the supreme adjudicators of the law, are loyalty and love for the Lord himself.

*Vengeance cometh speedily upon the inhabitants of
the earth, a day of wrath. . . . And upon my house shall it
begin, and from my house shall it go forth, saith the Lord; first
among those among you, saith the Lord, who have professed
to know my name and have not known me.*

DOCTRINE & COVENANTS 112:24–26

The apostle Peter wrote to the Saints scattered
abroad that the "time is come that judgment must
begin at the house of God; and if it first begin at us,
what shall the end be of them that obey not the gospel
of God?" (1 Peter 4:17). God will not be mocked. He
will not allow hypocrisy within the household of faith
to destroy the work of the kingdom or to tarnish the
good name of the Church. He will see to it that those
who have professed his name—who are supposedly
members in good standing and active in the Church—
but have blasphemed against him will be removed and
face the consequences of their actions. Those who
have spoken or acted in an impious, irreverent, disre-
spectful, and profane manner, those who sow discord
or proselytize others to share their cynicism, will be
revealed for who and what they are.

Verily I say unto you, the keys of the dispensation,
which ye have received, have come down from the fathers,
and last of all, being sent down from heaven unto you.
DOCTRINE & COVENANTS 112:32

For centuries before the Messiah came, righteous men and women looked forward to the day when all truth and authority would be brought together into a grand whole. The Former-day Saints spoke of the dispensation of the fulness of times as a day when all things would be gathered together in Christ (Ephesians 1:10). This final gospel dispensation is the ocean of revealed truth and power into which all of the rivers and streams of past dispensations have flowed. Adam had the gospel. So do we. Enoch baptized and confirmed. So do we. Noah ordained others to the priesthood. So do we. Abraham participated in eternal marriage. So do we. Moses received the highest blessings of the priesthood. Such also is our privilege if we remain true and faithful. We can thus humbly rejoice that "the keys of the kingdom of God are committed unto man on the earth, and from thence shall the gospel roll forth unto the ends of the earth" (D&C 65:2).

It is wisdom in my servant David W. Patten . . . that he may
perform a mission unto me next spring. . . . For verily thus saith
the Lord, that inasmuch as there are those among you who
deny my name, others shall be planted in their stead.
DOCTRINE & COVENANTS 114:1–2

David W. Patten was a member of the original Quorum of the Twelve Apostles in this dispensation. Fearless and faithful unto the end of his days, he died a martyr in Zion's cause in the Battle of Crooked River in the fall of 1838. Doctrine and Covenants 114 had been revealed to the Prophet Joseph the previous spring. The Lord knew Elder Patten's mission was to continue on the other side of the veil, where the valiant are likewise needed. Sadly, when apostasy infected some Saints in 1838, several leaders were excommunicated—they chose not to follow Elder Patten's example of faithfulness. But the work of the Lord rolls forth. If we fail to do our appointed task, if we fall into sin and rebellion, others will be prepared, called up, and given our place. The work of the Restoration is greater than any one person. It is the work of Almighty God. He will not let it fail.

For thus shall my church be called in the last days, even
The Church of Jesus Christ of Latter-day Saints. Verily I say
unto you all: Arise and shine forth, that thy light may
be a standard for the nations.

DOCTRINE & COVENANTS 115:4–5

Before the revelation recorded in Doctrine and
Covenants 115 was received, the Church had been called
by various names. At a conference held in Kirtland in
May 1834, the Saints gave it the name "'The Church of
the Latter-day Saints.' All these names, however, were
by this revelation brushed aside, and since then the official name given in this revelation has been recognized
as the true title of the Church. . . . The appropriateness
of this title is self evident, and in it there is a beautiful
recognition of the relationship both of the Lord Jesus
Christ and of the Saints to the organization" (Smith,
History of the Church, 3:24). Anciently, members of the
Christian Church were called Saints. They were
Former-day Saints; we are Latter-day Saints. Like them,
we too are followers of the Lord Jesus Christ, the Son
of God, the Savior of the world, the chief cornerstone
of the Church, and the central figure in all our worship.

Spring Hill is named by the Lord Adam-ondi-Ahman, because, said he, it is the place where Adam shall come to visit his people, or the Ancient of Days shall sit, as spoken of by Daniel the prophet.

DOCTRINE & COVENANTS 116:1

At the end of his life, Adam called all of his righteous posterity together in "the valley of Adam-ondi-Ahman and there bestowed upon them his last blessing" (D&C 107:53). Adam-ondi-Ahman is the Valley of God, a place—known in the 1830s as Spring Hill, Missouri—where Adam will come to visit his descendants before Christ appears in glory to the world. The Prophet Joseph said that Adam "is the father of the human family, and presides over the spirits of all men, and all that have had the keys must stand before him in this grand council" (*Teachings of the Prophet Joseph Smith,* 157). At this conference, Adam, whom Joseph Smith identified as the Ancient of Days, and others will render an accounting of their stewardships. Father Adam, in turn, will deliver up his stewardship to Christ. This magnificent congregation of faithful Saints in Adam-ondi-Ahman will help prepare the way for the return of our Lord in glory.

Let them repent of all their sins, and of all their covetous desires, before me, saith the Lord; for what is property unto me? saith the Lord.
DOCTRINE & COVENANTS 117:4

God is our Principal, and we are his agents. And we are expected to do things the way he wants things done and according to his timetable (D&C 64:29). When he commands a people to settle in a particular area, they would do well to settle there. When the Omniscient One directs that a people move to a new gathering place, it would be wise so to do. The Saints had been commanded to relocate to Far West, Missouri, but some of the Church leaders found themselves preoccupied with the profits they could acquire through the sale of properties in Kirtland. Here the Lord reminds William Marks and Newel K. Whitney that some things matter more than others. True Saints never allow themselves to be possessed by their possessions. Rather, their highest ambition is to learn and live the will of God.

*Is there not room enough on the mountains of
Adam-ondi-Ahman, and on the plains of Olaha Shinehah,
or the land where Adam dwelt, that you should covet that which is
but the drop, and neglect the more weighty matters?*
DOCTRINE & COVENANTS 117:8

We all need to be reminded from time to time that
the more weighty matters should always be given top
priority. Sometimes we focus so intently on things of
little worth, things of little consequence, that we neglect that which truly matters most. The Lord wants us
to put first things first and turn to him in righteousness; he wants us to "be ashamed of . . . all [our]
littleness of soul" before him (D&C 117:11). Anything
that shrinks our soul, entices us to do evil, and diverts
our attention from everlasting things should be
rejected. We are to give heed to the counsel of the
Lord as it is given through his anointed prophet.
Nothing should take precedence over faithfully keeping our covenants and humbly doing our duty.

*Let my servant Newel K. Whitney be ashamed of the
Nicolaitane band and of all their secret abominations, and of all his
littleness of soul before me, . . . and be a bishop unto my people.*
DOCTRINE & COVENANTS 117:11

Newel K. Whitney had been called as the second
bishop of the Church (D&C 72) and as such had
responsibilities to be with and care for his flock.
Instead, he yielded to the temptation to spend his
time and energies upon treasures that are temporary.
To dramatize the seriousness of his sin, the Savior
compared Bishop Whitney's double-mindedness to
the Nicolaitane band spoken of in the Apocalypse
(Revelation 2:6, 15), a group of Church members who
were trying to maintain their standing in the Church
while at the same time yielding to the pull of the world
(McConkie, *Doctrinal New Testament Commentary,* 3:446).
The Lord described this character flaw as "littleness of
soul," an indication that someone of Bishop Whitney's
spiritual stature should not allow his head to be so easily turned by the fanciful and the fleeting.

*I remember my servant Oliver Granger. . . . his name shall be
had in sacred remembrance from generation to generation. . . . let
him contend earnestly for the redemption of the First Presidency
of my Church . . . ; and when he falls he shall rise again, for his
sacrifice shall be more sacred unto me than his increase.*

DOCTRINE & COVENANTS 117:12–13

Oliver Granger was appointed by the Prophet
Joseph Smith as his agent in Kirtland to attend to
unfinished business. Although relatively few members
of the Church today know who Brother Granger was,
he fulfilled his task with exactness. He remained true
and faithful and died secure in his testimony. His posterity has inherited a legacy of loyalty and can find
great comfort in the Lord's tender words to their fore-
bear. Like Brother Granger, all of us will fall and make
mistakes. The Lord's counsel is to pick ourselves up,
dust ourselves off, and move on. From God's eternal
perspective, our sacrifice (our complete submission
and surrender to the Almighty) is more significant
and sacred than our increase (the amount of good that
could be accomplished through our good deeds). We
will be judged by the desires of our hearts as well as by
our works (Alma 41:3; D&C 137:4). Far more important than our geography is our direction.

Let the residue continue to preach from that hour,
and if they will do this in all lowliness of heart, in meekness and
humility, and long-suffering, I, the Lord, give unto them a
promise that I will provide for their families; and an
effectual door shall be opened for them.

DOCTRINE & COVENANTS 118:3

Doctrine and Covenants 118 is a revelation given through the Prophet Joseph in Far West, Missouri, in July 1838 in response to the supplication, "Show us thy will, O Lord, concerning the Twelve" (headnote). The Lord responded that the vacancies in the Twelve as a result of apostasy should be filled, and he gave the names, manifesting that those who are appointed are called by the Lord, not by man, to be his witnesses. The Lord promised the Twelve that doors would open for them and their families would be provided for if they were diligent, meek, humble, and long-suffering in their callings. They were given a precise date for departing for their mission the following year (26 April 1839)—the only revelation in the Doctrine and Covenants that has a day, month, and year prescribed by which time certain things were to be accomplished. It was thus fulfilled. Then, as now, the faithful apostles were obedient and diligent in their callings as special witnesses.

NOVEMBER

*Joseph Smith, the Prophet and Seer
of the Lord, has done more, save Jesus only,
for the salvation of men in this world, than
any other man that ever lived in it. . . . He
lived great, and he died great in the
eyes of God and his people.*

DOCTRINE & COVENANTS
135:3

[They] shall pay one-tenth of all their interest annually; and this shall be a standing law unto them forever. . . . it shall come to pass that all those who gather unto the land of Zion . . . shall observe this law, or they shall not be found worthy to abide among you.

DOCTRINE & COVENANTS 119:4–5

President Gordon B. Hinckley has said: "We *can* pay our tithing. This is not so much a matter of money as it is a matter of faith. . . . The fact is that tithing is the Lord's law of finance. . . . It is a divine law with a great and beautiful promise. . . . It is applicable to the widow in her poverty as well as to the wealthy man in his riches. . . . One need only compare it with the income tax to recognize the simplicity that comes of the wisdom of God in contrast with the complexity that comes of the wisdom of men" (*Teachings of Gordon B. Hinckley*, 655). Tithing is a principle with a promise: The Lord will open the windows of heaven to those who are honest in paying their tithes and offerings, and there shall not be room enough to receive the promised blessings (Malachi 3:10). Those who faithfully obey the law of tithing testify that the Lord keeps his promise.

The time is now come, that it shall be disposed of by a council,
composed of the First Presidency of my Church, and of the bishop
and his council, and by my high council; and by mine
own voice unto them, saith the Lord.

DOCTRINE & COVENANTS 120

The disbursement of tithing funds is supervised by a priesthood council consisting of the First Presidency, the Quorum of the Twelve Apostles, and the Presiding Bishopric. This Council on the Disposition of the Tithes distributes these sacred funds for building and maintaining temples, meetinghouses, and other facilities, as well as for various programs of the Church. The council works unanimously as they are directed by "[the Lord's] own voice" (D&C 120). Our tithes and offerings belong to the Lord. The appointed council of his servants decides how they should be used. How comforting and reassuring to know that these consecrated funds are disbursed by inspired priesthood holders whose sole desire is to bless people and move the work of the Lord forward. Our great opportunity to obey the law of tithing manifests our true conversion and provides us a protective shield both temporally and spiritually (D&C 64:23–24).

*O God, where art thou? And where is
the pavilion that covereth thy hiding place?*
DOCTRINE & COVENANTS 121:1

The Prophet Joseph Smith's letters from Liberty Jail to
the Saints are among the most touching and inspiring in
our literature. It is difficult to imagine spending several
months in such confined, filthy, and degrading quarters.
The Prophet of the Restoration cried out, as surely each
of us would have, to the God of all creation and pleaded
for comfort, direction, and deliverance. Every one of us at
one time or another wonders where God is, wonders
why good does not prevail, wonders why the vile and the
vicious seem to prosper in this terribly unfair world.
Although perhaps none of us would volunteer to endure
Joseph's hardships in order to learn Joseph's lessons, each
of us can benefit from the lessons themselves. Liberty Jail
proved to be a season of sanctification, an era of unusual
enlightenment, a spiritual gestation period for the man
called to lead the final dispensation. Liberty Jail was, as
Elder B. H. Roberts observed, a "Prison-Temple" (*Comprehensive History of The Church,* 1:527–28).

*My son, peace be unto thy soul; thine adversity
and thine afflictions shall be but a small moment; and then,
if thou endure it well, God shall exalt thee on high;
thou shalt triumph over all thy foes.*

DOCTRINE & COVENANTS 121:7–8

For the Prophet Joseph, Liberty Jail proved to be a school of sanctification. The Lord, with perfect empathy, offered him comfort and encouragement. Followers of Christ are promised not freedom from tribulation but strength to endure it: "I will . . . ease the burdens which are put upon your shoulders, . . . that ye may know of a surety that I, the Lord God, do visit my people in their afflictions" (Mosiah 24:14). Three months after his experience in Liberty Jail, the Prophet wrote: "After a person has faith in Christ, repents of his sins, and is baptized for the remission of his sins and receives the Holy Ghost, . . . then let him continue to humble himself before God. . . . When the Lord has thoroughly proved him, and finds that the man is determined to serve Him at all hazards, then the man will find his calling and his election made sure" (*Teachings of the Prophet Joseph Smith,* 150).

*Thy friends do stand by thee, and they shall hail thee
again with warm hearts and friendly hands. Thou art not yet as
Job; thy friends do not contend against thee, neither charge
thee with transgression, as they did Job.*

DOCTRINE & COVENANTS 121:9–10

The accounts of the lives of faithful Job and Joseph are instructive and inspiring. Unlike Job, Joseph Smith's wife, family, and true friends loved and supported him in his tribulations. Unlike Joseph, Job's suffering ceased, his fortunes were restored, and he lived out a long life of prosperity. We are each given customized challenges so that we might be tutored and refined to develop the attributes of godliness. In a real sense, we're all in this together. As we struggle through life as "fellowcitizens with the saints, and of the household of God" (Ephesians 2:19), what a difference kind words make; how sweet the sound of a loyal friend's voice; how comforting the loving words and deeds of those who care. There is no smooth surface from shore to shore, from season to season, for anyone. But the trials of life are more bearable, the burdens less heavy, the joys more rich, with friends and loved ones by our side.

NOVEMBER 6

Cursed are all those that shall lift up the heel against mine anointed, saith the Lord, and cry they have sinned when they have not sinned before me, saith the Lord, but have done that which was meet in mine eyes, and which I commanded them.

DOCTRINE & COVENANTS 121:16

An awful irony is associated with those, whether within or outside the faith, who stand on the sidelines and attack, insult, or accuse the men charged to guide the destiny of the Lord's kingdom. Elder Harold B. Lee reminded us to "[m]ark well those who speak evil of the Lord's anointed for they speak from impure hearts" (Conference Report, October 1947, 67). Brother Joseph himself explained: "That man who rises up to condemn others, finding fault with the Church, saying that they are out of the way, while he himself is righteous, then know assuredly, that that man is in the high road to apostasy; and if he does not repent, will apostatize, as God lives" (*Teachings of the Prophet Joseph Smith,* 156–57). So often, therefore, we learn far more about the accusers of the Brethren than we do about the Brethren. Such attacks are generally autobiographical, not factual.

As well might man stretch forth his puny arm to stop
the Missouri river in its decreed course, or to turn it up stream,
as to hinder the Almighty from pouring down knowledge from
heaven upon the heads of the Latter-day Saints.

DOCTRINE & COVENANTS 121:33

The enemies of the Church tried unceasingly to stop the marvelous work of the Lord by persecuting and imprisoning the Prophet Joseph. These denizens of darkness thought that if they could separate the Prophet from his people, either the Saints or the Prophet would weaken and falter. But they knew not God or his purposes—or his anointed prophet. The Lord's adversaries failed to place the Prophet beyond the reach of heaven. Revelation from on high continued to flow unto the Prophet in prison, thus making his place of confinement a sanctuary of inspiration, a temple of truth. The enemies of righteousness were powerless to impede the work of the Lord's kingdom—then and now. Oh, they may occasionally win victory over a soul who lets go of the iron rod, but the work of the Lord moves on and grows, unhindered, unobstructed, unstoppable. In the end, the war will be won by the Lord, his prophet, his Saints.

*Their hearts are set so much upon the things of this
world, . . . that they do not learn this one lesson—that the rights of
the priesthood are inseparably connected with the powers of
heaven, and that the powers of heaven cannot be controlled
nor handled only upon the principles of righteousness.*

DOCTRINE & COVENANTS 121:35–36

So very often we live beneath our spiritual privileges
because we become too attracted by the allurements
and treasures of this world. The powers of heaven can
only be exercised by one who communes with the
heavens regularly, one whose aspiration is for divine
approbation, not the applause of the fickle and the
fading. The powers of God cannot be summoned by
one who strives to specialize in the powers of earth.
Righteousness leads to power. Humility results in
strength. Submission and surrender bring about the
ultimate victory over the stumbling blocks of this
telestial tenement. As we "grow up unto the Lord"
(Helaman 3:21; D&C 109:15), we become more dis-
criminating—our spiritual senses long for association
with eternal things. In short, the powers of godliness
are channeled only through the God-fearing.

When we undertake to cover our sins, . . . or to exercise
control or dominion or compulsion upon the souls of the children
of men, in any degree of unrighteousness, behold, . . . the Spirit
of the Lord is grieved; and when it is withdrawn, Amen
to the priesthood or the authority of that man.

DOCTRINE & COVENANTS 121:37

If a priesthood holder becomes unrighteous in his life or in the exercise of priesthood authority, his power in the priesthood ends and becomes instead a source of condemnation rather than blessing. "Unworthiness impairs a man's ability to bless others through his priesthood. Nevertheless, if an unworthy person is called upon unknowingly to perform an ordinance, the ordinance is valid because the individual performs it not so much by his own authority as by his having been duly appointed as an agent for the Church. Basing the validity of ordinances on the worthiness of the officiator would inevitably raise questions and create confusion. Hence the efficacy of ordinances depends on the worthiness of those receiving them rather than on the worthiness of those performing them" (Cowan, *Answers,* 138). Those who exercise their priesthood upon principles of righteousness will be chosen for an inheritance of eternal life.

We have learned by sad experience that it is the nature and disposition of almost all men, as soon as they get a little authority, as they suppose, they will immediately begin to exercise unrighteous dominion.

DOCTRINE & COVENANTS 121:39

An angel taught King Benjamin that "the natural man is an enemy to God, and has been from the fall of Adam, and will be, forever and ever, unless he yields to the enticings of the Holy Spirit" (Mosiah 3:19). Fallen (unredeemed) man is self-seeking, self-congratulatory, and, in the end, self-destructive. Not having rendered his heart unto God, he sees things not as they are but as he is. He is subjected to his own myopic will. Such a person is also power-hungry, eager to get ahead and to have more than his neighbor. He thus easily resorts to exercising unrighteous dominion. On the other hand, individuals who are washed clean in the blood of the Lamb enjoy the refining influences of the Holy Spirit, look to the good of others, reach out to lift one who has fallen, and find their greatest happiness in the success of their fellowman.

*No power or influence can or ought to be maintained by
virtue of the priesthood, only by persuasion, by long-suffering,
by gentleness and meekness, and by love unfeigned.*

DOCTRINE & COVENANTS 121:41

Those called to bear the holy priesthood of God are
also called to bear it with fidelity and devotion, to lead
and direct and lift others in the process. Righteousness
cannot be demanded. Conformity cannot be coerced.
And the ends of the leader, even noble ends, cannot
be achieved by virtue of the priesthood or by virtue of
position or power. Those who exercise righteous
dominion have righteous motives, and such persons
never need to compel obedience. People feel to follow
a humble leader, for such a leader functions after the
fashion of the Good Shepherd.

*Reproving betimes with sharpness, when moved
upon by the Holy Ghost; and then showing forth afterwards an
increase of love toward him whom thou hast reproved,
lest he esteem thee to be his enemy.*

DOCTRINE & COVENANTS 121:43

Occasionally, the righteous leader is required to reprove "betimes with sharpness" (D&C 121:43). That means to reprove or correct early in the process, at the earliest possible moment, and to do so sharply, meaning specifically or pointedly. It is not difficult to detect the motive behind a reproof. Certain questions come to mind: Has the reproving one truly been moved upon by the Holy Ghost? Is love for the one reproved the true motive for reproof? Does the person being reproved feel loved? Does an expression of love for the one reproved flow easily or is such an effort labored? Is the one reproving motivated more by saving the soul of another or saving face for himself? Truly, as the apostle Peter observed, "charity preventeth a multitude of sins" (JST 1 Peter 4:8). It is no accident that the world's greatest leader was the One who loved the world the most.

Let thy bowels also be full of charity towards all men,
and to the household of faith, and let virtue garnish thy thoughts
unceasingly; then shall thy confidence wax strong in the presence
of God; and the doctrine of the priesthood shall distil upon
thy soul as the dews from heaven.

DOCTRINE & COVENANTS 121:45

Power in the priesthood comes from the pure love of
Christ dwelling in the heart; it comes from chastity and
fidelity, from pure hands and clean thoughts. Priesthood
holders—although mortal and imperfect—can have
the confidence that comes of worthiness, the sweet
assurance that comes of righteousness. Confidence in
the Lord is the very opposite of smugness and self-
righteousness. Worthy priesthood holders have the confidence in the Lord born of humility and meekness, the
courage and strength in the Lord born of submissiveness.
This confidence is a result of applying the principles of
righteousness in their lives. Though men have the rights
of the priesthood conferred upon them, they will not
reap its eternal blessings if they are unworthy or use the
priesthood for unrighteous purposes. Those who hold
this power and authority are inheritors of eternal life if
they exercise their priesthood in righteousness and serve
in the kingdom with an eye single to the glory of God.

The Holy Ghost shall be thy constant companion, and thy scepter an unchanging scepter of righteousness and truth; and thy dominion shall be an everlasting dominion, and without compulsory means it shall flow unto thee forever and ever.

DOCTRINE & COVENANTS 121:46

A worthy priesthood holder has the companionship of a member of the Godhead to guide and protect him constantly. A worthy priesthood holder draws others to his goodness as he leads with integrity and blesses all with whom he comes in contact. The power promised to a righteous priesthood holder in mortality will continue with him everlastingly, for he will attain unto eternal life and preside in righteousness forever. Nevertheless, these supernal blessings are not for the priesthood holder alone. He is blessed only in relation to others. Priesthood is love—love in action. One cannot give a priesthood blessing to oneself. It is in the moments of daily living—associating with neighbors and ward members, serving in callings in the Church—that we develop attributes of godliness and learn what it means to hold and honor the sacred priesthood power of God. The blessings of the priesthood are inseparably connected to the principles of righteousness.

The ends of the earth shall inquire after thy name,
and fools shall have thee in derision, and hell shall rage against
thee; while the pure in heart, and the wise, and the noble, and the
virtuous, shall seek counsel, and authority, and blessings
constantly from under thy hand.

DOCTRINE & COVENANTS 122:1–2

In the dank, dark dungeon of oxymoronic Liberty Jail, the Lord reassured the Prophet Joseph that the Restoration he had commenced would continue to roll forth. The Lord's comforting words to his prophet continue to be fulfilled. All gospel roads lead through Joseph Smith to Jesus Christ. All individuals, whether now or at some future date, will be called to account for where they stand with reference to the Prophet and his divine mission. Either he was a prophet of God called to usher in the dispensation of the fulness of times and restore gospel light to a darkening world, or he was an imposter. Was Joseph Smith a prophet of God? The honest in heart, the virtuous and meek, will drink at the well restored by the Prophet's hand and testify that Joseph Smith was, without equivocation, a prophet of God. We honor his name and seek counsel and authority and blessing from him who now wears that prophetic mantle.

Know thou, my son, that all these things shall give thee experience, and shall be for thy good. The Son of Man hath descended below them all. Art thou greater than he?
DOCTRINE & COVENANTS 122:7–8

Few men have been called on to suffer more than did Joseph Smith," stated President Joseph Fielding Smith. "His entire life was spent in the midst of persecution by the hands of his enemies. No doubt he wondered many times why this had to be. In this revelation the Lord tells him. . . . There is great experience in tribulation that brings to pass much good. The person who goes through life without pain or sorrow, and who is not called upon to sacrifice comforts and partake of hardships, never receives the full value of life. We came here for experience, the benefits of which are not to be limited to this mortal life" (*Church History and Modern Revelation,* 2:181). No one has ever suffered more than did the Lord. In our agony, let us always remember his condescension, and look to Christ and live. In our tribulation, let us follow the Savior and endure it well.

Therefore, hold on thy way, and the priesthood shall remain with thee; for their bounds are set, they cannot pass. Thy days are known, and thy years shall not be numbered less; therefore, fear not what man can do, for God shall be with you forever and ever.

DOCTRINE & COVENANTS 122:9

The Lord said, "I will try you and prove you herewith" (D&C 98:12). Life is a school and testing ground in which we learn and prove ourselves worthy of celestial inheritance. Enemies of righteousness abound all during life. Our days are filled with customized challenges for optimal opportunities for growth. "We are continually being tried and tested as individuals and as a church," said President Spencer W. Kimball. "There are more trials yet to come, but be not discouraged nor dismayed. Always remember that if this were not the Lord's work, the adversary would not pay any attention to us. If this Church were merely a church of men and women, teaching only the doctrines of men, we would encounter little or no criticism or resistance—but because this is the Church of Him whose name it bears, we must not be surprised when criticisms or difficulties arise" (*Ensign,* May 1981, 79). Let us go forward with faith in the Lord and his purposes.

There are many yet on the earth among all sects, parties,
and denominations, who are blinded by the subtle craftiness of
men, whereby they lie in wait to deceive, and who are only kept
from the truth because they know not where to find it.
DOCTRINE & COVENANTS 123:12

There are good men and women throughout the earth. Many of them are members of particular religious denominations; while others have chosen not to associate themselves officially with a church but to do their best to maintain a life of morality, decency, and integrity. The need to look to and worship a higher power is instinctive, but it is often unfulfilled. Some individuals' formal association with a religious body does not seem to bring personal satisfaction and fulfillment. Even though the restored gospel is spreading throughout the earth, the Latter-day Saints remain a small proportion of the earth's population. One matter that ought to provide continuing motivation for missionary work is our understanding that many noble souls seek after the truth, even the fulness of the truth, but do not know where to find it. Our task is to search them out and help them fulfill their deepest unmet needs.

A very large ship is benefited very much by a very small helm in the time of a storm, by being kept workways with the wind and the waves. Therefore, dearly beloved brethren, let us cheerfully do all things that lie in our power.

DOCTRINE & COVENANTS 123:16–17

Membership in the Church calls forth a determination to serve," declared President Thomas S. Monson. "A position of responsibility may not be of recognized importance, nor may the reward be broadly known. Service, to be acceptable to the Savior, must come from willing minds, ready hands, and pledged hearts. Occasionally discouragement may darken our pathway; frustration may be a constant companion. In our ears there may sound the sophistry of Satan as he whispers, 'You cannot save the world; your small efforts are meaningless. You haven't time to be concerned for others.' Trusting in the Lord, let us turn our heads from such falsehoods and make certain our feet are firmly planted in the path of service and our hearts and souls dedicated to follow the example of the Lord" (*Ensign,* March 2004, 5). As we do our part, we can find comfort in the Lord's promise: "Be not weary in well-doing" (D&C 64:33).

*How shall your washings be acceptable unto me, except ye
perform them in a house which you have built to my name? . . .
that those ordinances might be revealed which had been
hid from before the world was.*

DOCTRINE & COVENANTS 124:37–38

In the revelation recorded in Doctrine and Covenants
124, the Lord began to unfold to the Prophet Joseph
Smith principles and doctrines and practices of temple
worship that had not been made known at the time of
the dedication of the Kirtland Temple. In May 1842
the Prophet began to reveal the temple endowment as
we now know it (*Teachings of the Prophet Joseph Smith*,
237). We learn from Doctrine and Covenants 124 that
whenever the priesthood of God is upon the earth and
whenever the people of God are prepared to receive
it, our Father in Heaven instructs his living oracles
to build temples and introduce to the Saints the
covenants, ordinances, and teachings that have always
been kept from the world. By this means, individuals
and families are sealed and bound into eternal family
units, thus allowing the earth to fulfill its foreordained
purpose (D&C 2:2–3).

When I give a commandment to any of the sons of men to do a work unto my name, and those sons of men go with all their might . . . , and their enemies come upon them . . . , it behooveth me to require that work no more at the hands of those sons of men.

Some prophecies are unconditional: They will come to pass no matter what. For example, Lehi taught that the Savior would come to earth six hundred years from the time his family left Jerusalem (1 Nephi 10:4). Likewise, Samuel the Lamanite prophesied that the resurrected Savior would visit the Nephites in five years (Helaman 14:2). Finally, the time of the second coming of the Lord in glory is set, fixed, and established; it may not be postponed or hastened (McConkie, *Millennial Messiah*, 26–27, 405). On the other hand, most prophecies are conditional: They have been uttered under the influence of God's Spirit, but their fulfillment depends in large measure upon circumstances. For instance, although the Saints were told that a temple in Jackson County "shall be reared in this generation" (D&C 84:4; see also v. 31), the enemies of the Church persecuted them to such extent that the people of the covenant were forced to leave Independence without having built the temple.

David Patten I have taken unto myself; behold,
his priesthood no man taketh from him; but, verily I say unto
you, another may be appointed unto the same calling.
DOCTRINE & COVENANTS 124:130

When Elder David W. Patten was martyred and entered the world of spirits, he did not lose his priesthood nor did he change quorums. "The same priesthood exists on the other side of the veil," President Wilford Woodruff taught. "Every man who is faithful is in his quorum there. When a man dies and his body is laid in the tomb, he does not lose his position. The Prophet Joseph Smith held the keys of this dispensation on this side of the veil, and he will hold them throughout the countless ages of eternity." President Woodruff also said that "every Apostle, every seventy, every elder, etc., who has died in the faith, as soon as he passes to the other side of the veil, enters into the work of the ministry, and there is a thousand times more to preach there than there is here" (*Discourses of Wilford Woodruff,* 77). Thus, whatever callings we magnify here will have a bearing upon what we are called to do hereafter.

*And a commandment I give unto you, that you
should fill all these offices and approve of those names which I have
mentioned, or else disapprove of them at my general conference.*

DOCTRINE & COVENANTS 124:144

We gather in general conference twice each year
from the far corners of the earth to be instructed and
edified by the Lord's servants. "For all things must be
done in order, and by common consent in the church,
by the prayer of faith" (D&C 28:13). We assemble to
transact Church business and learn the current condition of the Church. We meet to worship the Lord in
thankfulness and to be strengthened in our testimonies and determination to serve him. We come
together to hear the voice of warning from the Lord's
inspired leaders. And we gather to raise our hands to
manifest our solemn covenant to sustain those leaders. Our positive participation in the sustaining vote
is a demonstration of our desire to support the Lord's
authorized representatives; to support them means
that we humbly, willingly, follow their counsel and
heed their words. In word and deed, we stand in faithfulness to the Lord and his apostles and prophets.

If those who call themselves by my name and are essaying to be my saints, if they will do my will and keep my commandments concerning them, let them gather themselves together unto the places which I shall appoint unto them by my servant Joseph.

DOCTRINE & COVENANTS 125:2

In the early decades of the Church, members had been commanded to gather in various locations (Ohio, Missouri, Illinois, Utah). Faithful Saints knew the importance of following the prophet in gathering where the Lord commanded. Today it is the same—the places of gathering are still being revealed through the Lord's living prophet. Members gather to the household of faith in a ward or branch, stake or mission, wherever they live around the world. Each is assigned a place of membership within the geographical boundaries where he or she resides. We do not gather now to Nauvoo or Salt Lake City. The Saints build up the Church as they gather in love and unity in cities and towns across the nations of the earth. We gather to serve one another, to receive priesthood ordinances and renew covenants, and to strengthen each other in faith and testimony as we face the temptations and tribulations of life.

*Dear and well-beloved brother, Brigham Young, verily
thus saith the Lord unto you: My servant Brigham, it is no more
required at your hand to leave your family as in times past,
for your offering is acceptable to me.*
DOCTRINE & COVENANTS 126:1

Brigham Young was president of the Quorum of the
Twelve Apostles in 1841 when the revelation recorded
in Doctrine and Covenants 126 was given. He had just
returned to his family and the Church at Nauvoo after
serving a mission to Great Britain. The Lord, who had
seen Brigham Young's untiring "labor and toil in jour-
neyings for my name" (D&C 126:2), instructed him to
leave his family no more but to send the Lord's word
abroad and provide for his family (D&C 126:1, 3).
President Young needed to take care of his family, to
be with the other leaders of the Church, to learn more
from the Prophet Joseph, to direct missionary efforts,
and to prepare himself to be Joseph's successor just
three years hence. O, to be called dear and beloved of
the Lord! The Master loves those who labor faithfully
in his name. Their efforts and sacrifices, as well as
those of their families, are acknowledged by the Lord.

*And as for the perils which I am called to pass through,
they seem but a small thing to me, as the envy and wrath of
man have been my common lot all the days of my life.*

DOCTRINE & COVENANTS 127:2

Joseph Smith spent his life from the age of fourteen until he was martyred at age thirty-eight suffering persecution and affliction. He had many faithful associates and constant friends, but he also knew much anguish and betrayal. His enemies' relentlessness was mysterious to him, but he understood that it was preordained for him from before the foundation of the world. At peace with himself, he was content to let God judge his life and allow others to do the same. "Judge ye for yourselves. God knoweth all these things, whether it be good or bad. But nevertheless, deep water is what I am wont to swim in. It all has become a second nature to me; and I feel, like Paul, to glory in tribulation" (D&C 127:2). Joseph knew that he would triumph over all his enemies, and in the end the gospel would continue to roll forth without hindrance to fill the whole earth in preparation for the second coming of Jesus Christ.

As I stated . . . that I would write to you from time to time and give you information in relation to many subjects, I now resume the subject of the baptism for the dead, as that subject seems to occupy my mind, and press itself upon my feelings.

DOCTRINE & COVENANTS 128:1

The Lord uses a myriad of ways to reveal himself to his children. He who is omnipotent and omniscient is hardly limited in how he speaks or makes known his mind and will. As recorded in Doctrine and Covenants 8:2–3, the Spirit can reveal things to our mind (in the form of thoughts) and to our heart (in the form of feelings), and these two can serve as a kind of balance for one another. The revelations of God are almost always what we would call rational. It is impressive to note that someone as seasoned and experienced in the things of the Spirit as the Prophet of the Restoration should identify as revelation that which God had caused to occupy his mind and press upon his feelings. It is a great lesson to those who aspire to perfect communion with the heavens: We will never outgrow the simple and straightforward manifestations of the Holy Ghost.

The book which was the book of life is the record which is kept in heaven; the principle agreeing precisely with the doctrine which is commanded you in the revelation . . . that in all your recordings it may be recorded in heaven.

DOCTRINE & COVENANTS 128:7

Neither our good deeds nor our participation in saving ordinances on this earth will be undetected and unrecorded in what we call the Lamb's book of life. President Brigham Young explained: "We receive the gospel, not that we may have our names written in the Lamb's book of life, but that our names may not be blotted out of that book. . . . My doctrine is—that there never was a son and daughter of Adam and Eve born on this earth whose names were not already written in the Lamb's book of life, and there they will remain until their conduct is such that the angel who keeps the record is authorized to blot them out and record them elsewhere" (*Journal of Discourses,* 12:101). In short, our desire is to have our names "recorded in the book of the names of the sanctified, even them of the celestial world" (D&C 88:2).

Now, what do we hear in the gospel which we have received? A voice of gladness! A voice of mercy from heaven; and a voice of truth out of the earth.

DOCTRINE & COVENANTS 128:19

The gospel is a message of good news and happiness, of glad tidings, of great joy and good things; it is a testament of truth and a message of mercy to all the earth (D&C 128:19). It is all this to both the living and the dead. "This isn't a gospel of gloom, it is a gospel of gladness," said President Gordon B. Hinckley. "We ought to be happy in it. We ought to be smiling about it. Oh, there is worry once in a while, but then there is prayer to take care of that. . . . I just stand back once in a while and marvel at it all—at the things we are trying to do as a Church to make the world a better place in which to live, a more informed place. We are trying to do a great work, the work of the Savior" (*Teachings of Gordon B. Hinckley,* 246). We who have the gospel are richly blessed.

*That same sociality which exists among us here will
exist among us there, only it will be coupled with eternal glory,
which glory we do not now enjoy.*

DOCTRINE & COVENANTS 130:2

Men and women are social creatures, and they cannot realize the fulness of their potential until they open themselves to relationships with others in society. If a member of the Church should become so enamored with the study of the scriptures, for example, that he spends inordinate periods of time alone and begins to view other people as distractions and interruptions to more important things, he is walking on shifting sand. The scriptures affirm that the more we become like our Master, the more people-centered we become. The apostle Paul taught that one of the signs of spiritual growth is the "fruit of the Spirit" (Galatians 5:22), those qualities and gifts and manifestations that evidence our growing love for our Father's children and our heightened desire to serve them. Heaven will be heaven hereafter, not just because of the power and glory we possess but mainly because of the continuation of sweet associations that we developed in this our second estate.

DECEMBER

*All who have died without a knowledge of
this gospel, who would have received it if they
had been permitted to tarry, shall be heirs of
the celestial kingdom of God; also all that
shall die henceforth without a knowledge of
it, who would have received it with all their
hearts, shall be heirs of that kingdom.*

DOCTRINE & COVENANTS
137:7–8

The appearing of the Father and the Son, in [John 14:23],
is a personal appearance; and the idea that the Father and the Son
dwell in a man's heart is an old sectarian notion, and is false.
DOCTRINE & COVENANTS 130:3

The Spirit of God may come upon us and dwell in us, but because the Father and Son are physical beings, they cannot personally dwell in our hearts. Once we have cultivated the spirit of revelation in our lives (the First Comforter) and have demonstrated by sacrifice that we are willing to give all things for the kingdom's sake, the Lord then makes our salvation secure; we then open ourselves to the possibility of additional revelation with the first and second members of the Godhead. "If a man love me, he will keep my words: And my Father will love him, and we will come unto him and make our abode with him" (John 14:23; see also v. 21; Smith, *Teachings of the Prophet Joseph Smith,* 149–50). This transcendent blessing is not, however, one that we can produce, program, or bring about ourselves; it will be "in [God's] own time, and in his own way, and according to his own will" (D&C 88:68).

If a person gains more knowledge and intelligence in this
life through his diligence and obedience than another, he will
have so much the advantage in the world to come.

DOCTRINE & COVENANTS 130:19

True intelligence is reflected in our acquiring light and truth (D&C 93:36). It is manifest as we diligently live in obedience to the truth. Intelligence, which has been defined as the righteous application of knowledge, is clearly more than academic degrees or amassing information and facts. So much of the knowledge of this world is worthless. Intelligence is God's truth and light; it is in knowing and putting first things first; it is in living in accordance with the new and everlasting covenant. This supernal intelligence comes from obedience to the commandments of God and diligence in being true to the truth and keeping close to the Church. The light and truth of intelligence forsake the power of the adversary (D&C 93:37) and are among the few things that remain with us when we die. Those who apply themselves in this life with faithfulness and sincerity in seeking light and truth will obtain greater advantages in the world to come.

There is a law, irrevocably decreed in heaven before
the foundations of this world, upon which all blessings are
predicated—and when we obtain any blessing from God, it is
by obedience to that law upon which it is predicated.

DOCTRINE & COVENANTS 130:20–21

Blessings are received through obedience to law. Whether the law of the Sabbath, the law of tithing, the law of chastity, or other laws, blessings come to those who follow the first law of heaven: obedience. If we obey the commandments and keep the law, we are promised the blessing (D&C 82:10). God does not lie or deceive. "Who am I, saith the Lord, that have promised and have not fulfilled?" (D&C 58:31). His blessings are sure. "He that hath my commandments, and keepeth them, he it is that loveth me: and he that loveth me shall be loved of my Father, and I will love him, and will manifest myself to him" (John 14:21). God's blessings—large and small—are given to those who place their will submissively on God's altar. Some blessings come soon, some come later, but they do come to those who obey.

*The Father has a body of flesh and bones as tangible
as man's; the Son also; but the Holy Ghost has not a body of flesh
and bones, but is a personage of Spirit. Were it not so, the
Holy Ghost could not dwell in us.*

DOCTRINE & COVENANTS 130:22

There are three distinct beings in the Godhead. The
Father and the Son are resurrected beings with bodies of flesh and bones, and when they appear, they are
seen as exalted men. Centuries of doctrinal confusion
and speculation were clarified in the early spring of
1820 when young Joseph Smith saw "two Personages,
whose brightness and glory defy all description, standing above me in the air. One of them spake unto
me, calling me by name and said, pointing to the
other—*This is My Beloved Son. Hear Him!*" (Joseph
Smith–History 1:17). The third member of the
Godhead, the Holy Ghost, is a personage of spirit and
does not have a tangible body of flesh and bones.
Sometimes the term *Holy Ghost* is used to refer to the
power or gift of that member of the Godhead, rather
than to his actual Personage. The three Personages are
united as one—one in spirit, one in mind, one in intelligence and truth, one in all godly attributes.

*In the celestial glory there are three heavens or degrees;
and in order to obtain the highest, a man must enter into this
order of the priesthood [meaning the new and everlasting covenant
of marriage]; and if he does not, he cannot obtain it.*
DOCTRINE & COVENANTS 131:1–3

The doctrine of eternal sealings of husband and wife, parents and children, the living and the dead—has come to the Latter-day Saints line upon line, precept upon precept. We learn through the Vision (D&C 76), received in February 1832, that there is more than a heaven and a hell hereafter. As a result of Joseph Smith's vision of the celestial kingdom (D&C 137) in January 1836, we learn that every person will have an opportunity to hear and accept the fulness of the gospel, whether here or hereafter. Through instructions given by the Choice Seer in 1843, we learn of degrees within the highest heaven: "Except a man and his wife enter into an everlasting covenant and be married for eternity, while in this probation, by the power and authority of the Holy Priesthood, they will cease to increase when they die; that is, they will not have any children after the resurrection" (Smith, *Teachings of the Prophet Joseph Smith*, 300–301).

He may enter into the other [lesser kingdoms], but
that is the end of his kingdom; he cannot have an increase.
DOCTRINE & COVENANTS 131:4

Although God knows all things and thus "the past, the present, and the future were and are, with Him, one eternal now," he is an eternal optimist (Smith, *Teachings of the Prophet Joseph Smith,* 220). He points us upward and onward, riveting our attention to the highest glories, the grandest rewards, and the most transcendent inheritances. The scriptures and the prophets have not made known, for example, what persons will inherit the other two degrees in the celestial kingdom, and it is fruitless to speculate. Rather, we know that receiving and abiding by the new and everlasting covenant of marriage opens one to the highest degree of salvation. Further, we know that our Father in Heaven is merciful and gracious, that "there is no Latter-day Saint who dies after having lived a faithful life who will lose anything because of having failed to do certain things when opportunities have not been furnished him or her" (Snow, *Teachings of Lorenzo Snow,* 138).

DECEMBER 7

*The more sure word of prophecy means a man's knowing
that he is sealed up unto eternal life, by revelation and the spirit
of prophecy, through the power of the Holy Priesthood.*
DOCTRINE & COVENANTS 131:5

Receiving the more sure word of prophecy" is
essentially the same as being "sealed by the Holy Spirit
of promise" (D&C 76:53), "seal[ed] up unto eternal
life" (D&C 68:12), or making our "calling and election
sure" (2 Peter 1:10). Joseph Smith taught that achiev-
ing this supernal spiritual grace prepares us to enjoy
the subsequent transcendent blessing of receiving the
Second Comforter: meeting the Savior face to face
(D&C 67:10). The Prophet said, "Go on and continue
to call upon God until you make your calling and election sure for yourselves, by obtaining this more sure
word of prophecy, and wait patiently for the promise
until you obtain it" (*Teachings of the Prophet Joseph Smith,*
149–50, 299). Humbly and patiently we are to strive
to pass the tests of mortality and receive the assurance
of eternal life.

It is impossible for a man to be saved in ignorance.
DOCTRINE & COVENANTS 131:6

In the hierarchy of truth, some truths matter more than others. It's useful to know the various "truths" of this world—from science to mathematics to engineering. But it's absolutely essential to know the truths that stand the test of time, that are eternal and unchanging. As children of God, we cannot be saved in ignorance of his plan of happiness and salvation. We cannot be saved in ignorance of the saving principles of the gospel, without faith in the Lord Jesus Christ, without accessing the power of the infinite atonement in putting off the "natural man" (Mosiah 3:19). We may "know" many things—and miss the whole point and purpose of life. The devil knows many things, but his knowledge does not redound unto salvation. Ignorance and apathy toward everlasting things gets us nowhere. We are here in mortality, away from our heavenly home, to acquire an education in the things of eternity.

*Behold, I reveal unto you a new and an everlasting covenant;
and if ye abide not that covenant, then ye are damned; for no one
can reject this covenant and be permitted to enter into my glory.*

DOCTRINE & COVENANTS 132:4

The revelation setting forth the doctrine of eternal marriage is one of the most significant by God to man in this final dispensation. In the early verses of the revelation (note especially verses 6–8), the Lord teaches a vital principle: All things, including covenants, ordinances, and any and every rite associated with the gospel, must be entered into with the Holy Spirit of Promise and ultimately sealed by that Spirit. That is to say, they must be entered into worthily, so that the Holy Spirit, promised to the Saints, can ratify, accept, and place his divine stamp of approval upon the covenants, thus allowing them to have efficacy, virtue, and force in and after the resurrection. As an illustration of this principle, the Savior chooses the doctrine and practice of marriage: Only a marriage that meets the appropriate criteria (performed in the right place by the right person holding the right authority) becomes an eternal union.

*If that covenant is not by me or by my word, . . . and is not
sealed by the Holy Spirit of promise, through him whom I have
anointed . . . , then it is not valid . . . when they are out of the
world . . . ; they cannot, therefore, inherit my glory.*
DOCTRINE & COVENANTS 132:18

Marriage can endure for eternity when we comply
with the conditions the Lord has set. All the wishful
thinking in the world will not bind us together as an
eternal couple without the sealing keys of priesthood
power, without the ratifying seal of approval from the
Holy Ghost, without worthiness on the part of
the couple as they both wholeheartedly strive to live
the gospel. Some have thought that the power to perform a marriage is available through sources that are
not authorized by the Lord. But these marriages end
when death comes. Satan deceives many couples into
thinking that either their love or God's mercy will
keep them together hereafter, or marriage will be
unnecessary in the next life. Both are deceptions.
"[God's] house is a house of order" (D&C 132:18).
The glory of everlasting life together as a couple is
reserved for those who live the law of celestial
marriage.

*If a man marry a wife by my word, which is my law, and
by the new and everlasting covenant, and it is sealed unto them by
the Holy Spirit of promise, by him who is anointed, . . . it shall be
said unto them—Ye shall come forth in the first resurrection.*

DOCTRINE & COVENANTS 132:19

The new and everlasting covenant of marriage is
part of the path that leads to eternal life. God's greatest gift to us is the quality of life that he himself lives
and is reserved for those worthy of the celestial kingdom. There the family unit continues through eternity, and we inherit the fulness of the glory of the
Father. Eternal life means to be "saved in the everlasting kingdom of the Lamb" (1 Nephi 13:37), to qualify
for the resurrection of the just and to come forth in
the morning of the first resurrection, clothed with
glory, immortality, and eternal lives. Those who abide
the new and everlasting covenant of marriage "shall
pass by the angels, and the gods, which are set there,
to their exaltation and glory in all things, . . . which
glory shall be a fulness and a continuation of the seeds
forever and ever" (D&C 132:19). What sweet peace
the doctrine of celestial marriage brings!

*Then shall they be gods, because they have no end; therefore
shall they be from everlasting to everlasting, because they continue;
then shall they be above all, because all things are subject unto
them. Then shall they be gods, because they have all
power, and the angels are subject unto them.*

DOCTRINE & COVENANTS 132:20

It is clearly taught in the New Testament that we should strive for perfection, just like our Heavenly Father (Matthew 5:48); that we can be joint heirs or co-inheritors with Christ to all the Father has (Romans 8:16–17); that we become partakers of the divine nature (2 Peter 1:4); and that through becoming the sons and daughters of God by regeneration, we will, in the resurrection, see God as he is, for we will have become like him (1 John 3:1–2). This mind-stretching doctrine of deification was taught at least into the fifth century by such post-apostolic notables as Irenaus, Clement of Alexandria, Justin Martyr, Athanasius, and Augustine. The scriptures declare that eternal life consists of inheriting and possessing the fulness of the glory of the Father and enjoying the continuation of the family unit eternally (D&C 132:19). Beyond that, we do not fully comprehend what it means to become like God.

Except ye abide my law ye cannot attain to this glory. For strait is the gate, and narrow the way that leadeth unto the exaltation and continuation of the lives, and few there be that find it, because ye receive me not in the world neither do ye know me.

DOCTRINE & COVENANTS 132:21–22

The law of celestial marriage is a gate through which a couple must enter to receive the blessings of eternal marriage. We proceed along the path to exaltation by faithfulness in keeping the covenant made in connection with this holy order of matrimony. To experience eternal lives is to experience God's life; it is a continuation of the seeds (children) forever; it is for a worthy and eternally sealed couple to be given all that God has (D&C 132:19–24). This doctrine comforts and inspires all who love their spouse here and wish to remain at each other's side hereafter. It is a rational doctrine that a loving Father would provide the means for his children to inherit all that he has and live in an eternal family unit. It is a profound doctrine that changes and expands the way we see God, ourselves, our spouses, and the potential we have together. Celestial marriage is the gate to the everlasting happiness of exaltation.

If a man marry a wife according to my word, and they are sealed by the Holy Spirit of promise, . . . and if they commit no murder . . . , yet they shall come forth in the first resurrection.

DOCTRINE & COVENANTS 132:26

Few scriptures have been wrested, twisted, and distorted from their intended meaning more than has Doctrine and Covenants 132:26. Some have taught that because they have been married in the temple, nothing can prevent them from obtaining eternal life. Others have even suggested that following their temple marriage they need only avoid murdering someone in order to gain the highest of rewards hereafter. Yet, the burden of scripture is that all are required to adhere faithfully to their covenants to the end of their mortal lives—to live the gospel, to attend church and partake worthily of the sacrament, to love and serve one another, to keep the commandments of God. The Almighty "cannot look upon sin with the least degree of allowance" (D&C 1:31), and so only the penitent, the repentant, the God-fearing can enjoy association with Gods and angels hereafter.

The blasphemy against the Holy Ghost, which shall not be forgiven in the world nor out of the world, is in that ye commit murder wherein ye shed innocent blood, and assent unto my death, after ye have received my new and everlasting covenant, saith the Lord God.

DOCTRINE & COVENANTS 132:27

Most people identify the expression "shedding innocent blood" with murder, the premeditated taking of a human life. In counseling his errant son, Corianton, Alma declared that sexual immorality is "most abominable above all sins" except murder and denying the Holy Ghost (Alma 39:5). There is, however, another way these words are employed in scripture. Note Paul's language: "For it is impossible for those who were once enlightened, and have tasted of the heavenly gift, and were made partakers of the Holy Ghost, and have tasted the good word of God, and the powers of the world to come, if they shall fall away, to renew them again unto repentance; seeing they crucify to themselves the Son of God afresh, and put him to an open shame" (Hebrews 6:4–6). In short, those who sin against the Holy Ghost have essentially, through their defection to perdition, shed once again the blood of the only truly innocent being in eternity: Jesus Christ.

Abraham received concubines, and they bore him children; and it was accounted unto him for righteousness; and because they did none other things than that which they were commanded, they have entered into their exaltation, . . . and are not angels but are gods.

DOCTRINE & COVENANTS 132:37

To state that Abraham, Isaac, and Jacob "did none other things than that which they were commanded" (D&C 132:37) is to indicate that they were obedient both to the letter and the spirit of the commandments of God. On the one hand, they did not take license with gospel liberty and strive to rationalize a paltry offering. On the other hand, they did what God called upon them to do and did not reach beyond the mark of propriety; they lived a sane and balanced life. As a result, they, with their wives, came forth from the graves in a glorious celestial resurrection and attained godhood. They now preside over an endless posterity as kings and queens, priests and priestesses.

*David also received many wives and concubines, and also
Solomon and Moses my servants, as also many others of my servants,
from the beginning of creation until this time; and in nothing did
they sin save in those things which they received not of me.*

DOCTRINE & COVENANTS 132:38

Doctrine and Covenants 132:38 is a modern
prophetic commentary on the condemnation sounded
in the Book of Mormon against David and Solomon's
practice of plural marriage (Jacob 2:23–24). The
problem was not plural marriage per se, for others of
the ancients had been commanded to have more than
one wife. The problem was with the *unauthorized* practice. David's adultery with Bathsheba (2 Samuel
11–12) and Solomon's taking of foreign wives who
turned his heart away from the worship of Jehovah (1
Kings 11) were not sanctioned by those who held the
keys of the priesthood and certainly not sanctioned by
the Lord himself. Joseph Smith taught that *"no man shall
have but one wife at a time, unless the Lord directs otherwise"*
(*Teachings of the Prophet Joseph Smith,* 324). "For if I will,
saith the Lord of Hosts, raise up seed unto me
[through plural marriage], I will command my people"
(Jacob 2:30).

I am the Lord thy God, and will be with thee . . . through all eternity; for verily I seal upon you your exaltation. . . . I have seen your sacrifices, and will forgive all your sins. . . . I make a way for your escape, as I accepted the offering of Abraham of his son Isaac.

DOCTRINE & COVENANTS 132:49–50

The Prophet of the Restoration received the consummate promise of eternal life and exaltation through the voice of the Lord. That is, he passed the tests of mortality and advanced, as it were, the day of judgment. His salvation was secure. Why? Because he was perfect? No, only the Lord Jesus has attained perfection. Because he did all things right and had no flaws within his character? No, for the perfect work of the Lord goes forward through the instrumentality of dedicated but imperfect people. The promise of eternal life came to Brother Joseph for the same reason it will come to Brother Johnson and Sister Farrington and Brother Hendrickson and Sister Alexander: because they have given themselves, without let or hindrance, at all hazards, to the Savior and sought to maintain an eye single to his glory. They have obtained the promise of the highest heaven because they have been willing to sacrifice all for the truth's sake (D&C 97:8).

*Go ye out from Babylon. Be ye
clean that bear the vessels of the Lord.*
DOCTRINE & COVENANTS 133:5

Those who come unto Christ and gather with the sheep of his fold are instructed to leave behind the tinsel and transcience of Babylon. They are called to come unto Zion, the society of the pure in heart, the city of God. They are called to eschew the actions and agenda of those who have taken up lodging in the great and spacious building, to ignore the taunts of the vocal citizens of the city of man. As possessors of the gospel, as bearers of the holy priesthood, as persons who have received the ordinances of salvation, and as receptacles of God's directing and sanctifying Spirit, they "bear the vessels of the Lord" (D&C 133:5). They strive to keep their hands (actions) clean and their hearts (desires) pure (Psalm 24:3–4). They have forsaken the god of this world (2 Corinthians 4:4) and now "shew forth the praises of him who hath called [us] out of darkness into his marvellous light" (1 Peter 2:9).

Go ye out from among the nations, even from Babylon,
from the midst of wickedness, which is spiritual Babylon . . .
and he that goeth, let him not look back lest sudden
destruction shall come upon him.
DOCTRINE & COVENANTS 133:14–15

The righteous flee the worldliness of Babylon and gather to Zion. "For this is Zion—THE PURE IN HEART; therefore, let Zion rejoice, while all the wicked shall mourn" (D&C 97:21). We are to go forth with hands firmly on the iron rod as we separate ourselves from worldly wickedness. This life is the time to exercise our agency to make righteous choices. Some attempt to leave Babylon, but the enticements and temptations of pride, power, and possessions keep them from purifying their hearts and gathering to Zion. Others come to Zion for a time but look back longingly to carnality and immediate gratification. Zion is a protected and joyous place, a place where all who come do so of their own free will, a place for those who have drawn upon the infinite atonement, had their hearts purified, and entered into a covenant relationship with Christ. Let us flee Babylon and gather with the righteous in Zion.

*The Lord shall be red in his apparel. . . . And so great shall
be the glory of his presence that the sun shall hide his face in
shame. . . . And his voice shall be heard: I have trodden the wine-
press alone, and have brought judgment upon all people.*
Doctrine & Covenants 133:48–50

Red is symbolic of victory—victory over the devil,
death, hell, and endless torment. It is the symbol of
salvation, of being placed beyond the power of all
one's enemies (Smith, *Teachings of the Prophet Joseph Smith,*
297, 301, 305). Christ's red apparel will symbolize both
aspects of his ministry to fallen humanity—his mercy
and his justice. Because he has faced the awful alienation of the Atonement on his own, has trodden the
winepress alone, "even the wine-press of the fierceness
of the wrath of Almighty God" (D&C 76:107;
88:106), he has descended below all things and mercifully taken upon him our stains, our blood or our sins
(2 Nephi 9:44; Jacob 1:19; 2:2; Alma 5:22). In addition,
the Lord of Hosts, the Lord of armies, comes in dyed
garments as the God of justice, even he who has
trampled the wicked beneath his feet and brought
peace to a troubled world.

*We believe that governments were instituted of God
for the benefit of man; and that he holds men accountable
for their acts in relation to them, both in making laws and
administering them, for the good and safety of society.*
DOCTRINE & COVENANTS 134:1

In 1835, by unanimous vote at a general assembly in
Kirtland, the Saints adopted a declaration of belief
regarding governments and laws in general. That declaration is now Doctrine and Covenants 134: "We believe
that no government can exist in peace, except such laws
are framed and held inviolate as will secure to each individual the free exercise of conscience, the right and control of property, and the protection of life" (v. 2).
Governments are to preserve freedom of conscience and
freedom of worship and to protect life and private property. We are to uphold such governments and obey the
law. As Latter-day Saints, "we believe in being subject to
kings, presidents, rulers, and magistrates, in obeying,
honoring, and sustaining the law" (Articles of Faith 1:12).
We can support honorable individuals in elections, get
involved in our communities to promote freedom and
strengthen the family, and be upstanding citizens who
obey the law, teaching our children to do the same.

Joseph Smith, the Prophet and Seer of the Lord, has done more, save Jesus only, for the salvation of men in this world, than any other man that ever lived in it. . . . He lived great, and he died great in the eyes of God and his people.

DOCTRINE & COVENANTS 135:3

Joseph Smith presides over the time when the Spirit of the Lord is being poured out upon all flesh (Joel 2:28–29), both in the conversion of souls as well as in the rapid intellectual, scientific, and technological developments from the Industrial Revolution to our own Age of Information. Most of what we know today in doctrine has come through Joseph Smith. In addition, the Prophet oversees the monumental labor of performing the saving ordinances for all humankind in all ages of the world. The work of redeeming the dead began with the visit of the disembodied Savior to the postmortal spirit world. Though the preaching of the gospel continued in the world of spirits during the Great Apostasy on the earth, not until priesthood authority was restored through Joseph Smith could the physical labor of redeeming the dead begin, a labor that will ultimately see to the salvation of billions of people.

[Joseph and Hyrum] will be classed among the martyrs of religion; and . . . every nation will be reminded that the Book of Mormon, and this book of Doctrine and Covenants of the church, cost the best blood of the nineteenth century to bring them forth for the salvation of a ruined world.

DOCTRINE & COVENANTS 135:6

Joseph and Hyrum Smith willingly gave their lives for the latter-day kingdom of God. "They lived for glory; they died for glory; and glory is their eternal reward. From age to age shall their names go down to posterity as gems for the sanctified" (D&C 135:6). They were guiltless of any crime, but they were persecuted and jailed by wicked men. Their innocent blood calls to the honest people among the nations as a beacon of righteousness (D&C 135:7). These two brothers, Prophet and Patriarch in the last and greatest gospel dispensation, united themselves in purpose and blood to usher in the return of the Lord Jesus Christ. Two greater brothers and martyrs never lived. Long may their truth stretch across the earth until the Lord returns in glory and every tongue confesses that Jesus is the Christ and that Joseph and Hyrum Smith were innocent sufferers in His cause. They lived great and died great in the eyes of God and the faithful (D&C 135:3).

And this shall be our covenant—that we
will walk in all the ordinances of the Lord.
DOCTRINE & COVENANTS 136:4

Jesus the Christ is our Exemplar, our Teacher, our Benefactor, and our Redeemer. If he had not come into the world and offered himself as a sinless sacrifice, a ransom for the souls of men and women, no amount of good on our part could make up for the loss. He is the Center of all things: We measure time by his birth, goodness by his impeccable life, and truth by his teachings. The gospel is the good news, the glad tidings that deliverance from death and sin and ignorance is available through covenant with Christ. As we accept him as Lord and Savior and thereafter strive to "walk in all the ordinances of the Lord," we enjoy a birth, a rebirth within our souls (D&C 136:4). We exult in the birth of the Son of God in Bethlehem. And we rejoice even more when he is born in our individual hearts and we thereafter begin to manifest his image in our countenances.

*If thou art merry, praise the Lord with singing,
with music, with dancing, and with a prayer of praise and
thanksgiving. If thou art sorrowful, call on the Lord thy God
with supplication, that your souls may be joyful.*
DOCTRINE & COVENANTS 136:28–29

The gospel of Jesus Christ is a gospel of joy and happiness, a message of peace and contentment. From earliest times to our day, believers have raised their voices in worshipful praise to the Giver of life and every good thing in the world. They have made a joyful noise and danced in pure delight for the bounteous goodness of our God. These gladsome expressions are always done in thanksgiving and humility—a sincere prayer from the heart. With music and dance appropriate and respectful of the Lord and everlasting things, joy and praise and music and dance all come together wonderfully when hearts are tuned to the God of heaven, when the spoken word alone does not quite capture our joy, when we cannot give utterance to all that we feel.

*My people must be tried in all things, that they may
be prepared to receive the glory that I have for them, even
the glory of Zion; and he that will not bear chastisement
is not worthy of my kingdom.*

DOCTRINE & COVENANTS 136:31

So much about life can be harsh and unfair. We may
have to endure trials more terrible than we think possible. Also, the myopia of mortality makes it difficult
to see things as they really are. The heavenly veil may
seem more like a brick wall, when the light of eternity
is left behind in the pressing demands of the here-
and-now. Often there are times we simply must "be
still, and know that [he is] God" (Psalm 46:10).
Patient endurance is required; humble submission is
needed. Indeed, God "trieth [our] patience and [our]
faith. Nevertheless—whosoever putteth his trust in
him the same shall be lifted up at the last day" (Mosiah
23:21–22). We must draw near unto the Lord and
prove ourselves worthy of the kingdom of God. Trusting submissiveness is the key that opens the door to
the celestial halls of everlasting peace.

*Let him that is ignorant learn wisdom by humbling himself and
calling upon the Lord his God, that his eyes may be opened . . . ;
for my Spirit is sent forth into the world to enlighten the humble
and contrite, and to the condemnation of the ungodly.*

DOCTRINE & COVENANTS 136:32–33

We might expect an ignorant person to be counseled to study or search or discuss with knowledgeable parties, all of which are extremely valuable enterprises. In Doctrine and Covenants 136:32–33, however, the Master teaches a grand and seldom appreciated truth: The first and most fundamental step to gaining spiritual knowledge is humility—the simple recognition of one's weakness, ignorance, or inability to grasp the truth without divine assistance. The apostle Paul wrote: "I take pleasure in infirmities, in reproaches, in necessities, in persecutions, in distresses for Christ's sake: for when I am weak, then am I strong" (2 Corinthians 12:10; compare Ether 12:27). As we acknowledge our weakness, we open ourselves to the Master's sanctifying strength as well as his supernal truths.

All who have died without a knowledge of this gospel,
who would have received it if they had been permitted to tarry,
shall be heirs of the celestial kingdom of God.
DOCTRINE & COVENANTS 137:7

In vision in the Kirtland Temple, the Prophet learned that salvation is available to those who died without a knowledge of the gospel while in mortality and yet would have embraced it. He also learned that God knows the hearts of all people and whether they would have endured faithfully to the end (D&C 137:8–9). The living cannot neglect their responsibilities in this life, expecting someone else to perform their work when they are gone. "This life is the time for men to prepare to meet God" (Alma 34:32). Also reconfirmed to the Prophet was a doctrine he had learned earlier from the Book of Mormon—that little children shall live eternally in celestial glory (D&C 137:10). These blessed truths provide perfect evidence of an omniscient and loving God—no eternal blessing or opportunity will be withheld from any who would have accepted the gospel.

The Son of God appeared, declaring liberty to
the captives who had been faithful; and there he preached to
them the everlasting gospel, the doctrine of the resurrection
and the redemption of mankind from the fall, and from
individual sins on conditions of repentance.

DOCTRINE & COVENANTS 138:18–19

Isaiah prophesied that the Messiah would not only
"preach good tidings unto the meek" but also "bind up
the brokenhearted, . . . proclaim liberty to the captives," and open "the prison to them that are bound"
(Isaiah 61:1). To a great extent, Jesus did these things
during his three-year ministry on earth. His ministry
did not end, however, when he gave up the ghost on
Calvary's hill. As his physical body took its last breath,
his spirit entered paradise, the abode of the righteous
in the postmortal spirit world. There he taught the
gospel to "an innumerable company of the spirits of
the just" (D&C 138:12) and organized the prophets
and righteous Saints to bridge the gulf between paradise and hell (vv. 29–30). "And the chosen messengers
went forth to . . . proclaim liberty to the captives who
were bound, even unto all who would repent of their
sins and receive the gospel" (v. 31). The justice and
mercy of God are thereby manifest.

*I beheld that the faithful elders of this dispensation,
when they depart from mortal life, continue their labors in the
preaching of the gospel of repentance and redemption . . . among
those who are in darkness and under the bondage of sin in
the great world of the spirits of the dead.*

DOCTRINE & COVENANTS 138:57

The work of the Lord goes forward on both sides of the veil, and it may not matter a great deal which side we are working on. Those who leave this life with a knowledge of the gospel and have been valiant in the testimony of Jesus continue in the work of redeeming souls, including proclaiming the truths of salvation in the next sphere. Thus, our efforts here to learn the gospel, to apply its principles in our lives, and to come to embody its transforming truths are but preparatory for what lies ahead hereafter. We have the assurance that no person will be denied the opportunity to receive and bask in the light of the gospel, in order that the Almighty may level the playing field of life and that all "might be judged according to men in the flesh, but live in the spirit according to the will of God" (JST 1 Peter 4:6).

SOURCES

Ashton, Marvin J. *Ensign,* May 1992, 19.

Backman, Milton V. *Joseph Smith's First Vision: Confirming Evidences in Contemporary Accounts.* 2d ed. Salt Lake City: Bookcraft, 1980.

Ballard, M. Russell. *Ensign,* May 1999, 86–87.

Benson, Ezra Taft. *A Witness and a Warning.* Salt Lake City: Deseret Book, 1988.

———. *New Era,* January 1988, 6.

Christensen, Joe J. *Ensign,* May 1999, 10.

Cowan, Richard O. *Answers to Your Questions about the Doctrine and Covenants.* Salt Lake City: Deseret Book, 1996.

Dew, Sheri L. *Go Forward with Faith: The Biography of Gordon B. Hinckley.* Salt Lake City: Deseret Book, 1996.

Faust, James E. *New Era,* July 1998, 4.

First Presidency [Ezra Taft Benson, Gordon. B. Hinckley, Thomas S. Monson]. *Ensign,* January 1993, 80.

———. "The Family: A Proclamation to the World." *Ensign,* November 1995, 102.

———. Letter, 11 February 1999.

Grant, Heber J. *Gospel Standards.* Compiled by G. Homer Durham. Salt Lake City: Deseret Book, 1976.

Hinckley, Gordon B. Conference Report, April 1984, 73.

———. *Ensign,* April 1986, 5; May 1987, 48; May 1992, 53; November 2001, 73; November 2003, 82, 84.

———. *Stand a Little Taller.* Salt Lake City: Deseret Book, 2001.

———. *Teachings of Gordon B. Hinckley.* Salt Lake City: Deseret Book, 1997.

Hymns of The Church of Jesus Christ of Latter-day Saints. Salt Lake City: The Church of Jesus Christ of Latter-day Saints, 1985.

Kimball, Spencer W. *Ensign,* May 1981, 79.

———. *Faith Precedes the Miracle.* Salt Lake City: Deseret Book, 1972.

Lee, Harold B. Conference Report, October 1947, 67; October 1972, 17.

———. *Teachings of Harold B. Lee.* Compiled by Clyde J. Williams. Salt Lake City: Bookcraft, 1996.

Lewis, C. S. *The Great Divorce.* New York: Collier Books, 1984.

———. *The Weight of Glory and Other Addresses.* New York: Touchstone, 1996.

Ludlow, Daniel H. *A Companion to Your Study of the Doctrine and Covenants.* 2 vols. Salt Lake City: Deseret Book, 1978.

McConkie, Bruce R. *Doctrinal New Testament Commentary.* 3 vols. Salt Lake City: Bookcraft, 1965–73.

———. *Ensign,* May 1982, 33.

———. *The Millennial Messiah: The Second Coming of the Son of Man.* Salt Lake City: Deseret Book, 1982.

———. *A New Witness for the Articles of Faith.* Salt Lake City: Deseret Book, 1985.

———. *The Promised Messiah: The First Coming of Christ.* Salt Lake City: Deseret Book, 1981.

McConkie, Joseph Fielding, and Craig J. Ostler. *Revelations of*

SOURCES

*the Restoration: A Commentary on the Doctrine and Covenants
and Other Modern Revelations.* Salt Lake City: Deseret
Book, 2000.

McKay, David O. *Gospel Ideals.* Salt Lake City: Improvement
Era, 1954.

Monson, Thomas S. *Ensign,* March 2004, 5.

Otten, L. G., and C. M. Caldwell. *Sacred Truths of the Doctrine
& Covenants.* 2 vols. Springville, Utah: LEMB, 1982–83.

Packer, Boyd K. *Ensign,* November 1986, 17; November 1994,
61; November 1998, 22.

———. *Memorable Stories and Parables.* Salt Lake City: Bookcraft,
1997.

———. *Memorable Stories with a Message.* Salt Lake City: Deseret
Book, 2000.

Roberts, B. H. *A Comprehensive History of The Church of Jesus
Christ of Latter-day Saints.* 6 vols. Salt Lake City: Deseret
News Press, 1938.

———. Conference Report, April 1906, 14–15.

Robinson, Stephen E., and H. Dean Garrett. *A Commentary
on the Doctrine and Covenants.* Vols. 1 and 2. Salt Lake City:
Deseret Book, 2000–2001.

Romney, Marion G. Conference Report, April 1945, 90.

Scott, Richard G. *Ensign,* May 1996, 25.

Smith, Joseph. *History of The Church of Jesus Christ of Latter-day
Saints.* Edited by B. H. Roberts. 2d ed. rev. 7 vols. Salt
Lake City: The Church of Jesus Christ of Latter-day
Saints, 1932–51.

———. *Lectures on Faith.* Salt Lake City: Deseret Book, 1985.

Teachings of the Prophet Joseph Smith. Compiled by Joseph
Fielding Smith. Salt Lake City: Deseret Book, 1976.

——. "The Vision." *Times and Seasons* 4, no. 6 (1 February 1843): 82–83.

Smith, Joseph F. *Gospel Doctrine.* 5th ed. Salt Lake City: Deseret Book, 1939.

Smith, Joseph Fielding. *Church History and Modern Revelation.* 4 vols. Salt Lake City: Council of the Twelve Apostles, 1946–1949.

——. *Doctrines of Salvation.* Compiled by Bruce R. McConkie. 3 vols. Salt Lake City: Bookcraft, 1954–56.

Snow, Lorenzo. *The Teachings of Lorenzo Snow.* Compiled by Clyde J. Williams. Salt Lake City: Bookcraft, 1996.

Talmage, James E. *Jesus the Christ.* Salt Lake City: Deseret Book, 1915.

Wirthlin, Joseph B. *Ensign,* November 1998, 27.

Woodruff, Wilford. *The Discourses of Wilford Woodruff.* Selected by G. Homer Durham. Salt Lake City: Bookcraft, 1969.

Young, Brigham. *Journal of Discourses.* 26 vols. London: Latter-day Saints' Book Depot, 1854–86, 3:205, 12:101.

About the Authors

Robert L. Millet and Lloyd D. Newell are members of the Religious Education faculty at Brigham Young University and coauthors of *Jesus, the Very Thought of Thee,* and *When Ye Shall Receive These Things.*

Brother Millet, professor of ancient scripture and former dean of Religious Education at BYU, has served with Church Public Affairs and the Materials Evaluation Committee of The Church of Jesus Christ of Latter-day Saints. He is the author of numerous books, including *Grace Works, More Holiness Give Me,* and *Alive in Christ.* He and his wife, Shauna Sizemore Millet, are the parents of six children.

Brother Newell teaches classes at BYU in the department of Church History and Doctrine and in the School of Family Life. He has served as the announcer and a writer for the Mormon Tabernacle Choir broadcast "Music and the Spoken Word" since 1990 and is the author of two books, *The Divine Connection* and *May Peace Be with You.* He and his wife, Karmel H. Newell, are the parents of four children.